ANIMALS AND THEIR MORAL STANDING

'To say that everyone interested in the ethics of our relations to animals will want to read Animals and their Moral Standing is true, but it doesn't make clear enough the significance of Stephen Clark's new book. Clark writes from a profound recognition of how our own wish to control "how things should go" distorts human life, besides imposing great suffering on our animal kin. Drawing on cultural traditions largely ignored in debates about animal rights, Clark communicates a vision of "cosmic democracy". The book is stimulating, original, insightful.' Cora Diamond, University of Virginia

'At the core of Clark's controlled passion is an acute sense of the violation of the laws that an ideal Creator-God would make (or has made) for the world - the laws of decency, humility and integrity. The essays collected in Animals and their Moral Standing are uncompromising in their exposure of the intellectual confusions, the perversions of once honourable ambitions, and the sheer hypocrisy of those who would deny or reduce that standing.'
David E. Cooper, University of Durham

Stephen R. L. Clark is an international authority on animal rights. His major writings over twenty years are now brought together for the first time in one volume as a record of his pioneering work. Over the last decade or more, animal rights has become an issue of genuine and outspoken public concern, following the work of philosophers, scientists and welfarists who have raised awareness of the issue. Renowned for *The Moral Status of Animals* and *The Nature of the Beast*, Clark's writings have been central to this debate; this collection traces the development of 'animal rights'. *Animals and their Moral Standing* tackles issues such as the calculation of costs and benefits; the 'rights' of wild animals, and of ecosystems; problems with our understanding of animal behaviour, and the faults of specism. Written with clarity and insight, these essays are core reading for anyone interested in the debates around animal rights, as well as an invaluable collection for philosophers and scientists.

Stephen R. L. Clark is Professor of Philosophy at the University of Liverpool and sometime fellow of All Souls. He has written extensively on animals; his books include *The Moral Status of Animals*, *The Nature of the Beast*, and *How to Think about the Earth*.

ANIMALS AND THEIR MORAL STANDING

Stephen R. L. Clark

London and New York

First published 1997
by Routledge
11 New Fetter Lane, London EC4P 4EE

Simultaneously published in the USA and Canada
by Routledge
29 West 35th Street, New York, NY 10001

© 1997 Stephen R. L. Clark

Typeset in Garamond by Routledge
Printed and bound in Great Britain by T. J. International Ltd,
Padstow, Cornwall

British Library Cataloguing in Publication Data
A catalogue record for this book is available from the British
Library

Library of Congress Cataloguing in Publication Data
Clark, Stephen R. L.
Animals and their moral standing/Stephen R. L Clark
Collection of essays previously published from 1977 to 1994.
Includes bibliographical references.
1. Animal rights 2. Animal welfare – moral and ethical aspects.
3. Animal psychology. I. Title.
HV4711 C58 1997
179'. 3-dc21
96-39502
CIP

ISBN 0–415–13559–1 (hbk)
ISBN 0–415–13560–5 (pbk)

CONTENTS

Acknowledgements   vii

1 INTRODUCTION   1

2 HOW TO CALCULATE THE GREATER
GOOD (1978)   9

3 THE RIGHTS OF WILD THINGS (1979)   16

4 AWARENESS AND SELF-AWARENESS (1981)   31

5 HUMANS, ANIMALS AND 'ANIMAL
BEHAVIOUR' (1983)   42

6 HUME, ANIMALS AND THE OBJECTIVITY
OF MORALS (1985)   55

7 ANIMALS, ECOSYSTEMS AND THE LIBERAL
ETHIC (1987)   70

8 THE DESCRIPTION AND EVALUATION OF
ANIMAL EMOTION (1987)   87

9 UTILITY, RIGHTS AND THE DOMESTIC
VIRTUES (1988)   97

10 ETHICAL PROBLEMS IN ANIMAL
WELFARE (1989)   112

11 THE REALITY OF SHARED EMOTION (1990)   121

12 THE CONSCIOUSNESS OF ANIMALS (1991)   139

13 MODERN ERRORS, ANCIENT VIRTUES (1994)   154

Stephen R. L. Clark: Publications   169
Notes   175
Bibliography   183
Index   190

ACKNOWLEDGEMENTS

1. 'How to Calculate the Greater good' was originally published in *Animal Rights*, eds, Richard Ryder and David Paterson (Centaur Press 1978), pp. 96–105, and is reprinted with the permission of Jon Wynne-Tyson.

2. 'The Rights of Wild Things' was originally published in *Inquiry* 22. 1979, pp. 171ff, and is reprinted with the permission of the Scandinavian University Press.

3. 'Humans, animals and "animal behavior" ' was originally published in *Ethics and Animals* eds, Harlan B. Miller and W. H. Williams (Humana Press 1993), pp. 169ff, and is reprinted with the permission of Humana Press.

4. 'Hume, animals and the objectivity of morals' was originally published in *Philosophical Quarterly* 25.1985, pp. 117–33, and is reprinted with the permission of the Editors of the *Philosophical Quarterly*.

5. 'Awareness and self-awareness' was originally published in *Self-awareness in domesticated animals* eds, D. G. M. Wood-Gush, M. Dawkins, R. Ewbank (UFAW 1981), pp. 11–18, and is reprinted with the permission of the Universities Federation for Animal Welfare.

6. 'Animals, ecosystems and the liberal ethic' was originally published in *Monist* 70.1987, pp. 114–33, and is reprinted with the permission of the Editor of the Monist.

7. 'The description and evaluation of animal emotion' was originally published in *Mindwaves* eds, C. Blakemore and S. Greenfield (Blackwell 1987), pp. 139–49, and is reprinted with the permission of Blackwell Publishers.

8. 'Utility, Rights and the Domestic Virtues' was originally published in *Between the Species* 4.1988, pp. 235–46, and is reprinted with the permission of the editors of *Between the Species*.

ACKNOWLEDGEMENTS

9. 'Ethical problems in animal welfare' was originally published in *The Status of Animals* eds, D. Paterson and M. Palmer (CAB International 1989), pp. 5–14, and is reprinted with the permission of CAP International.

10. 'The Reality of Shared Emotion' was originally published in *Interpretation and Explanation in the Study of Behavior* eds, M. Bekoff and D. Jamieson (Westview Press 1990), vol. I, pp. 449–72, and is reprinted with the permission of the Editors and Westview Press.

11. 'The Consciousness of Animals' was originally published in *The Pursuit of Mind* eds, R. Tallis and H. Robinson (Carcanet Press 1991), pp. 110–28, and is reprinted with the permission of Carcanet Press.

12. 'Modern Errors Ancient Virtues' was originally published in *Ethics and Biotechnology* eds, A. Dyson and J. Harris (Routledge 1994), pp. 13–32, and is reprinted with the permission of Routledge.

The editors of those various volumes, and their original audience, are to be thanked for whatever clarity or cogency I have achieved. I must also thank both critical and sympathetic readers over the years, especially Gillian, Samuel and Alexandra Clark.

1

INTRODUCTION

A large part of my published work over the last twenty years has dealt with ways of understanding and treating 'animals'. My first book on the subject, *The Moral Status of Animals*, was written in Oxford and in Glasgow, and variously denounced as too extreme, or rude, or insufficiently grounded in clear fundamental principles. The second, *The Nature of the Beast*, attempted to deal with information from ethologists and animal psychologists about the way 'beasts' thought and felt. Chapters in subsequent books (*From Athens to Jerusalem, Civil Peace and Sacred Order, A Parliament of Souls, God's World and the Great Awakening, How to Think about the Earth*) made further suggestions about global politics, and about the implications of evolutionary theory for philosophy of mind, and for political theory. I shall soon be attempting, in *Biology and Christian Ethics*, a larger and more systematic study of the relationship of biological theory, ethics and religion.

I have not included some very recent papers in this volume, notably 'Enlarging the Community'[1] and 'Apes and the Idea of Kindred'.[2] I have also omitted some related work, on environmentalism, on the roots of moral feeling, and on philosophy of biology. The papers I *have* collected here were written (usually on request) as descants or diversions. They chiefly deal with particular issues about our treatment of animals, or about our understanding of them: in both cases, the animals in question will include the human ones. These papers were composed for many different audiences, and in different styles, but they all belong to a single conversation: with myself, my friends and my opponents. Sometimes I have written sentences with which I don't agree – and never did agree: they were written as imagined criticisms or suggestions that I went on to rebut or qualify. Sometimes what I have written is only half of what I really think (and thought), and there are unvoiced qualifications lurking in a different paper. Too many modern philosophers (and other readers) neglect the historical moment, and report (with sorrow or with joy) that (for example) Clark says this and also that (which is a contradiction). The truth, most often, is that Clark (perhaps) *said* this, and on another occasion *that*. Maybe in neither case did he endorse it; maybe he has changed his mind (for what seemed some good reason, or by inattention). There is no reason why a collection of papers written over twenty years should always be consistent. There is even less reason to expect them all to say exactly the same thing (why bother, then, to publish more than one?).

On the other hand, I do see some consistencies, and some repeated themes. In trying to think about the 'rights' of animals I began to view the state rather differently: if 'rights' are natural interests such that everyone can count on lawful authority to defend or guarantee them, what might they be once 'everyone' is 'every animal'? In trying to think about the sort of beliefs and practices to be expected of a variety of placental mammal (namely, us), I began to see the attractions and the dangers of a fully naturalised epistemology. The papers printed here will therefore often have links to books and papers other than the ones explicitly about non-human creatures.

When I began thinking and writing about the way we dealt with 'animals' I concluded that anyone who wanted to defend that way would have to show that 'animals' didn't mind at all about their treatment. That is indeed the route that many took: they denied, that is, that 'animals' could think or feel or wish at all. Some such neo-Cartesians based their claims on biological assumptions: it has been part of the 'scientific mindset' for a century that 'anthropomorphism' is a deadly sin, and that any ascription to an 'animal' of a property possessed by people is 'anthropomorphic'. The thesis is absurd, and regularly rebutted by biologists themselves. Only creationists could make a plausible case for such a gross dichotomy – and creationists are almost more despised in biological circles than zoophiles! Other neo-Cartesians are philosophers, and found their flat rejection of the moral considerability of 'animals' on their 'not having language'. Because they cannot talk (it is said), they cannot think; because they cannot think, they cannot wish or feel. Oddly, such philosophers rarely conclude that all present legislation about animal welfare should at once be repealed (as pointless): somehow they still think it wrong 'to be cruel to animals' while absolutely right to hunt, imprison, experiment upon and kill them. Even more oddly, some neo-Cartesians (or Wittgensteinians) also reject the older philosophical division between natural facts and conventions. What is true is only what 'we' will affirm – but 'we' (bizarrely) always excludes anyone who gives weight to 'animal' experience. Philosophers who write against 'animals' also seem quite unwilling to discover what biologists, of any school, could tell them. Biologists who write against them are as unwilling to read philosophers. As a philosopher with an abiding interest in biology (quite apart from my moral interest in the matter) I find this upsetting.

Those who write in the defence of animals, of course, are not united. Some (most obviously, Peter Singer) are utilitarian: others (including me) most certainly are not.[3] Some are avowedly secular moralists, rejecting all 'religious' contexts: others (including me) write from within a strongly theological tradition.[4] Some believe that human beings are only animals, and animals in turn are only 'biological': others (including me) are ready to reckon that 'biology' (as ordinarily defined) is not the whole story, either about mice or men. Most of us are realists: we think, that is, that there really is an external world, and creatures like and unlike us in it. A few (for example, Hearne 1987) have been persuaded into the anti-realist camp, and argue largely about animals 'as they are for us'. Some are not content merely to write or argue, and have taken to various forms of direct action in defence of 'animals'. Others (including me) are far too conscious of the fragility of civil peace, and the improbability that our cause would win in open war, to endorse even such actions as do not injure innocents.

Notoriously, argument about 'animals' and our treatment of them can (or even must) be heated. The discussion is not of trivialities, nor all one-sided. How we remake our culture to accommodate the old, and modern, insight, that there are no boundaries in nature, and no exact natural kinds, is a serious, and a difficult, issue. 'Animal rightists' (so to call us) do not claim – or certainly should not claim – that hunters, vivisectors and the rest are crazed killers. Nor do they deny that all those people may have moral virtues. Whoever supposed, except the terminally stupid, that good men never serve bad causes, or that bad causes cannot have any attractive features? How easy life would be if that were true! The problem 'animal rightists' see is not that certain people (but not us) are wicked, but that all of us inherit a way of life, a set of attitudes, that rest in the end on a mistake. Correcting that mistake, and learning better ways, needs courage and courtesy and imagination. We cannot always avoid harsh language – but the harsher the language the more likely it is that we ourselves are in the dock, and know it.

Seeing a creature whole (and not simply as a set of different aspects, tools or meanings) is a difficult moral exercise. Sometimes we manage it by realising our affinity, by seeing it as a creature rather like ourselves, and therefore beginning to treat it rather as we would ourselves wish to be treated. But there is another mode of recognition, movingly described by Roy Willis, in a concluding chapter of *Signifying animals: human meaning in the natural world* (Routledge 1993). Encountering a – very dangerous – cobra, his 'overwhelming emotion was awe at its strange beauty'. That too is a moral exercise – to see a thing as Other, and unlike ourselves, and not a creature to be tamed or beaten. Maybe it is easier to meet that moment with a thing we see as 'wild': seeing a 'tame' creature in that way would be to understand at once that we are wrong to think it merely mutton. Even the creatures we have bred and coached (including people) are not things we have ourselves created, and they are not *ours*.

One way of testing these intuitions is to ask how those who really strike us as spiritually alive and saintly beings, those most alive to the presence of that Other, treat the natural world.[5] Saints, of course, come in many guises, and many who have the title for political or ecclesiastical reasons are not convincingly saintly. They also come in many different traditions. If I emphasise the Jewish, Christian and Islamic traditions in what follows (broadly, the Abrahamic), it is not from any lack of respect for Buddhist or pagan sensibilities.[6] The most convincing saints characteristically welcome the non-human, greet them as fellow-strugglers and worshippers of the most high, not because they have any naive or sentimental belief about what, say, a skylark believes, but because they see the lark's fulfilment of its God-given nature as at once a pledge and an example. John the Divine heard

> every created thing in heaven and on earth and under the earth and in the sea, all that is in them crying: Praise and honour, glory and might, to him that sits upon the throne and to the Lamb for ever and ever.
>
> (*Revelation* 5. 13)

Too many of us, too much of the time, see the natural world as merely a vast heap of more or less usable material, having no significance until the handyman has arrived to make something of it. The saint understands him- or herself to live within a meaningful and orderly universe, even if its meaning is sometimes simply that our action is needed. To interfere too radically in the natural order, to forget our own nature as terrestrial mammals and demand the right to remake all things only in our own image, for our own purposes, is to corrupt the text.

Saintliness requires that we respect the natures of our fellow creatures, and the order of which we are all a part. Some saints have concluded, in practice, that they should live in complete and open dependence, fitting themselves entirely into the natural order, and so offending the squeamishness of ordinarily decent people. It is a minor irony that Christ's own sardonic instruction to rely upon the Lord who remembers the falling sparrow, who clothes the anemones and finds the ravens their food, is usually quoted to 'prove' that he thought people – or at least his followers – more valuable than sparrows, and so licensed to take unfair advantage of sparrows, anemones and ravens. But saints live within the promised covenant, 'with the beasts of the field and the fowls of heaven, and with the creeping things of the land' when God shall have broken the bow and the sword and the battle out of the land and made them to lie down safely (*Hosea* 2. 18). The beasts will be at peace with us, said an early commentator on the Gospel of Mark, 'when in the shrine of our souls we tame the clean and unclean animals and lie down with the lions, like Daniel'.[7]

Most religious traditions, unsurprisingly, have found a place not only for these saints but for the mass of pious and more or less well-intentioned persons. How shall we, who do not yet feel called to go out into the wilderness, singly or in groups, think and act toward the natural order? It is, as Aldo Leopold remarked, the temptation of town-dwellers to think that food comes from the grocery store, and heat from the boiler. It is easy to believe that we do not live 'in nature' but in human culture, although everything we have and are is a transformation of a natural product. We need above all to remember that we do not live in a human technosphere, surrounded by an 'environment' that we may take a casual interest in if we choose. In the *Book of Job* 'Yahweh describes himself as the wisdom that makes for the survival of the wild ass, the hamster, the eagle, the ostrich, of all living nature, and the wisdom that uproots mountains and annihilates angels' (Kallen 1969). The vision of things before which Job at last bowed his head, and repented in dust and ashes, was one that Philo of Alexandria also approved: a sort of cosmic democracy, in which each creature gets its turn, and is allowed its own integrity. So far from dictating that we human beings should think all nature at our own disposal, the Bible constantly insists that humankind is not alone, not privileged above all others, not like God.

> Do you not know, have you not heard, were you not told long ago, have you not perceived ever since the world began, that God sits throned on the vaulted roof of earth, whose inhabitants are like grasshoppers? He stretches out the skies like a curtain, he spreads them out like a tent to live in; He reduces the great to nothing and makes all the earth's princes less than nothing. To whom then will you liken me, who set up as my equal? asks the Holy One.
>
> *(Isaiah* 40. 21ff)

Where humanist Christianity has borrowed from Stoicism the self-congratulatory notion that 'nothing irrational is capable of the beatifying friendship with God which is the bond of Christian love of neighbour',[8] and thence concluded that 'the irrational' is only material for our purposes, the Bible expects us to accept our place within the creation, to live by the rules God imposes, to take what we need, no more, and to give up our demands so that life may go on. Every seventh and fiftieth year the land must be unploughed, and all live together off its natural produce, citizen and stranger and the wild animals of the country (*Leviticus* 26. 6f). If the law is not kept the people shall be driven from the land, and 'the land shall enjoy its sabbaths to the full' (*Leviticus* 26. 34). None shall eat the life, which is the blood, of any creature, even if in the post-Noahic days meat-eating is allowed. This is not to say that the Bible contains many specific injunctions of a kind to appeal to zoophiles. It was a sterner world than ours, and the animals who shared the Israelites' land or houses could not have had an easier life than the Israelites themselves. But there was affection there, and acknowledgement of duty. A donkey fallen into a ditch must be hauled out even on the sabbath, and even if it is one's enemy's (*Deuteronomy* 22. 4). The poor man's pet sheep, whom Nathan the prophet used to shame King David (*I Kings* 12) was loved as a daughter (and no one had the brass nerve to say that he shouldn't have wasted good affection on a mere beast).

Northrop Frye, in his attempt to see the Bible whole, concludes that one of its messages is that we shall not regain the world we have lost, the world where we might easily live in nature, with all creatures as our friends, 'until [we] know thoroughly what hell is, and realise that the pleasure gained by dominating and exploiting, whether of [our] fellow man or of nature itself, is part of that hell-world'.[9] Things are not wholly at our disposal, and never will be, either in the sense that we can or that we ought to use them with an eye solely to our benefit, and avoid all inconveniences of this mortal life. We cannot by any technical means transform this world into a pleasure garden, nor ought we to try. Nor can we retreat within a denatured city, and imagine that we thereby fulfil the biblical prophecy of a world wholly suffused with humanly significant meaning, 'when there shall be no more sea', no more image of the unaccountable. The city that the Bible praises was imagined as part of the land within which it stood, the holy mountain where wolf shall dwell with lamb, leopard lie down with kid (*Isaiah* 11. 6), and the leaves of the trees serve for the healing of the nations (*Revelation* 22. 2).

No one who reads the Bible can doubt that its human authors were deeply conscious of the natural world, the creation, the land flowing with milk and honey. Where we see 'nature', the non-human environment ruled by powers alien to humankind, they saw God's creation, a world continually offering embodied images of the spiritual values they pursued.

> The God of Israel spoke, the Rock of Israel spoke of [David]: He who rules men in justice, who rules in the fear of God, is like the light of morning at sunrise, a morning that is cloudless after rain and makes the grass sparkle from the earth.
>
> (*2 Samuel* 23. 3f)

In the mouths of poets and prophets this is more than simile, more than a rather strained declaration that a just ruler is like the sun after rain. The prophet sees God's liberating justice in the light when God sets His rainbow in the sky 'sign of the covenant between [Himself] and earth' (*Genesis* 9. 14). 'As the hills enfold Jerusalem, so the Lord enfolds His people' (*Psalm* 125. 2).

> Once the Lord called you an olive-tree, leafy and fair; but now with a great roaring noise you will feel sharp anguish; fire sets its leaves alight and consumes its branches. The Lord of Hosts who planted you has threatened you with disaster.
>
> (*Jeremiah* 11. 16)

When Babylon the Great has fallen at last,

> there no Arab shall pitch his tent, no shepherds fold their flocks. There marmots shall have their lairs, and porcupines shall overrun her houses; there desert owls shall dwell, and there he-goats shall gambol; jackals shall occupy her mansions, and wolves her gorgeous palaces.
>
> (*Isaiah* 13. 20f)

The whole world has rest and is at peace; it breaks into cries of joy. The

pines themselves and the cedars of Lebanon exult over you; since you
have been laid low, they say, no man comes up to fell us.

(Isaiah 14. 7f)

The whole world, not merely human history, embodies God's purposes to the
prophetic eye, and no general distinction is drawn between human and non-
human. God's purposes, indeed, may be more fully and obviously embodied
in the non-human, and moral examples drawn from them: 'Mothers, cherish
your sons. Rear them joyfully as a dove rears her nestlings' (2 Esdras 2. 15).

Why, if all this is so, are there so few general injunctions to behave
decently to the non-human? The word of the Lord to Ezra:

> champion the widow, defend the cause of the fatherless, give to the
> poor, protect the orphan, clothe the naked. Care for the weak and the
> helpless, and do not mock at the cripple; watch over the disabled, and
> bring the blind to the vision of my brightness. Keep safe within your
> walls both old and young.

(2 Esdras 2. 20ff)

These commands could certainly be read as applying to non-human
creatures, but just as certainly were not. There were few occasions when the
Israelites could do much hurt to the wild things, unless by overhunting
them or keeping them away from the crops. The creatures they used for
sacrifice – which was the only licensed way of getting meat – were being
returned to God. And the prophets disapproved:

> your countless sacrifices, what are they to Me? says the Lord. I am sated
> with the whole-offering of rams and the fat of buffaloes; I have no
> desire for the blood of bulls, of sheep and of he-goats. Though you offer
> countless prayers, I will not listen. There is blood on your hands. Put
> away the evil of your deeds, away out of my sight. Cease to do evil and
> learn to do right, pursue justice and champion the oppressed; give the
> orphan his rights, plead the widow's cause.

(Isaiah 1.11, 15f)

The God of Israel, in short, is made known in the demand for justice, the
insistence that no human being is entitled to oppress God's creatures or
claim equality with God.

> For the Lord of Hosts has a day of doom awaiting for all that is proud
> and lofty, for all that is high and lifted up, for all the cedars of Lebanon,
> lofty and high, and for all the oaks of Bashan, for all lofty mountains
> and for all high hills, for all the dhows of Arabia. Then man's pride
> shall be brought low, and the loftiness of man shall be humbled.

(Isaiah 2. 12f)

So, far from lending support to the sort of humanism which puts its trust in

7

human resourcefulness, the Biblical tradition recognises that our powers are no different in kind from those of any other creature, and the Lord stands over all.

The first step then is simply not to aim too high, not to expect a pleasure garden, not to demand our human comforts at whatever cost, not to 'turn the world into a desert and lay its cities in ruins' (*Isaiah* 14. 17). If we cannot live in the land on the terms allotted to us, of allowing others their place, not disregarding the needs of the apparently defenceless, not claiming the right to decide how all things should go, then we shall find that we have lost the land. The natural historian of a future age may be able to point to the particular follies that brought ruin – chopping down the tropical rain-forests, meditating nuclear war, introducing hybrid monocultures, spreading poisons, financing grain-mountains and rearing cattle in conditions that clearly breach the spirit of the commandment not to muzzle the ox that treads out the corn (*Deuteronomy* 25. 4). The historian whose eyes are opened to the acts of God will have no doubt that we brought that ruin on ourselves, that it is God's answer to the arrogant. In those days our survivors will have to be saints, unless we have taken a step back from the furnace and consented to be ordinarily decent and God-fearing folk. 'How long must the land lie parched and its green grass wither? No birds and beasts are left, because its people are so wicked, because they say, God will not see what we are doing' (*Jeremiah* 12. 4).

Readers may regard those scriptural musings, if they wish, as metaphor. As a Christian philosopher, I think the warnings are straightforwardly, and even obviously, true. But the papers that follow are not directed only at Christians (or any other heir of Abraham). They are my attempt to think through the implications of a great discovery (call it a revelation): that the real world, the world that we are 'meant' to see, is one composed of many living creatures who are all, potentially, our friends.

2

HOW TO CALCULATE THE GREATER GOOD[1]

Those moralists who deny that non-human beings have rights generally mean that there is no moral reason to consider the feelings or wishes of those creatures. I myself agree with the early Cartesians, that if a creature has feelings then we ought not to torment and kill him or her.[2] Their absurdity in concluding that it would therefore be inhumane to think that animals had feelings does not discredit their initial insight. I am happy then to agree that animals have rights, and I shall not argue the point further in this chapter.

But moralists opposed to animal rights may have a slightly different point in mind. Certainly, they may say, we should not multiply animal suffering unduly, nor wantonly diminish animal delights. In that sense, animals have rights. But this admission is compatible with a strictly utilitarian treatment of non-human creatures which we are generally unwilling to extend to the human. Those who believe in human rights believe that human creatures have a right to a say in what is done to them and their world. Perhaps a sophisticated social engineer can see, and correctly see, that a certain policy will bring long-term advantage, yet he has no right to implement that policy if it conflicts with the standing rights of the human creatures affected. Perhaps I ought, for example, to give most of my goods to the poor, for utilitarian reasons, but yet I have a right not to do so, and no one else has a right to enforce the gift. It is this sort of right which orthodox moralists probably deny to the non-human.

Fully committed utilitarians, of course, must find such 'rights of autonomy' suspect: there are no works of supererogation in utilitarian morality. If I ought to do x then I have no right not to, I am not in the right if I don't. And on the other hand, fully committed zoophiles, such as myself, can think of no good reason to deny such 'rights of autonomy' at least to our closer kindred, or even to any sentient being. If I have no right to force my fellow adults, children or mental defectives to serve the greater good against their will, I do not see how I could acquire such a right against a chimpanzee, a cat or a cow. To say that they have no wills is neither more nor less correct than to say that children and mental defectives have no wills. Incidentally, even non-utilitarians may agree that my rights or alleged rights

9

cannot always hold out against the needs of the greater good: perhaps I have a right not to be robbed of my goods even to feed the starving, but if I have an enormous superfluity and the starving are desperate millions, I do not suffer much injury from such forcible appropriation. But where such gross inequality does not obtain, or holds in the opposite direction, I do not see that, for example, ten people have a right to seize on one to use his flesh or organs to aid their survival even if that one would be heroically virtuous if he exercised his right to self-sacrifice. And one further caveat: there may be moral rules of a non-utilitarian sort that forbid animal torture even for the greater good without attributing any rights of autonomy to the potential victim, but I am not now concerned with these.

I myself then do not believe that chimpanzees, rats and the rest should be sacrificed even for an acknowledged greater good: such sacrifice infringes their right to refuse. In my morality, all creatures with feelings and wishes should be thought of as ends-in-themselves, and not merely as means (see Raphael 1974). We may remember the efforts men have made in the past to make it seem that their animal victims went consenting. Their intuition, though not their techniques of 'persuasion', is also mine. However, I now wish to consider what moral effects follow from a determination to treat animals according to utilitarian, and people according to Kantian morality (see Nozick 1974, pp. 34f). Human beings must give their consent to operations either upon themselves or upon the human creatures in their tutelage and may not, at least in this country, give such consent in the latter cases unless the operation is, or is very likely to be, of direct benefit to the victim. We may not sacrifice our children even if assured that torturing one to death will enable doctors to save several. The child has a right to refuse, and since he (or she) cannot exercise this option in an informed manner we refuse on his behalf. My point is not that he *would* refuse if he were rational – we might know him to be good-natured enough to agree – but simply that as the operation cannot be carried out without his consent and as he has not consented, the operation cannot justly be carried out unless by failing to do so we infringe his right to our best help. Those who think, by the way, that children and mental defectives are not primary right-bearers, but are protected only for the sake of parental squeamishness, might like to explain why parents should not have the right to sell, say, brain-damaged or mongoloid or microcephalic children – you can see the posters already: 'A Parent's Right to Choose'.

Let us simply stipulate, for no good reason that I can see, that creatures of human descent have rights of autonomy and creatures of non-human descent do not. I do not know if this is intended to license acts of utilitarian violence against intelligent aliens: perhaps not, though if not, I do not see why at any rate chimpanzees, gorillas and perhaps dolphins should not be allowed the courtesies we would afford extra-terrestrials.

According to the view I am outlining, then, animals have rights in the sense that it is wrong to multiply their suffering, that their pain is an evil and their pleasure a good. If pain is not an intrinsic evil, nor pleasure an intrinsic good, by the way, much argument for, say, vivisection collapses, for it rests on the notion that (our) suffering is an evil. But that *is* by the way. Animals do not have rights in the sense that once we have demonstrated to our satisfaction that a particular act leads to the greater good of the greater number, including animals, we are at once entitled to perform that act however much our victim objects. How, then, are we to perform this calculation and what, in general terms, could it justify?

Classical utilitarians do include animal pains and pleasures in their calculation, though they generally add some, rarely argued, clause to the effect that animals experience less intense or fewer pleasures. Correspondingly, one would think, adult humans have more options open to them and suffer less from any single disappointment. Benthamite utilitarians work with a simple notion of quantity of pleasure or pain. Followers of Mill incorporate some notion of variety of pleasures, upon whatever excuse: better many pleasures than one pleasure, better a collection of entities variously pleased than a mass of the unanimously voluptuous. Better intellectual than sensual pleasures. These facts, with a little fudging, give a general bias towards the human, particularly the normal adult human. Better multiply such creatures than multiply, say, happy bees, and if we are to choose between having happily uniform animals and happily various humans, we should have the latter. Doubtless this point greatly exaggerates both human variety and non-human uniformity, but let it pass (particularly as it favours the vegan rather than the wholefood wing of ecologically-conscious politics).

Utilitarians make no difference between directly causing and merely allowing an event. To allow an event which one could have prevented is to be responsible for its occurrence. Common morality does not relish this: we think it one thing to save ten men at the cost of allowing another man to die, and quite another to kill one man in order to save the ten (unless the one man is himself the danger, potential assassin or plague vector). The moralists I am considering allow this distinction among human objects, but not among non-humans. If I forebear to experiment upon a baboon and thereby fail to acquire the knowledge that might enable me to save a human, I am guilty of that human's death, as I would not be guilty if the route to his survival was destructive experimentation on an unconsenting human victim. I repeat that I myself see no important difference between the cases, and do not consider myself or anyone else obliged to save any human being by causing pain, distress or death to an unconsenting 'person' – where 'person' is defined as a creature with whom one can have at least as much of a personal relationship as one can with an infant, a brain-damaged adolescent or a senile old man.

But let it be so. In judging whether an act of violence against an animal is required I must see whether doing it or not doing it will lead to an increase

11

of pleasure, or variety of pleasure, or a decrease of pain among those affected by my policy. In calculating the matter I must employ simple decision-theory: that is, I must attend both to the value and to the probability of the outcome. If the value accruing, though great in itself, is very unlikely, this may count for less in my calculation than a less valuable, but more likely outcome. The peculiarity, though not a failing, of utilitarianism is that I cannot perform the calculation afterwards, in full knowledge of what *did* happen. Perhaps what I did or failed to do resulted, by chance, in the greatest imaginable good, but unless I had some epistemological right to expect that outcome with the appropriate probability my action was not justified, and I ought not to have done it. Conversely I may be justified in acting so, even though in fact history goes against me. Neither the gains nor the losses of serendipity can enter into my calculation, for they are, precisely, incalculable. So in considering, say, whether or not to poison a baboon to death, or smash his leg with a sledge-hammer, or drive her, pregnant, into a brick wall, I must not simply weigh the distress caused by doing so against an imagined benefit to other entities. I must weigh the certain pain against the merely possible diminution of later pain. Otherwise I shall in the end simply be increasing pain (and we may note the steady increase in the vivisection industry over the last century): the less note is taken of the relative improbability of certain outcomes, the more violent actions are licensed, and the more often they result in no particularly valuable result. Of course some valuable results are in fact obtained that could not reasonably have been expected at the time, but that is not enough to justify the unreasonable act. The same argument applies against any 'rule-utilitarian' defence of the institution of animal torture, that to require proper discriminations of probability over any particular experiment would so hamper the scientist that the overall gains would not be as high as they might be if the scientists were allowed a completely free hand. Such an institution may increase profits; it also increases costs.

Strictly, there are two principles involved in utilitarianism: increase pleasure and diminish pain. Or even four, for we might add: do not decrease pleasure, do not increase pain. There are no clear utilitarian reasons for judging between these principles when they conflict: we cannot assess the consequences in terms of 'the greater good', for it is the nature of this goal which is in question. Shall we increase pleasure even by increasing or failing to decrease pain? Or shall we diminish pain even by decreasing or failing to increase pleasure? The second option leads to the paradox of negative utilitarianism, that we should commit genocide. The first, to the paradox of positive utilitarianism, that we should increase the population at every cost so long as that population has a few more pleasures at each generation. Other problems of utilitarian population control involve distinctions between the number of entities involved and the qualities of the lives they enjoy. All these problems, I think, require intuitionist solutions (that is, any solution

12

has to be based on an independent assessment of several moral principles without any principled way of choosing between those principles, or at least without any utilitarian way), thus weakening the initial plausibility of utilitarian morality as an unambiguous and monarchical system. In particular, shall we cause pain in order to diminish pain, or may we also do so in order to increase pleasure (where the absence of pleasure is no pain)? Shall we avoid pleasures in order to increase long-run pleasures or also to diminish pain? The second question seems plausibly answered by saying that we should forego pleasures in order to diminish pain, at least as long as there are some pleasures left. The first question may plausibly be answered by saying that we may cause pain in order to earn a long-run diminution of pain, but not so as to increase pleasure: if we decreed otherwise it would be *right* for a sadist to torture an animal to death if he thereby increased his own and his companions' sexual and gastronomic pleasures. Fortunately, these intuited answers agree.

So: as utilitarians we should forego pleasures if we thereby diminish or avoid increasing pain, and should not cause pains in order to increase pleasures. Of course, this does not apply to a calculus over an agent's *own* pains and pleasures: if we like to pain ourselves now to gain pleasures later, very well. But even here there is something amiss with us if we take pleasures now at the cost of a later increase in pain: our 'future self' should have more claim on what happens than that – he or she is entitled *not* to be pained. But this is to involve myself in a theory of rights once more.

Utilitarians are also, of course and essentially, concerned with the choice between alternative courses of action. The incurably polar bias of our species suggests to us that in any crisis there are only two actions: to do or not to do. But of course in reality there may be non-denumerably many available acts. Do x or do y or do z or do something else entirely. So the calculus should not simply assess the costs and benefits of doing or not doing x, as if omitting the one we are automatically barred from performing any other act. We must take the alternatives into account, as the Research Defence Society prevented Parliament from requiring laboratory scientists to do.[3] Of course, 'alternatives' are not merely those popularised by FRAME (Fund for the Replacement of Animals in Medical Experiments) or financed by the various trusts recently set up by anti-vivisection societies (which may have their own costs): the alternatives must include alterations in our diet and way of life, herbal remedies, and the application of elementary stoicism to the ills of the flesh rather than to the iatrogenic penalties of modern medicine. Medical practitioners and experimentalists have until recently been strangely averse to submitting their success rate to objective study. It seem very likely that changes in social custom, wealth and diet have had an enormously more beneficial effect on the health of the developed West than laboratory science and orthodox medicine, even if particular cases have unambiguously benefited from the latter (see Bates 1977). Some of these alternative courses of action, of course, are not directly in the power of, say, the individual scientist; he cannot decree that everyone stop smoking, and may consider himself justified in taking the actions of others and the way of life they actually lead as providing the boundary conditions for his calculations. Given that people will go on smoking, how best can he hope to reduce the cancer rate? The answer is obviously not by *increasing* the cancer rate among laboratory animals, particularly given our marked failure to solve the problem in this way so far. The laboratory scientists could perhaps use their knowledge to attack the given state of things: the more people realise the costs of their addiction, the more of them may stop.

One further difficulty: utilitarians are concerned with long-run advantage. But they cannot be concerned with too long a run, and there is no clear way of defining how many imagined consequences should be taken into account. First, because on a long view it is difficult to say what *is* the consequence of a given act: the more time elapses between the act and the outcome, the more alternative courses of history could have generated just that outcome (see Prior 1968). Blaming the blacksmith for the loss of a kingdom involves us in disregarding all the other agents, all the other causal factors that led to this dénouement. Second, because once we start reckoning long-run consequences we have no assurance that the value of the outcome will remain the same from one moment to the next. Perhaps the state of affairs at t^i is better than it would have been if action x had not been performed, but the immediately following state of affairs at t^{ii} is worse than it would have been if action x had not been performed. Probability theory will cope with some of these cases, of course: generally speaking, the more distant the consequence, the less ground could we have for expecting it.

Distant consequences of not performing destructive experiments must count for very little. But probability does not help us on one point: in the long run, as the saying goes, we're all dead. This is not an improbable, but an all-but-certain consequence of anything we do. In the long run any action will count for as much or as little good as any other. The differences of value will be ironed out by the centuries, and in the end we're all dead. Experimentalists sometimes speak as if paradise is just around the corner: only a few more acts of violence and we shall live, men and animals alike, a pain-free idyll that will last for ever. If we could be sure of this, and sure that the memory of our past behaviour would not stain our felicity, their utilitarian calculation might be justified. As I at least am sure rather of its opposite, that pain and frustration will be with us till the day of doom, that in the long run nothing earthly lasts, their calculation seems far from safe.

Accordingly, as utilitarians we should think ourselves justified in inflicting pain, or deprivation, on a sentient being only if we are justified in believing that the amount of pain will thereby in the not-too-long run be diminished to an extent that outweighs (preferably appreciably so) the certain pain we inflict, and if there are no alternative acts which would with

14

equal or greater probability lead to the same or nearly the same benefit. As far as agribusiness and meat-eating in general goes, the answer is now obvious: we are not justified, since the likely benefits accruing in terms of increased pleasure (to us) do not outweigh the costs (to the animals), and there are other, incidentally healthier, diets. This is a practical point for campaigners: it is no use complaining to an experimenter about the way he gets profit from a baboon, if he can retort that one is oneself going home to chomp a battery chicken. If the animals can be tormented for our purposes, they surely can be for his. As far as laboratory science goes, some acts of violence might be hereby justified, but certainly no such act is proper where there is an alternative available in a changed human life. We can do without cosmetics and the like: we can reduce the cancer rate by not smoking, eating more roughage, breast-feeding (where appropriate), and so on.

We can do this, and on utilitarian principles we should. But I may now return to my beginning. Ought we to be forced to prefer the option that is preferable? Do we have standing rights in the matter entitling us to ignore the greater good? In claiming that we do, we entirely abandon utilitarianism as an ethical policy, and reassert our rights (self-claimed) to treat non-human beings as we please. But if we are not utilitarians at this point we cannot make the distinction from which I began: we cannot claim to be considering animal pleasures and pains as morally relevant but deny animals human rights of autonomy. In hanging on to our 'rights' in this matter we implicitly deny animals all moral consideration.

I conclude that honest semi-utilitarians, even if their fundamental distinction between animals and men is allowed, must forego meat and other products of the factory farm, and refrain from or seek to halt most vivisection. If they claim a continuing right to ignore the results of utilitarian calculation in this matter they are implicitly denying that non-human animals have any moral standing at all.

3

THE RIGHTS OF WILD THINGS[1]

RITCHIE'S REDUCTIO

D. G. Ritchie, responding to Henry Salt's claim that at least some non-human animals had some rights in law, observed that were this so we should be obliged to enforce such rights even against other non-humans. If a mouse has a right not to be tormented, a cat ought not to torment him, and we ought, if possible, to restrain the cat. Ritchie's argument, of course, was intended as a *reductio ad absurdum*, his object to deny rights to non-human animals.

> Must we not put to death blackbirds and thrushes because they feed on worms, or (if capital punishment offends our humanitarianism) starve them slowly by permanent captivity and vegetarian diet? What becomes of the 'return to nature' if we must prevent the cat's nocturnal wanderings, lest she should wickedly slay a mouse? Are we not to vindicate the rights of the persecuted prey of the stronger? Or is our declaration of the rights of every creeping thing to remain a mere hypocritical formula to gratify pug-loving sentimentalists?[2]

Ritchie preferred to base 'our duty to animals' on the requirement to maintain a civilised, humanitarian, human society, though he acknowledged that we might, metaphorically, have duties towards domestic animals as 'honorary human beings'.

Even Ritchie, were he to be acquainted with present practices towards the non-human, in farms, laboratories, zoos, circuses, and the wild, might have agreed that such were not the customs of a humane society, and that our advocacy of 'kindness to animals' must only be a hypocritical formula if we always prefer our sensual gratification to the slightest realistic effort not to hurt our kindred. Even those who would deny that 'animals' have any 'rights', moral or legal, may agree that their suffering is an evil. A hurt is a hurt whoever has it. What Nozick has called 'utilitarianism for animals, Kantianism for people'[3] places the non-human on a lower level of moral concern, but actually — as I argued in the previous chapter — outlaws most of our present practices (at least if we consider the argument carefully). My object in this paper is not to defend vegetarianism but to try to disentangle the various kinds of right we might wish to impute to our kindred, and to help Utopian speculation a little further forward.

THE MORALISING RESPONSE

An immediate reply to Ritchie's argument might be that mice no more have rights against cats than they do against earthquakes, for neither danger has any duties. An event may injure or hurt a mouse but not infringe his rights, just as our rights are not infringed by epidemics, earthquakes, or tornadoes – unless those episodes are engineered by maleficent moral agents. One can have rights only against those capable of acknowledging them. This class, indeed, may be smaller than the class of moral agents. Harman's space-travelling anthropophages may perhaps recognise moral constraints in their dealings with each other, but are incapable of seeing our distress as any reason to refrain from action. There would at least be little point in demanding our rights from such oppressors.[4]

This reply makes use of an intuition often used against those disturbed by the thought of 'nature red in tooth and claw'. The hyena is not cruel in eating a zebra alive, for he is only seeking food, not the enjoyment of power or the distress of his victim. It is simply sentimental to be upset by such a sight. This is to say that it is moral and not physical evil which is to be denounced: not the victim's distress but the predator's character. What is evil, correspondingly, in our tormenting of the mouse is the cruelty or callousness we thereby display, not the mouse's distress. A cat shows no such fault of character, though maybe chimpanzees sometimes do,[5] and there is therefore no important evil in the cat's pursuit of mice. She is innocent.

This reply to Ritchie, however, plainly concedes his case: that human character and society is the proper object of concern, not the pain of the non-human. We should not behave to them as Harman's aliens or Soame Jenyns's demons[6] do to us, for we should not want to be like such oppressors. Nor should we salve our consciences by fantasising that as men hunt animals, so the spirits hunt men.[7] It is a part of a decent human life that it is susceptible to sympathetic distress. We should not be cruel or callous, but should not permit 'kindliness' to be our solitary virtue.

That the reply concedes Ritchie's point may itself be sufficiently counter-intuitive to count against it, but it has other faults. First, the laws against the torture or neglect of (some) animals are thereby revealed as laws of manners, acceptable to moralistic legislators, but not to anyone who refuses to let the law come between a man and his morals.[8] Should they then be repealed?

Second, it is surely quite unclear what could be wrong with cruelty or callousness if suffering were not itself an evil. Why should we object to these character traits except because they multiply physical evil? A Kantian may reply that we should object because the traits, once established, will tend to multiply human suffering. There may be some truth in this – the psychologists who have been happy to experiment upon the non-human are also implicated, as a profession, in gross deception and oppression of human victims. But they could be restrained by Kantian considerations, to the effect that humans are a quite different sort of creature from non-humans (all of them?), that human suffering is evil (perhaps) because it interferes with distinctively human activities: a migraine makes it difficult to do philosophy. It follows, of course, that medical efforts to reduce human suffering of a kind that is not interfering with the realisation of such capacities (because trivial, or because the patient has no such capacities) is misplaced, and many standardly emotive arguments for vivisection are thereby invalidated. Physical evil is evil in its own right.

A third difficulty with the moralistic response is that it does not even solve Ritchie's puzzle. If callousness is an evil, is it not displayed as well in watching a cat play with a mouse, a chimpanzee bashing out a baboon's brains, without any inclination to intervene? If susceptibility to sympathetic distress is a value, ought we not to be distressed by the behaviour of predators? And if we ought not, how are we obliged to be distressed by the behaviour of our fellow men? To be distressed only by moral evil and not by physical evil surely is, in the context, to be callous. Writers other than Ritchie have been more consistent in considering that animal pains and pleasures were morally indifferent, and no one obliged to take account of them.

Fourth, animal distress is surely an intrinsic evil in just the way that much human distress is, so that even if the cat has no duties towards the mouse, and the mouse therefore no rights against the cat, it may still be that the mouse has rights against *us*, to safeguard his life. McCloskey has argued that animals have no interests, and therefore no rights, just in that they are not subject to any obligations, even prudential ones, to preserve those interests (McCloskey 1965). Regan has replied that any prescriptive element in the having of interests may be embodied in a more general obligation, that those able to keep those interests in mind, ought to do so.[9] It would seem to follow that we ought to keep predators off their prey, even though the predators have no duty in the matter.

One final point against the moralistic response: it is by no means clear .that non-humans cannot violate rights. A bigger bird who drives a smaller from the latter's nest is not absurdly described as 'violating the victim's rights', for property is generally acknowledged by members of the same population.[10] Even butterflies appear to allow occupants of a patch of sunlight to have the moral edge over intruders: perhaps they could steal the patch?[11] A chimpanzee who grabs a young baboon with whom her own children have been playing, kills and eats her, is not implausibly described as doing what she ought not, at least to the same extent that a Yanomamo Indian who beats and mutilates his wife is 'doing what he ought not'.[12] If we ought to restrain injustice, perhaps we ought to restrain at least some predators. If that is absurd, perhaps it is also absurd to restrain human predation (inside or outside the state).

USEFUL CONSEQUENCES

Instead of denying that the situation of a mouse in a cat's claws is in any respect an evil, could we reject the inference from animal rights to a duty of general protection? Perhaps non-human animals have rights not to be treated in certain ways, but no right to our assistance against their enemies. We violate their rights in hunting them ourselves, but not in allowing them to suffer at the claws of predators.

This distinction is difficult to draw on any utilitarian ethic. If what is of moral concern is the suffering of the victim, and if some action of ours could diminish that suffering (without untoward consequences elsewhere in the system: see below), we ought to perform that action. It is not entirely clear why we should not, in that case, simply go around killing all creatures that otherwise suffer. Total genocide might have bad effects, perhaps removable by further slaughter, but something less than a total cull would apparently be obligatory (see Godlovitch 1971). There seems to be little room for animal *rights* in such a system, and my suspicion is that the rhetoric of rights is a little out of place in some recent pleas for animal liberation.

Utilitarians have their own problems, but perhaps not Ritchie's. Animal suffering is an evil, but not all such evils can be eliminated without introducing worse ones. Caribou may be spared the pain of wolves, or Inuits, but the consequent population explosion will lead to overgrazing, disease, famine and a population crash.[13] Ritchie would be ill-advised to interfere too much in the relations of prey and predators: but it does not follow that we are thereby entitled to inflict whatever suffering we please on our kindred. We should surely only inflict as much as is necessary for the fairly quick reduction, with high probability, of the total sum of suffering (a sum calculated on the basis of the amount of individual distress and the number of individuals distressed, though it is not obvious how this calculation is to be performed). How could this justify the capture, imprisonment, deprivation and slaughter of sentient creatures for merely gastronomic ends? Killing, itself, of course, would not necessarily be an evil, nor the infliction of suffering under circumstances that most people would think unjust if the victims were human.

Our ordinary moral code, criticised but not yet defeated by utilitarians, would wish to set up barriers against the use of humans for utilitarian advantage. Even if a particular action against the interests and wishes of a given man would result in an overall advantage to the common good, we do not consider that the man should be victimised without his consent (or even, sometimes, with it). We may be happier to avoid a massive disadvantage (which is not the same as a mere failure to obtain an advantage) to the commonwealth by imposing costs on an individual, but even here there is a standing intuition that the victim deserves compensation for his loss, that no one individual or class of individuals should be permanent victims, that some costs are too high. Some things should not be done even if they are advantageous. Some things should not be done even if not to do them is disadvantageous. Individual humans have a right not to cooperate: just as utilitarianism advances from egoistic hedonism to the realisation that pleasures are goods and pains are evils whoever has them, so the rights theorist allows that every agent has as much right as the utilitarian engineer to determine what shall be. The utilitarian has no right to overrule the judgment of his potential victims: they have rights of autonomy.

In this non-utilitarian setting, can we justify a distinction between rights not to be oppressed and rights to be protected? If the goal of our actions is to be the minimising of violated rights, then we cannot, nor can we rule out the possibility that it may be right to violate someone's rights in order to reduce the number of violated rights. This is surely to lose the point of having rights at all. If we follow Nozick's suggestion that rights are side-constraints, we may do better. 'The side-constraint view forbids you to violate those moral constraints in the pursuit of your goals'.[14] We ought not to injure, enslave or kill an individual right-bearer even if the commonwealth would, as we suppose, profit by these acts. We ought not to violate rights even to prevent the violation of rights.

We may not be entirely ready to agree that even human animals have such powerful rights. But if we do, it seems difficult to see any plausible reason why non-human animals might not also have them. It might be urged that non-human animals do not offer rival judgments of what ought to be done with as much claim to be enacted as the utilitarian engineer's. But in any sense in which many *human* animals present a rival programme, non-human animals may do so too. Rights of autonomy do not rest on the possession of a philosophically articulated moral system, but simply on having desires and preferences for an outcome perhaps different from the utilitarian ideal. If human animals have such (side-constraint) rights of autonomy, so do many non-human animals. And in that case Ritchie's argument may not convince us. We ought not to torment mice because mice have a right not to be tormented: a right that involves more than the intrinsic evil of their suffering, and which is not to be balanced against other evils. But equally we ought not to rescue the mice by restraining and thereby tormenting the cats (though we might surely bell the cat without undue injury?). We ought not to do evil that good may come, when the evil is a matter of violating the rightful autonomy of our victims.

It appears therefore that neither utilitarians nor side-constraint theories need allow Ritchie's *reductio*. On a utilitarian view, animal pains and pleasures must be taken into moral consideration. Our increase of their pains can be halted without serious costs; the pains of predation cannot usually be alleviated without making matters worse. On a side-constraint view we ought not to violate animal rights but are under no obligation always to prevent such violations. On neither view are animal 'rights' rendered absurd, whether the rights consist only in the requirement that their distresses be entered in the moral reckoning, or more seriously in a prima facie bar against utilitarian or other exploitation.

Unfortunately, these solutions do not work, or do not work satisfactorily. For Henry Salt and his fellow believers were not concerned only to refrain from animal torture themselves. They wished, as their predecessors in Parliament had wished, to restrain others from animal torture. Kleinig has remarked, in passing, that 'if we do not wish to ascribe rights to animals it is . . . because we do not consider their welfare interests important enough to justify securing them by force'.[15] But British law and other legal systems already embody the principle that the welfare interests of (some) animals do justify the use of force. It has not been true for over a century that people may do just what they please with 'their' animals. The fact that what would otherwise be illegal cruelty is permitted if performed under a licence granted under the act of 1876, while readying the creature to be killed and eaten, or in the course of hunting,[16] can be explained either by basing this legislation on moralistic grounds (it is not the animal's distress we regret but the human animal's goals), or more plausibly by recognising that we have not applied the realisation that 'animals have rights' at all consistently. But though our legislation is confused and inadequate, it does mark a readiness to enforce the welfare interests of the non-human.

When the first relevant legislation was being pushed through Parliament[17] there were clearly costs to be borne by drovers, farmers, hansom-cab drivers, and slaughterers. Their pleasures were sometimes diminished, their pains (for a time) increased. Of course, the end result was such as to be desirable on any 'reasonable' utilitarian calculation, but the route to that end was doubtless often difficult. So also was the route to the desirable end of abolishing the slave trade. Can the pleasures and problems of those engaged in an improper activity be reckoned into the utilitarian calculation on just the same terms as the pains of their victims? How could such utilitarianism avoid the problem of 'utility monsters', who derive greater pleasure from sadistic oppression than their victims lose, and who would suffer more from restraint than their victims suffer from tyranny?[18] If such considerations should deter us from enforcing the welfare interests of mice against cats, or caribou against Inuit, then it ought to have deterred the reformers from enforcing the rights of dogs, cats, horses and cattle against those who profited from their pains. At the least, even if the calculation which determined that, all things considered, it was worth forbidding some current practices, this conclusion would not match the moral seriousness of the reformers' case, which was not that there were possible worlds with a better pleasure–pain balance, but that there were some things that we should not do.

Utilitarianism is perhaps not the best basis upon which to demand better treatment for our kindred (or anything much else), but if it is right to bring about the pains consequent upon a successful reform movement in the name of an eventual improvement in the general good, then it is not out of the question that we should also bring about the pains involved in an over-all regulation of the relations of prey and predator. If slaughterers and circus managers should be restrained, then maybe cats should be as well. If the cost of restraining non-human predators are reckoned too high, perhaps the reformers should have reckoned the costs of restraining people to be too high as well.

Dissatisfaction with the inadequacies of common utilitarian theory may lead us to conclude that there are some pleasures I have no right to demand, and some pains I have no right to be spared. We ought not to take pleasure in another's pain, and any pleasure we do take cannot be held to compensate for that pain. These rules of casuistry are part of ordinary moral reasoning, and may help to make a difference between the non-human and the human predator. We do not violate anyone's rights in preventing them from violating another's rights when they could do otherwise, for no one has a right to violate another's rights. In restraining them from such assaults we ought not to violate the rights they do have (broadly, to decent treatment and happiness according to their kind), but if we can restrain them without such a violation we ought to do so. A human animal is done no violence if required not to oppress his kindred, for such oppression is no necessary part of his life. Non-human animals, very often, are obliged to oppress others if they are to live at all or to live in happiness according to their kind. We cannot be obliged to defend their prey against them if to do so is to violate their rights. They need to kill: we, very often, don't. In Plutarch's words, their killing is for sustenance and ours for relish.[19] Henry Salt, similarly, insisted that his principle was not to outlaw killing but only unnecessary killing, killing inessential to the agent's life. A wolf needs to kill and should not always be restrained from doing so: we in the developed West clearly need, at least, to kill far less than we do. Farmers and furriers alike have a tendency to claim that their activity is as much 'a part of nature' as the wolf's, but it is certainly not true that, as human activities or as activities of civilised persons, they are the products of natural necessity.

But why is necessity a proper justification? Why, if 'one must live', is that a reason for allowing predators to kill? If creatures have a right to life, then they ought not to be killed: why then is the predator not doing something that ought not to happen? Why should the stronger's needs be paramount? Why should our necessity give us a right to kill when our victim's equal necessity does not give him a right not to be killed? We may restrain predators when to do so involves no violation of right, but do predators have any right to go on living if they can only do so at another's expense?

WHY NOT DEFEND MICE?

If we cannot seriously doubt that animal suffering is an evil, nor that we ought to do our best to limit it; if we cannot doubt that non-humans may have rights of autonomy, rights to live their lives out according to their kind, and a corresponding claim on such help as we can justly give, then we cannot · rule out the possibility that we may have a duty to help prey-animals. Why should we not defend victims against their oppressors?

Can we avoid Ritchie's *reductio* by denying that it is *ad absurdum*? What is wrong with the conclusion that we might indeed be required to defend the weaker party? Is his complaint that this would be very difficult? To this we might justly reply that this is no more than Cornford's Wedge: 'that you should not act justly now for fear of raising expectations that you will act still more justly in the future – expectations which you are afraid you will not have the courage to satisfy'.[20] It is sometimes easy to act rightly, and sometimes not. Should we omit the easy right actions merely because we would find it too difficult to do the difficult ones? Our failure to help the human victims of earthquake and famine to the utmost of our ability can hardly license us to create still more disasters. Ritchie might be claiming that one who fails to do what his professed principles require except when it is easy can hardly speak with authority when condemning others' compromises. The point is indeed a standard one: anyone who speaks against animal experimentation, fur-trapping, or circuses is open to an obvious *tu quoque* as long as he himself helps to finance the factory farm. It is a just retort, but one who makes it, as I have pointed out in a passage fiercely denounced as self-righteous by reviewers who have not troubled to read it, should remember that we are all, variously and uneasily, in rebellion against our own principles.[21] Our admitted failures do not require us to deny that some of our duties are quite easy.

Perceived difficulty, in any case, may not betoken a mere failure on our part. It might be said that though we should, in the abstract, defend prey against predators, any realistic attempt to perform this abstract duty would grossly interfere with our performance of our other duties. There is a limit to the positive action any of us can take. Merely to abstain from flesh-foods, cosmetics and unnecessary medicaments is not generally an enterprise that diverts energy from other goals. Veganism, in the present state of society, perhaps does; and even vegetarianism, as both Buddhist and Christian missionaries have concluded, may interfere with the performance of one's mission under some circumstances.[22] Most of us, not being wandering preachers, can be vegetarians quite easily. Some of us can be vegans. But very few of us can wholeheartedly devote ourselves to the defence of mice.

Ritchie's argument does better if he is seen to be saying that defending mice would be not merely difficult, but wrong. If a mouse has rights, we ought not to let him be tormented by a cat; but it is not the case that we ought not to let him be tormented, so a mouse has no rights. But why is it not the case that we ought not to let him be tormented? Presumably we do not have that obligation because we have an obligation to let the *cat* live a natural life after her kind. If mice have a right to life, so do cats.

But what sort of *reductio* is this? All this shows is that prima facie rights conflict: where they do, one right may defeat another, either because it is more important or because the winner can bring other rights into the game. If two humans have an equal right to life I may still save my wife with justice because she has additional rights against me. Such conflicts do not prove that the creatures concerned have no rights: how could they? Ritchie cannot plausibly argue that we should not describe animals as having rights because to do so would commit us to doing them grievous harm. If it is wrong to cause them grievous harm, they have rights. Would it sound plausible to argue that we should not speak of human animals' having rights because we thereby commit ourselves to interfering injuriously with the internal affairs of other nations and tribes? We are perhaps more cautious than Ritchie in rushing to defend 'human rights' at whatever cost, but our recognition of the likely costs is itself an acknowledgement that humans have rights. So also 'animals'.

THE BIOLOGICAL BACKGROUND

Before considering what rights human animals may have if non-humans have any, can we clarify the appeal to 'nature'? Many vegetarians have laid stress on the fundamentally frugivorous nature of our species, insinuating that flesh-eating was a relatively late corruption to which we are only imperfectly adapted. It was perhaps a natural response to the converse claim that 'nature intends us to eat flesh': a natural response and not an entirely ill-founded one. Gorillas and chimpanzees are chiefly plant-eaters, though chimpanzees will also eat such small animals as they catch. The enormous popular appeal of fantasies about 'Man the Mighty Hunter' should certainly be corrected by a reminder that most modern hunter-gatherers get almost all their food from plants (though eggs and small animals may be gathered up as well), and certainly eat nothing like the amount of flesh consumed in the developed West. We know practically nothing about our hominid ancestors, but what little we can guess gives as good a case for thinking they were grain-eaters as that they were predators.[23] We certainly know that human beings can survive well and happily without eating flesh or drinking non-human milk: more healthily, in some respects, than omnivores.

The picture of 'the murderous ape, our ancestor' has been well mocked by Elaine Morgan, quoting Robert Ardrey on the baboon.

> 'He is submissive as a truck, as inoffensive as a bull-dozer, as gentle as a power-driven lawn-mower. He has predatory inclinations and enjoys nothing better than killing and devouring the new-born fawns of the delicate gazelle. And he will steal anything...' And so on. While [Ardrey's] male reader avidly polishes his spectacles and thinks: 'Yeah, that's me all right. Tell me more about the bull-dozer and how I ravaged that delicate gazelle'.[24]

As Morgan observes, it is clearly very attractive to some people (mostly males, or mostly American males, perhaps) to think that 'all that power and passion and brutal virility is seething within him, just below the skin, only barely held in check by the conscious control of his intellect'. But there is every reason to doubt the diagnosis. E. O. Wilson remarks that any Martian zoologists might well conclude that 'we are among the more pacific mammals as measured by serious assaults or murders per individual per unit time, even when our episodic wars are averaged in'.[25] The wish to think ourselves predators also occurs in the form of supposing it important to be at the 'top' of the food chain, though that is obviously the narrowest and most uncertain perch of all, a quite unsuitable one for so huge a population of hominids.[26]

It is perfectly reasonable, then, to insist that the human animal is calmer, more companionable, and less committed to a grossly predatory way of life than some have supposed. The 'natural' life is a baseline against which we can gauge unhealthiness and unhappiness, a moral norm, and the life 'natural' to our kind need not be a predatory nor a violent one. But if 'natural living according to one's kind' is what we should be engaged in and encouraging, then the cat should presumably be encouraged to catch mice. We ought to consider animals in a kindly fashion because it is part of our normative nature so to do. We ought to be kindly, but for the sake of human life and society, not because of animals' rights. Cats should not be kindly. And once this position is taken as our own we may consider ourselves justified in doing as other animals do, employing creatures of another kind to sustain and improve their own lives.

This attempt to make 'natural living' the proper criterion of moral health is supported by a naive assumption that 'whatever is, is right'. If animals behave in a certain way without obvious signs of divine disapproval, it must be all right. If it were wrong to have sex in religious sanctuaries the gods wouldn't let animals do so.[27] If fish eat fish, so may we. This approach is often associated with the claim that whereas animals respect their conspecifics they do not respect those of another kind. From this it is deduced that we are under obligation only to honour humans, not those of another kind. It is natural to be speciesist.

25

Even if we accept that non-human animals are good exemplars in this (and why should we not rather conclude that is in *our* nature not to be speciesist?), the data are debatable. 'The ethics of "speciesism" has no proper basis in evolutionary biology'.[28]

First, we are wrong to think that non-human animals always respect their conspecifics. The groups within which they live are much more limited: conspecific strangers are rejected, and of small account. When Zeno urged that 'we should regard all men as our fellow countrymen and fellow citizens, and there should be one life and one order like that of a single flock on a common pasture feeding together under common law',[29] he was openly urging us to feel in a way that as a rule we do not. Our natural loyalties and affections are directed to those of our own flock: humanism is an attempt to stretch our sympathies beyond their natural reach. We are not likely to have been equipped, by natural selection, with any impulse to seek the good of our species, any more than has any other animal kind.

Species are interbreeding populations, and formed very often by the preferences and pursuits of individual organisms. But conspecifics are united by mutual antagonism much more than mutual affection. Territorial rivalry is between members of the same species, and the owner of a territory is concerned to exclude conspecifics, and not true aliens: it is conspecifics, after all, who are rivals for food, mate and nesting place. It is relatives who are most in danger from mammalian aggression, and 'murder is far more common and hence "normal" in many vertebrate species than in man'.[30] We cannot live with our kindred, but neither can we live without them. Where aggression is so high as to exclude affection, new species, new breeding populations, will eventually form out of the old. If we are willing to follow the Stoics in recognising that conspecifics not of our local group are nonetheless worthy of our respect, it is no less natural to extend our concern a little further.

Sexual affection and family affection have doubtless been consolidated in the genetic tradition because they facilitate the multiple transmission of just such traits. It does not follow that only conspecifics benefit from them. Altruism, self-sacrifice for another's benefit, will be stabilised in the gene-pattern if those benefiting from the sacrifice are likely to be carrying the same genes. It does not follow that the altruist only sacrifices himself for those who are in fact his relatives. As long as the beneficiary has the properties which are usually associated with close relatives (such as appearance, smell, familiarity) the altruist's self-sacrifice is no offence to evolutionary logic. There are insects 'who have broken the code of the social insects' and live companionably in ant-colony or bee-hive.[31] Cuckoos exploit the parental impulses of other birds. The domestication of the dog possibly began in mutual exploitation,[32] but has long since progressed to a mutual socialisation: of men as the dogs' pack-leaders, of dogs as 'honorary human beings'. Creatures of different species can find mutually advantageous modes of life,[33] and can feel affection and loyalty to their social partners.

In short it is natural (i.e. it is almost bound to happen) that we should in general feel a primary loyalty to our most immediate families, even when those families are made of creatures not all of one species. A rhetoric of animal rights is an attempt paralleling the Stoics, to extend our nexus of associations beyond that local group. Justice begins with parental feeling, concern for the small and defenceless creatures put into our hands,[34] a concern that can also be awoken for creatures of another kind. If natural law is properly defined as *'quod natura omnia animalia docuit'*[35] (what nature has taught all animals), then one of its principal dictates is that parents should care for their children, or those socialised as such.

LOCAL ATTACHMENTS AND EARTH HOUSEHOLD

The drive to extend our concern has been expressed in rhetoric drawn from ecological science, talk of 'the land' as a community of which we are a part.[36] Passmore has criticised this:

> Ecologically, no doubt, men form a community with plants, animals, soil in the sense that a particular life cycle will involve all of them. But if it is essential to a community that the members of it have common interests and recognize mutual obligations then men, plants, animals and soil do *not* form a community.[37]

This seems an unnecessarily rigid concept of a community, and such as to exclude (deliberately?) all but rational adult humans from membership. It does not indeed follow from common membership of a community, a network of relationships, that members' interests never conflict, nor that there is any way of settling disputes in a manner recognized as just by all participants. What exists ecologically is not, and probably never will be, a moral community with agreed rules of procedure. Neither is the human species 'a single flock upon a common pasture under one law', and probably never will be. But even if there is never a World State, and even though such a State would legislate for humans who were incapable of participating in its decision-making process (and hence not strictly citizens of that State), the Stoics were right to remind us that we can enter into social relationships with other people, have some common interests, and manifold sympathies. So also, *mutatis mutandis*, are advocates of Earth's Household.

In the household of earth and heaven, Aristotle taught, the free men have more responsibilities than those incapable of moral deliberation.[38] This is the sort of intuition on which Darling's ethics of 'noblesse oblige' is raised: that we are, within limits, able both to minimise our own destructive impact on the world, and to help creatures cope with natural disaster (Darling 1970).

27

For though it does seem harsh, or even silly, to ask of us that we should protect creatures against predators, it is clearly not felt to be extraordinary that we should take steps to preserve wild things from flood, famine and pestilence, even if we also reckon that the vital interests of our own immediate households have first call on our resources. Conservationists have made stumbling attempts to justify this intuition in terms of the preservation of beauty, or potentially useful resources, or less anthropocentrically by talk of the rights of whole species. This second sort of justification has been held to license the killing or disturbance of individual animals, as though a population of animals were something other than those very animals taken together. A more satisfactory solution may be to say the individual animals do indeed have some right to our assistance but that these rights *require* our action only when the lives of many creatures are in question. We do not step outside our borders even to defend or avenge the rape or murder of a *human* being, even when local authorities are doing nothing – but we may take that dangerous step, at last, if very many are being raped or murdered without recourse.

Rights are rights to a 'natural' existence, a life not seriously maimed by factors outside the usual conditions of mortal life. Animals (human and non-human) have some right to be protected from unusual dangers (if we can protect them). But they may perhaps be expected to endure (as may we), usual dangers, even of a predatory kind, which could not easily or ever be eliminated. It is not absurd to help them even in such cases, but there are bound to be limits to the dutifulness even of decent aristocrats.

Stoic theory offers us the ideal of the World State in which men have rights just as men, that is as citizens or subjects of the World State (though it is far from clear that Stoics would really have included literally *all* human beings as equals). But this ideal is far from actual, and it may sometimes be wise to remember the rights we have as, say, Britons, rather than our *human* rights. Nations which think themselves potential founders of the World State may reasonably be subject to suspicion, for the thought encourages them to interfere in the doings of other communities whenever their moral opinions are sufficiently outraged. It may be that a World State is too high a price to pay for the universal realisation of human rights.[39] It may be similarly that Earth's Household could only be actualised by massive interference in the ways and preferences of our separated kindred. 'There is not a beast upon the earth, nor a bird that flies, but is a nation like to you'.[40] In the absence of an agreed international law, agreed between all the nations of the earth, we should perhaps attend to the regulation of our own immediate households and not seek to actualise our conception of animal rights throughout the world.

Just as Burke preferred the rights of Englishmen to the rights of men just as such, so we may maintain and seek to extend the rights of, as it were, British beasts. Some non-human animals are members, though not citizens,

28

of our immediate society, and have rights in law to our care and protection. They pay for those rights by the advantages we gain from them, and should certainly in natural justice be paid far more (or else pay far less). Some advantages we cannot seek from them without violating their rights as members of our society. Wild animals, to which condition those animals whom we cannot employ without injustice should be allowed to return, have rights not to be mistreated, but have no necessary call on our resources – though where their danger is great, we may have a moral obligation that passes beyond the law. In short, wild things are like Nozick's independents, who have hired no protection agency: 'The dominant protection agency's domain does *not* extend to quarrels of non-clients among themselves'.[41]

The agency, like any other moral agent, may have a moral responsibility to protect those unjustly treated (within the limits I have already sketched), but it should not use this as an excuse to extend its hegemony, nor interfere where there seems to be a settled relationship. But though the agency should not necessarily defend baboons against chimpanzees, it is bound to defend its own clients, human and non-human, against the wild things. And since it thereby denies the independents the right to settle things by their own methods, it must compensate them at least by protecting them against its own clients. 'Undoubtedly, the least expensive way to compensate the independents would be to supply them with protective services to cover those situations of conflict with the paying customers of the protective agency'.[42]

Wild things should be protected against us and against our non-human clients, because we insist on being protected against them. It is as well not to seek to protect them against each other, because if we do we shall easily slip into thinking that they owe us something for which they should pay. Where there is massive and unusual danger we should act; where it is our own clients who are the danger we may at least try to mute that danger. The rules are not very different from those we should apply to the troubles of human independents.

None of this is to say that the claims of wild things are of less importance than the slightest claim of members of our own society. On the contrary, we should not go to war against the other 'nations' unless for the most important of our interests, and perhaps not even them. The rights of wild things are fewer than the rights of those socialised as members of our society, but they are entirely real. 'If I say that I am more interested in preventing the slaughter of large whales than I am in improving housing conditions for people, I am likely to shock some of my friends',[43] but those who are shocked have been deluded by the rhetoric of humanism into thinking that the comfort of our own conspecifics should always count for more than the very life of our more distant kin. Neither the moral paradigm of Earth's Household nor the legal, of the minimal state, allows the claim.

My examination of Ritchie's argument has taken me a long way round. As always, there is more to be said. But my present conclusion is that non-human animals may have rights, even rights of welfare, without any absurd implication. For Ritchie's conclusion either does not follow, or follows in the abstract but not in practice, or is not absurd. Our clients we should protect, and sometimes even non-clients, but for the most part we should leave well enough alone. We have done enough remaking.

4

AWARENESS AND
SELF-AWARENESS[1]

People sometimes tell me that they do not believe in morality. As they are usually well-behaved and conscientious people, who keep their word and give to those in need, this is puzzling. What they turn out to mean is that they do not believe in 'objective moral facts' that must constrain our serious preferences. It is irritating for a philosopher that so many people assume that all philosophers believe in such 'moral facts' and that without them moral discourse founders. Neither is true: the existence (or not) of objective moral truths is a metaphysical question to which many answers can be given; it does not bear directly on our ordinary moral debates. Whether they exist or not we can still discuss what is to be done.

Again: there are philosophers who have doubted whether the material world exists. But the doubt is not a neurotic hesitation as to the firmness of the earth beneath, nor a lunatic conviction that we can walk through walls. It is a metaphysical question, and the answers to it do not bear directly on our ability to distinguish between real and phantasmal elephants.

I could continue the list. What needs to be remembered is that the metaphysical and broadly empirical levels of argument are distinct. Metaphysical questions cannot be answered by empirical methods, because any empirical observations or practices are compatible with any of the standard metaphysical alternatives. This is not to say that such questions are unimportant or even unanswerable.

And so to my topic. We can ordinarily distinguish those things in the world that we call 'aware' and those we don't. A sleeping man is not aware of what is going on around him, or not very aware. Anaesthetists discriminate quite carefully. Some things, like stones, are never aware; others, like the higher animals, often are. With some uneasiness we can stretch the concept to cover primitive robots, that respond discriminatingly to their surroundings, but machines are usually the plainest cases of things that are not aware. We test for awareness by seeing how the entity responds to what we perceive to be going on. But of course it has long been clear that, in a sense, the observations are bound to be incomplete: we cannot 'directly' sense another creature's awareness, cannot enter into its being aware to confirm that there is such a thing. It has been said that everything that we can sense being done (moving limbs, blinking eyes, uttering sounds) could be replicated by a machine (defined as something that is not aware). Insofar as we could be deceived in attributing awareness on the basis of what we sense, we have only 'really' sensed those motions. How then could we argue to a real awareness 'behind' the motions? Only if I am acquainted with a conjunction of smoke and fire can I argue from smoke to an unseen fire: how can I argue from seen motions to unseen awareness if I have never seen awareness and motion so conjoined? If the argument is based on an analogy with my own case it is a shockingly weak one. Accordingly, let us (or rather me) regress to solipsism.

I hope the line of argument is familiar. Philosophers have usually debated it in the context of doubt about the existence of other human minds, but the arguments involved bear directly on the wider issue of animal awareness. Fortunately, there is a lot that is wrong with it. First of all, notice that it is exactly parallel to the standard argument for the non-existence of material objects: all that we directly perceive (direct perception is what is required if my seeming to sense something is to necessitate that thing's being there) are phenomena, appearances, colours and shapes, and sounds and textures. At best the material objects cause these appearances, but as we have no experience of such causality (even less than in the mental case) we have no right to posit such non-phenomenal causes of phenomena. There have been thinkers bold enough to take the step to pure solipsistic phenomenalism, and to define all the terms they use purely operationally, in respect of the phenomena they could expect to perceive, notably the physicist P. W. Bridgman, for whom all science was his own private science (Bridgman 1936). But most of us continue to use the realistic language into which we have been initiated, and to believe, if pressed, that there really are material objects with at least the structural properties that we sense. To say that all such objects are, metaphysically, phantoms is to draw on an empirical concept as a metaphor. Similarly, to say that the very objects we ordinarily reckon aware are 'really' empty automata is to venture on metaphysics.

Second, all such arguments rest upon the concealed premise that our proper method should be to start from what is essentially indubitable – not merely what I, being what I am, cannot doubt, but what could not be denied without self-contradiction – and add as few entities or principles as are needed for consistency. The strength of the arguments is precisely that these methodological rules seem self-evidently rational. Unfortunately, it has proved impossible to justify these rules on their own terms: they are not essentially indubitable, and the history of Cartesian philosophy has convinced most professional philosophers that if we try to start where Descartes did, from the luminous self-evidence of our own existence, we shall not only never get anywhere else, but will have great difficulty even formulating our starting conviction. We can never get anywhere else, because we need Descartes' arguments for God and His truthfulness to bridge the gap between our convictions and the truth, and those arguments rely on premises that Descartes cannot validly affirm.[2] It is more important, however, that the starting point is flawed.

The arguments against other mental or material existence that I have sketched require that there are things that I directly perceive, that we can speak of pure egocentred consciousness and hence fail to infer the existence of a non-phenomenal world. But the whole language in which this argument is conducted is a public one geared to publicly identifiable things. I can be mistaken as to whether something is genuinely red, genuinely middle C, genuinely silky or warm. If I claim, to save my credit, that in calling something 'red' I mean only that it strikes me as what now I call 'red', I am progressively eliminating any content from my claim: for me to say 'this is red' means no more than 'I'm now inclined to say "red"'. There are no criteria by which I could be mistaken, and that is to say that I haven't said anything, for to speak at all is to enter into a rule-governed domain. A wholly private language – I do not mean one that I have made up and you could learn – is one without rules or identifiable references, and that is no language at all. Correspondingly the 'ego' which Cartesian thinkers have reckoned the most secure of entities, the self separable from body and social role, turns out to be a non-entity. 'I' is a term drawing attention to the speaker. If I point to myself, I point to this body, not at some non-spatial privately cognisable mind. (For an accessible account of these arguments see Kenny 1973 and also Midgley 1978.)

Our language, and the fundamental context of all our enquiries, is a public one. We do not begin from an indubitable certainty of self, and then find it impossible to ground a belief in other minds and bodies on that self-knowledge. We begin from the social network into which we have been growing from childhood. We perceive public objects, and communicate with other minds. We can make mistakes, but they are found to be mistakes within that public realm.

This does not make the metaphysical question senseless, the question whether this public framework is really veridical. But that is not a question that can be asked within the framework, and there is no reason to insist that it be answered by Cartesian methods. Our methodological rule has often got to be 'Believe it until it is proved wrong' and not 'Disbelieve it until it is proved right' (see Chisholm 1957).[3]

The sceptical arguments, you remember, suggested that what we really and directly see are phenomena, or else (illegitimately) mere motions of material bodies. But why should we accept this restriction? It is certainly not what we expect our children to see, and someone who really was aware of nothing else than the motions of material bodies would have a very odd reputation. We learn, perhaps we instinctively recognise, a great many behaviour patterns: we see our mother's smile, not merely a mechanical lifting of the mouth's corners. We recognise and respond to anger, affection, lust or plaintiveness. I can as truly say that I see my son's anger as that I see his body's motions: if I insist that I only directly see certain coloured shapes in motion, then both his body and his mind are on the far side of an unbridgeable gulf. But in fact his mind and body are just the sort of things that I do, ordinarily, see; that is what seeing is, being acquainted with entities publicly identifiable and discussable, through the medium of vision. The words we use get their meanings from just this sort of situation. Because I can recognise his anger I can teach him the formulae which in this society can accompany and encapsulate what he is feeling; because he can recognise my anger, and my recognition of his, he can grasp what I am talking about.

There is no hope of science's either establishing or subverting this framework of mutual discourse and endeavour. Without the framework science is impossible, for scientists are engaged in a cooperative endeavour which requires that they be able to recognise each other's intentions and moods and meanings. If they allowed themselves the heady metaphysical doubt that maybe no one was using the words in the same sense as they, science would collapse, Bridgman's operationalism notwithstanding. In using our ordinary framework scientists are not indulging an illicit animism, postulating superfluous minds over and above the observed motions: they are describing in the most direct way possible to us just what is going on. D. O. Hebb recounts that an attempt at a zoo to replace ordinary mentalistic description by purely material modes foundered just because the zoo-keepers could not satisfactorily communicate about their charges without using terms like 'nervous', 'hates human beings', 'affectionate but tricky' and so on (Hebb, 1946, Matthews, 1978).

For the framework which enables us to recognise and describe human behaviour (including our own) also extends to non-humans. It is possible indeed that we have been selected, in part, for our capacity as hunters and agriculturalists to form ideas of the character and likely conduct of our dogs and cattle. Indeed this is quite possibly the natural root of our concern for animals, and our moral confusions on the topic – for we have had to understand and care for them in order to be able to get a profit out of their deaths. T. O. Ingold, writing on the Lapps and their reindeer, points to the understanding the Lapps have of their reindeers' character and likely conduct as a necessary part of the as-it-were compact between the two groups (Ingold 1974). We can understand them. The fact that we also make mistakes proves no more than the fact that we also make mistakes about merely material objects. We find out our mistakes, in both cases, by learning better. We may find, for example, that a bird has much less concern than we thought about her eggs as prospective young, for she will ignore her own eggs in favour of larger, or even artificial eggs. Their ways are not always ours. But there is no a priori reason to suppose that their ways are wholly undiscoverable. Far too many students of animal behaviour equate the strange (to us) with the stupid, or the predictable with the unfeeling.

By interpreting mentalistic descriptions in this way, as shorthand for the behaviour to be expected, I may seem to be ignoring something of importance: namely, the sheer inwardness of the mental. Surely we can describe a machine as 'cranky' or 'irritable' or 'knowing its master's touch', and may be able to manage our machines better if we treat them as if they had genuine intentions, genuine feelings, although we do not seriously think they do. That a chimpanzee is likely to bite you may not, it might be said, mean that she is now feeling anything. Is my behavioural account of character and motivation a covertly behaviouristic one, that says there is nothing of importance 'behind the scenes'?

If it is, it is so for everyone, us humans included. But I don't think it is. My point has been that ordinary discourse precisely distinguishes things that merely move and things that behave: 'behaviour' is only possible for a creature with an inward dimension, with its own real perception of the world; in Uexkuell's terminology, an *Umwelt* (Uexkuell 1957). Within that framework we do not see merely material motions, but rather the embodiment of character and feeling in a material mode.

Nonetheless it is worth emphasising that inwardness which, as I think, we have the equipment to recognise. It is a thing so close to us that we have difficulty spelling out what exactly it is: roughly, there is something it is like to be a cow, as there is not to be a tractor. Tractors don't have points of view, cows do: there is a way things look to a cow. Now I can agree that we are unlikely ever to guess just how things look to a cow: obviously, they wouldn't look like that to us unless we were cows. Any guesses we make can be checked only against their success in predicting what the cow will do, and all the cow's overt behaviour may be such as to allow several different pictures of the cow's world-view. Things may be better than they sound because we have theoretical assumptions as to what sort of creature the cow is, and therefore discount many of the theoretically possible world-views. The case isn't really very different from the difficulties faced by physicists: notoriously, observations never wholly determine us to one particular theory of things as they are. To reduce the number of possible theories to manageable numbers we employ theoretical assumptions that cannot themselves be deduced from rationally self-evident principles. How, if at all, those assumptions can be grounded is a topic too large to discuss here.

I have been playing with the categories of the mental and the merely material. Nothing I have said is to imply that material objects can't have mental properties. I am not asking you to believe that there are objects called minds in addition to those called bodies (though there may be). My point is that some material entities are rightly described in mentalistic terms. Stones can't be bored or cross or joyful; dogs and pigs and cattle can. To say that all the variety of entities with which we are acquainted are really just like stones, that there is only an appearance of another dimension, is grotesque. We can no longer believe, if we take recent philosophical advances seriously, that the 'self' is the only point where awareness in the rich, subjective sense joins the material world. Such a supposition would destroy my very idea of a material world, and of my own identity: I am a continuing bodily presence among others in a world whose idea is socially maintained.

But there is a difficulty. The mental, in the sense of that inner dimension of which each of us is indeed directly aware, may not be the ground of our knowledge, but it is real. Unfortunately for naturalistic evolutionary theory it appears to be wholly unnecessary. Given our knowledge, such as it is, of how living things, as complex kinetic systems, are replicated, there seems no reason to expect that an object with an inner life would be better replicated than one without. Of course it may be useful to organisms to have internal models of what is likely to occur, but such modelling is not the same as inner life, only a part of the internal milieu which modifies the motions of the bodies concerned. There seems no need for consciousness in evolutionary biology. Indeed it is very difficult to connect material and mental modes at all: if we accept that atoms are not themselves aware then the awareness of a complex creature is a strictly emergent property. It just so happens that when you put atoms together just so then you get awareness: maybe that is satisfactory, but we are usually inclined to seek rather more than a bare constant conjunction in nature – we want the newly apparent property to be explicable in terms of the old, to be more of the same, to be the sum of whatever composes it. The explosion of two lumps of uranium when they are put together is only apparently emergent; really the two lumps were doing just what the larger one now does, only rather more slowly. So the awareness of a complex organism ought, we fee!, to be a similar resultant, and either atoms are already conscious or else consciousness is only a misleading label for neural impulse (Nagel 1979).[4]

There are many respectable positions on this issue. Interestingly, there are structural parallels between this case and the problem about morality from which I began this chapter. Are there moral or mental facts? If there are, are they different from empirical facts, or can we identify the moral rightness of an act with its evolutionary success, the mental inwardness with neural impulse? My own feeling is that neither identification can be made. Moral facts cannot be the same as empirical ones, for it always makes sense to deny that, for example, it is morally obligatory to propagate one's kind.[5] Similarly, the sheer subjectivity of awareness cannot be identified with any neural impulse, for it is admittedly quite possible, in logic even if not in the actual world, for the one to subsist without the other. The issue is a large one. My object in mentioning it here is to suggest to you that something like panpsychism is a real option: consciousness, if it is here now (and it is), must have been here from the beginning. There are ways, I agree, of evading the conclusion, but they have as many counter-intuitive effects as panpsychism itself.

Returning to the ordinary framework of our enquiries, what can be said of self-awareness? That the animals with which we are most familiar are aware, that they respond and yearn and fear, have characters of their own and a way that the world looks to them, is an established part of our common framework which I can see no non-metaphysical reason to deny. But are they aware of themselves? Recall that self-awareness does not require any awareness of the Self, as a non-empirical entity only contingently linked to the body, as Descartes would have it. Self-awareness is awareness of the being that is aware, the psycho-physical organism that is engaged in doing things in the world.

In discussions of self-awareness animals generally appear only as dummy figures: that is, they are treated as a single homogenous class, all of which we know, without argument, not to be self-aware. It is sometimes, indeed, declared that they 'have no selves', which appears to mean that they have no picture of themselves, no ideal which they acknowledge as their own, no long-term purposes. No 'serious person' would think that rats made choices except, if at all, 'on the basis of the relative expected utilities of the alternatives in terms of simple intrinsic and extrinsic gratifications' (McCall 1977), which means, in English, that rats, as paradigm animals, at best only do what they currently find most attractive. Normal humans, on the other hand, quite often choose what to do on the basis of what is expected of them, or what they prefer themselves to be. Human beings accept commitments over time; they can distinguish their own actions from mere events in the world. It is usually assumed that all these capacities are related to or summed up in our species' particular excellence, rational thought and language.

My own feeling is that 'self-awareness' is far from a simple or a single thing. A self-awareness that requires an ability to use some self-referring expression in a systematic way is clearly beyond all but the higher primates even on a charitable interpretation of the performance of such chimpanzees and gorillas as are marginally competent at American Sign Language. If Washoe is correctly reported as having identified her own image in a mirror as 'Washoe: that's me' the root of language is there. But as far as I know it has not yet been claimed that any Ameslan ape has managed the transformations between 'I bit you' and 'You were bitten by me' and 'Someone bit you and I am that someone' and so forth. I see no good reason either to exaggerate or to minimise the apes' achievements. We are the heirs of millennia of selection for linguistic ability; that they can manage as much as they can is a reminder of what must have preceded human language, a preverbal grasp of situations and connections. There have been those who deny the possibility of such a preverbal, practical grasp of what must follow from what, or what is going on, but if this were so it would be impossible ever to acquire a language at all.

But can there be any non-verbal ways of demonstrating an awareness of self? At various levels, yes. First, the creature can demonstrate a capacity to locate him- or herself in the world. This may seem so obvious a requirement for all locomotive creatures as not to need mentioning. But in fact it does not seem that a tick, to use Uexkuell's example, need do this: she has only to sit on a grass-stalk, for up to eighteen years, until the scent of butyric acid pulls her towards a mammal. She does not need to know where she has come from nor where she is going: it doesn't matter – all she has left to do is suck some blood, drop to the ground and lay her eggs. I must emphasise that there are not two mutually exclusive accounts, one that she is enticed by the scent of butyric acid and the other that she is pushed by the chemical properties of that acid: physical causation and goal-directed awareness are not incompatible with each other – witness our own case. But I can agree that the tick's *Umwelt* is a very attenuated one: it is aware of very little, at least, of the things of which we are aware, and can for much of the time be supposed to be a more or less efficient as-it-were machine. Organisms with more to do, which are more aware of what is going on, may well get great advantage from forming a cognitive map of the world, wherein they can locate themselves. They can realise that they are on the fringes of the world they know, can relocate a place from a new direction, though they may show their good sense by being chary of unfamiliar paths. They may identify or respond to things not merely in virtue of what they look like but in virtue of how they were reached, or how they are related to other things. Rats seem particularly adept at learning complex mazes, as might be expected of burrow-dwellers. Primates too display a grasp of the world's stability within which they move, except when they have been maimed by cerebral lesion: one possible interpretation of the behaviour of a brain-damaged rhesus is that she is reduced to seeing things in purely phenomenal, not operational terms (Menzel 1973, Humphreys 1974).

But this level of self-location is not the end. To relocate the same places and things is a great step, but its application at a social level is more important. Philosophers have recognised at least since Hegel that there can be one person only if there are several: we can be persons, beings conscious of our own existence, only if we can identify others as persons, as the same persons from one occasion to another. This indeed is the theme I have been labouring: we find ourselves within a social network. I am told that rats fail to perform this manoeuvre of re-identifying what we take to be the same individual, but treat each other with the superb impartiality of the Stoic moralist. Even a creature which does seem to re-identify other individuals may not be doing quite what we think, but rather responding to a particular manifestation of some universal quality – witness such creatures as do not seem to recognise their mates if some trivial-seeming element is altered by the humorous ethologist. Uexkuell coined the term 'companion', or 'kumpan', for such cases where a creature responds to others by virtue of their current role, without, it seems, forming any concept of the individual creature that takes those roles. Witness a mallard duck that responds protectively to a complaining duckling not of her kind, only to turn and peck at him when he attempts to join her flock. It is worth remarking before we are overcome by pride in human awareness that such 'kumpan' role-fillers are not unknown among our own acquaintance, and that the concept of 'individual' which such a duck lacks need not necessarily be one that an entirely truth-seeking intelligence would require.

Nonetheless, the realisation that this is the very individual who has, say, proved that he can beat me, despite disguise or change of role, is a step toward self-awareness. The sort of example I have in mind is provided by recent work with vervet monkeys: mother vervets not only recognise their own offspring's cry, but identify the mother whose offspring seems to be crying (and do so from the mere sound, not even the sight) (Cherfas 1980). But the real centre of such a self-concept is the degree of commitment and admitted responsibility that the creature displays: the extent of its time-binding faculty. It is probable that most non-humans (and many humans) attempt only locally maximising projects: that is, they prefer immediate gains to long-term gains via immediate losses, except where the crucial evolutionary disadvantages of such short-sightedness have allowed relatively stereotyped behaviour patterns to grow up. Once a particular pattern is begun the creature tends to continue with it even if this involves events that would, in the abstract, count as costs. Experimental psychologists seem to be somewhat surprised that animals can ignore what they would normally find painful when engaged in serious activities like sex, hunting, escaping or play. It would, on the contrary, be very surprising if they didn't. Such behaviour patterns are relatively stereotyped, and are not necessarily engaged in with a view to their natural consequences: humans can marry to have children to have supporters in their old age. Non-humans, it is usually supposed, mate, and then have children, and then do whatever comes next. Birds do not brood to hatch eggs, but just as the thing to do. Wasps do not put paralysed caterpillars with their eggs in order to provide food for their offspring. Their views are much more local (as are ours on most occasions). Once again, do not misunderstand: too many ethologists operate with a wholly misguided dichotomy between intentional action and stereotyped response, concluding from the locally maximising behaviour of most animals that they are merely as-it-were machines. This does not follow: I am not a mere machine because I sometimes engage in mating behaviour without any intention of bringing about the natural consequences of the act. We do not do everything we do merely to obtain something else. Some things we do for their own sakes. The fact that animals are aware, feeling and responsive creatures is not called into question by the playful experiments of ethologists (such as substituting plaster eggs). But their failure, or at least their apparent failure to take account of the long-term consequences of what they do, of what reaches beyond the pattern, does make it difficult to think that they have any strong concept of their own selfhood. Our nearer kin may be closer to us: a young chimpanzee who walks away from a luxury which he, unlike his tribe, has spotted, and so leads them away, returning on his own a little later, does seem to be improvising plans in expectation of a future success. So do those Japanese macaques who relinquish wheat-grains and sand to the sea in order to retrieve more grains than they could have picked up separately. Not a very long-term project certainly, but there is some reason to think that even humans find long-term prudence something of an artificial virtue: hunter-gatherers have no need of it – it is agriculturalists who have had to practice prudence. Once again, by the way, that an act is intentional is not refuted by pointing to the neurological episodes that accompanied it nor to its evolutionary function nor to its general predictability.

Having a longer grasp of our identity we can take up attitudes to our immediate impulses. We do not simply do what we want: sometimes we do not want to want what we do want, and can engineer situations to take us past temptation. We can do more than regret a situation we have brought about: we can rebuke ourselves for having done so. The *New Scientist* reported some time ago that an Ameslan gorilla had expressed her sorrow for having bitten her trainer three days before, she didn't remember why.[6] The claim is sufficiently disputable for me to rest little upon it. But most of us probably find it easy enough to suppose that dogs, say, (but not cats) 'know' when they are doing wrong, or have done wrong – know, that is, when they are headed for trouble, and can sometimes show some effort to restrain themselves. Having a less well-organised structure of preferences than at least some human beings they may be very unstable. The chimpanzee described by Goodall as hesitating between bananas and a desirable mate is instanced by Fromm as showing what would in humans be diagnosed as 'obsessional doubt' (Fromm 1974). A creature that can see several options before her, but lacks the power to devise a stable architectonic structure of desire is probably doomed to violent swings of mood. Oddly, there is an experiment with pigeons which seems to show that even such relatively stupid birds can recognise and avoid temptation. Rachlin and Green (1972) set pigeons to peck at lighted green and red keys. Given the choice of an immediate small reward or a later larger one, they chose the smaller. But given the option of either a ten-second delay and then a choice of immediate small or later large reward, or else a fourteen-second delay and a large reward, they chose, it seems, to put it out of their power to be tempted later by a small reward. Fourteen seconds isn't very long, of course: I don't instance the case as proof of long-term identity, but only as the beginnings of a grasp of one's own central purposes, and aversion to temptation.

Finally, in my analysis of self-awareness, there is the strand which involves seeing ourselves as others see us. To be self-aware is to take the observer's angle on one's own endeavours, and not simply an abstract observer's, but the angle of one's social peers. To understand that I can be the object of another's attentions, that I and they together are of a kind, subject to the same natural and moral laws, is one of the most important roots of science and of morality.

To see that you are another 'I', that we start equal, is vital to our sanity. Presumably only social animals are likely to take this step. Some have argued that it can only really be taken by language-users, equipped to use personal pronouns, but I doubt this: my son for a long time treated 'You' as his name, and of course might have continued to do so if suitably brought up. He would still have needed to know how others might see his actions, needed to know that we are all of a common subjective kind. Vernon Reynolds (1976) has asserted that there is every reason to doubt that animals ever consider how their actions look to others. As he does not name a single one of these multiple reasons, and as it seems to me very unlikely that a social and intelligent animal should be so obtuse I beg leave to doubt the claim. I have discussed this and related matters in *The Nature of the Beast* (Oxford University Press 1981).

In brief, there is reason to think, within the framework of educated assessment and empathy, that animals who live in social groups, with relatively long lives and a need to resist temptation in an environment where purely stereotyped behaviour will be maladaptive, will have some degree of self-awareness. Awareness itself does not have any clear evolutionary rationale, but self-awareness does. It does not 'pay' such aware creatures as do not need to live long and varied lives if they are to leave genetic replicas to have any self-awareness. It does 'pay' aware creatures that need to regulate their actions in accordance with relatively long-term goals and under the eyes of their fellows. Accordingly some non-human animals are self-aware. Attempts to reject this conclusion come down all too often to the blank assertion that 'animals' can't be self-aware. I think we should be readier to recognise that we are not alien monsters. We are terrestrial animals, and everything we do and feel must be something – obviously – that animals of our kind can do and feel. We have specialised in the use of language and of imaginative pictures and stories. We have, with agriculture and industry, obliged ourselves to adopt long-term views of a kind that hunter-gatherers have not needed. No one can reasonably deny our extraordinary capacities, but part of the very self-awareness of which I have spoken is the recognition of a self (even, if you like, a sleeping self) in others. The road to our self-awareness as human beings is to see how we might look to those others. We are all, in Leopold's phrase, 'fellow voyagers in the odyssey of evolution'. Even if there are no moral facts, I at least think that we should remember our strange fellowship, and act accordingly (Leopold, 1966).

5

HUMANS, ANIMALS AND 'ANIMAL BEHAVIOUR'

THE UTILITARIAN AND THE STOIC

Utilitarian theory proposes that pleasure is good and pain evil, and that actions are right insofar as they lead to pleasure, wrong insofar as they lead to pain. In sum, we should act so as to achieve 'the greatest happiness of the greatest number'. How this is to be calculated, and how far the principle's specious simplicity is real, are matters beyond my present brief. What concerns me is that the classical utilitarians included non-human animals in their calculations, and were attacked for so doing (Whewell 1852, cf. Mill 1852).

> The morality which depends upon the increase of pleasure alone would make it our duty to increase the pleasure of pigs or of geese rather than those of men, if we were sure that the pleasure we could give them were greater than the pleasures of men.
>
> (Whewell 1852, p. 223)

Such an approach, Whewell believed, disregarded the distinctively human attributes that were the proper objects of moral endeavour. Virtue, not pleasure, should be the end of action.

I have some sympathy with this criticism. There are notorious problems about taking pleasure, just as such, to be the only good. If that were so, for example, any pleasure produced by sadistic cruelty would compensate for the victim's suffering, and might even be so great as to outweigh that suffering. The case is not improved by hurried appeals to long-term imponderables. Not all pleasures are worth pursuing, and a worthwhile activity is not simply one that produces the best available ratio of pleasure to pain, either in the individual or in the universe.

But though I sympathise with Whewell's attack on naive utilitarianism, and think the question of our duty, or supposed duty, to increase the happiness of non-human animals is a real one, I do not share his disdain for non-human animals and for 'animal' pleasures. Nor do I share Kant's fears (1963, p. 164): 'Sexuality exposes us to the danger of equality with the

42

beasts.' And vice versa. To think of 'animal pleasures' as of moral significance is to 'lower ourselves' to the animal level. To recognise non-humans as seriously deserving of our consideration is to acknowledge their goals as ones we could share. To be concerned for animal welfare is to be a libertine. Really moral persons are not to sympathise with the trivial, ignoble, or disgusting aims of our non-human kin. Strangely, these aims are often perceived as sexual. Almost the only animals permanently in rut, and almost certainly the only ones ever to make a life's work of it, are humans, but sexual desire in particular is held to turn people into beasts. A rather similar sequence of thought results in the belief that males who like the company of women are effeminate. True manhood is displayed in disregarding the softer, soggier feelings of women, and non-humans, and the male's own feelings. To give in to a woman is, for a male, to give in to his own lower nature. Spinoza attributed concern for animal suffering precisely to womanish sentimentality (Spinoza 1982, 4.37.1).[2] Interestingly, again, it is women who are traditionally held to be sexual beings, and males supposed to be tempted by them against their own real natures. Traditional oppression of women is linked with fear of their sexuality and distrust of 'womanish' sentiment. The male embodies passionless reason, if only he is not corrupted by bad company.

Utilitarian propaganda has played a part in the slow erosion of such value systems. We are readier to admit the value of innocent pleasure, readier to spare each other pain. The discovery of anaesthetics and analgesics, by making it possible to evade (some) pains, has decreased our need to imagine that pain is good for us. Whatever we have lost in the last century, we cannot now regret our increased susceptibility to sympathetic and other distress, our increased readiness to enjoy sexual and other delights. Although I think utilitarian theory has helped to excuse many evils, of realpolitik and laboratory science, I gladly acknowledge that utilitarians have helped to produce legislation on behalf of animals, children, women, and the poor that would have been laughable – was laughed at – two centuries ago. But perhaps something should be said on the other side.

What is paradoxical about the association of animal welfare and libertinism is that it contradicts the ancient association of animal welfare and asceticism. The charge made against zoophiles by nineteenth-century moralists was that they were libertines (Austin 1885), or at best sentimentalists. The charge made against them by Augustine was that they were Manichaeans, dedicated to the belief that the world and the flesh were evil (Augustine, *De Moribus Manichaeorum*, 35f, *Civitas Dei*, I.19). It is still quite commonly assumed that vegetarians in particular are always moved by sheer distaste for incorporating the unclean. The assumption is, of course, sometimes correct. I have seen vegetarianism advocated, by a schoolmaster, precisely on the grounds that meat enflames the passions of the animal boy. This was also one of Gandhi's reasons. Meat especially, perhaps: there was a

43

medieval tradition that fish (and barnacle geese) alone were to be eaten on Fridays and during Lent, since they were not sexually generated.

Ascetics have often adopted vegetarian ways as part of their progressive detachment from the luxuries and corruptions of this naughty world. Moral behaviour lies in controlling and frustrating the desires of the flesh, 'the beast within' (Plato, *Republic*, 589a–b). We should follow Reason, embodied in the moral law, and not concern ourselves with the desires and feelings we share with the non-human. It is the mark of a slavish man to follow out his animal desires (Aristotle, *Eudemian Ethics*, 1215634); good people have their beasts well-trained. Both Cynics and Academics were often vegetarian, and in refraining from the luxuries and medicaments of their day were sometimes enabled to *see* the animals they no longer needed to oppress. Such asceticism is not to be despised: I have no doubt that our health would be improved, our duties to the human world made easier, and our eyes opened to much of value if we made more effort to practise the moral discipline of our predecessors. It would also have some good effects for animal welfare. Cosmetics, furs, expensive meats would give way to simpler tastes, and fewer of our non-human kin would be oppressed to produce them. We might also manage to endure more readily the pains and problems of this mortal life, and cease to seek 'cures' and 'palliatives' with such casual brutality. The only recipe for a long and healthy life yet known to us is simply moral discipline (and even that is not a guarantee).

But though the general adoption of a more disciplined approach to living, the abandonment of the absurd pursuit of pleasure and avoidance of every slight distress, would have some good effects, the 'beast-controlling morality' has at least two drawbacks. First, that it involves a disrespect for what are taken to be 'animal' concerns. If we do not think *our* pains and pleasures are to be taken seriously, how can we trouble ourselves about theirs? Second, that we may find ourselves engaged in symbolic behaviour. Animals symbolise things to us, in particular human capacities. So indeed do our fellow humans. How many victims of rape or marital violence or child abuse were raped or beaten simply because of their actual, individual natures? It is at least likely that in raping or beating, the agent was conquering or hitting out at something for which the victim was only a symbol: personal weakness, insecurity, or memory of failure. The list is not exhaustive. A moral code that despises 'animal behaviour' may also lead to symbolic action against the animals that seem to us to embody that behaviour. Even self-hatred is a dangerous game, given the human capacity for projecting undesirable qualities onto an external object (Epictetus, *Discourses*, I.3.7ff):

> It is because of our kinship with the flesh that those of us who incline toward it become like wolves, faithless and treacherous and hurtful, and others like lions, wild and savage and untamed; but most of us

become like foxes, that is to say, rascals of the animal kingdom. For what else is a slanderous and malicious man but a fox, or something even more rascally and degraded? Take heed, therefore, and beware that you become not one of these rascally creatures.

Epictetus was concerned above all to seek the good and worthwhile in what is not shared with the non-human. All other creatures are made for our use, for they lack understanding (*Discourses*, II.8.6ff). Strictly, of course, they cannot then be treacherous, savage, or rascally: they are only following out their God-given natures. But since we should not give way to the sort of impulses that we think operate in them, it is easy to regard them as positively evil, and therefore as suitable objects of correction.

Popular moralists continue the tradition. To behave in a particularly hurtful, rapacious or lustful way is to behave 'like an animal'. Carnivores are 'vicious killers' for no better reason than they feel no particular compunction about killing their prey. Epictetus went somewhat further. It is not only the sensual or aggressive passions that work against true human dignity, but also sentiment and the body (Epictetus, *Encheiridion*, 3.26):

> If you kiss your own child or wife, say to yourself that you are kissing a human being; for when it dies you will not be disturbed. Some other person's child or wife has died; no one but would say 'Such is the fate of man'. Yet when a man's own child dies, immediately the cry is 'Alas, woe is me!'. But we ought to remember how we feel when we hear of the same misfortune befalling others.

There is of course some merit in this advice, but the general message is disturbing. We ought not to take special ties of affection seriously, but strive to view events and creatures as we would view any objectively similar event or creature. One way of doing this might be to practise universal love, but human creatures being what they are, a universal indifference is more likely.

We are born to contemplate God and His works, and should not allow passion or private affection or bodily needs to corrupt our vision. These things do not matter. 'On earth there is nothing great but man; in man there is nothing great but mind!' – a quotation from the journal of the British Research Defence Society, *Conquest*.[3] A few years ago I wrote that this was sub-Hegelian gibberish (*Moral Status of Animals*, p. 7), which was careless of me. In fact it appears as the epigraph of W. Hamilton's edition of the *Works of Thomas Reid* and is attributed by him (I, p. 217) to a 'forgotten philosopher'. It appears to be of Stoic origin, though I have not yet located the exact source.

> The Stoics...saw and said that in the world, after God, there is nothing so important as man, and in man nothing so important as mind.... They starved and blighted human nature by finding no place or function for passion and worshipping as their ethical ideal apathetic

wisdom. They shut their eyes to patent facts of experience in pretending to regard outward events as insignificant and pain as no evil. They silenced the voice of humanity in their hearts by indulging in merciless contempt for the weak and the foolish.

(Bruce 1899, p. 387)

This judgment is not entirely fair to the Stoics,[4] but it has an alarmingly exact application to the character and practice of some moderns. It is worth noting here that we do not, as Stoic or rationalist theory requires, call someone 'inhuman' because that person is stupid, but because he or she lacks certain fundamental emotional responses.

Like utilitarianism, Stoicism has its good points, as have the Thomist and Kantian philosophies that are its descendants. It has helped to inculcate courage and temperance in many generations sorely in need, as are we, of these virtues. Even the seemingly pathological alienation from the body that such philosophies sometimes produce has its uses (Epictetus, *Discourses*, I.1.23ff):

'Tell your secrets!' I say not a word, for this is under my control. 'But I will chain you.' What is that you say, man? Chain *me*? My leg you will chain, but my will not God Himself can chain. 'I will throw you into prison.' My paltry body, rather. 'I will behead you!' Well, when did I ever tell you that mine was the only neck that could not be severed? These are the lessons that philosophers ought to rehearse.

If philosophers, and others, did now rehearse them, our demands upon the environment, upon non-human animals and upon our human kindred would grow less, and our susceptibility to threat and blackmail likewise. Even if a Stoic community continued to regard animals as exploitable and contemptible material, it would still in fact exploit them only for the sake of knowledge, just as such, and quite apart from any sensual advantage. Human reason is operative in the pursuit and contemplation of Truth, and this is the ultimate value.

Utilitarians pursue Happiness, and Stoics Truth. Both offer objective codes of behaviour, and urge us to act to anyone as we would to everyone, leaving all private affection and subjective difference aside. Utilitarian theory concedes that pleasure and pain are not morally indifferent nor animals of quite a different kind from ourselves, but licenses the exploitation of animals for our pleasure and weakens our hold on virtue. Stoic theory reminds us of the need for virtue and bids us endure with equanimity the post to which God has appointed us, but conceives all non-rational creatures to be there entirely for our use and systematically disregards the non-rational impulses we share with them. Oddly, both tend to assume that only pleasure and pain are of any significance to our non-human kin. By criticising this last assumption we may work towards a more satisfactory moral system.

UNDERSTANDING ANIMALS

What are animals actually like? Kenneth Dover remarks in passing (1975, p. 75) that

> to judge from the pronouncements made throughout human history on the subject of animals, it would seem that ours is the first culture to observe animals in their natural state and perhaps the first to care whether what it says about them is true or false.

Understandably, he exaggerates a little: there have been exact observers in the past, and there are considerable confusions in our present understanding. It is really extraordinarily difficult to find out what animals are actually like, to move beyond the stereotypes and projections and sentimental misapprehensions to what the creature itself feels and desires. This is not a problem special to ethology. It is always difficult to disentangle our perception of a creature's quiddity from our own emotional involvement: if we desire someone, the erotic charge makes it very difficult not to see her or him as, precisely, inviting. If we like cuddling a furry animal, we tend to assume that the animal is cuddly. Lambs are sweet and innocent; cows are bovine (obviously); pigs are greedy. The problem is made worse with animals because our social conditioning is deliberately (I do not say 'cynically') unrealistic. It is very interesting to watch parents painfully coping with their children's immediate sympathy for animals when that sympathy comes too close to home. Our children's books are full of pretend-animals with whom our young can identify; we encourage them to care for 'pets', to take an interest in living creatures. Farms and zoos and circuses are presented as occasions for community with animals – but what happens when the child realises what he or she is eating, or what is being done to the animals so that he or she may enjoy their 'company'? Kantians are forced to dissimulate. For them, animals are a superior sort of toy, to be cared for only as practice for caring for people; but they cannot reveal this to the child without subverting the programme. The child must respond to, and care for, the animals it pets, but must not in the end take its own concern seriously. The result is a sort of schizophrenia well exemplified in C. S. Lewis' *Narnia* saga: on the one hand, talking animals to be respected as companions and helpers; on the other 'dumb' animals who can be killed and hunted at will (this is especially obvious in *The Silver Chair*). To be fair to Lewis, he was against causing even dumb animals to suffer, and perhaps never realised how much his supper had suffered in farm, lorry, and slaughterhouse.

It is entirely understandable that serious investigators have reacted against this sentimentalism (see Diamond 1978) by seeking to eliminate all identifications, emotional attachments, and fantasies from their observations of animals. It is a methodological rule amongst ethologists that descriptions of behaviour should be purely 'objective', without appeal to any mental element imagined into being. A better term would perhaps be 'impersonal': scientific or scholarly descriptions should obviously be 'objective' (i.e. realistic), 'objective' (i.e. referring to qualities that exist independently of our attitudes) and 'objective' (i.e. unbiased), but cannot hope to be 'objective' (i.e. lacking in any emotive force) when the facts described are such as to move any normal person. There is no necessary conflict between objectivity and emotive force. It is not obvious that such description should exclude all reference to the motives and attitudes of the creatures described. But the policy is understandable, and it is also understandable that laboratory scientists, and even some of the laity, have drawn the Cartesian conclusion that animals are merely mechanisms. If we do not need the hypothesis of subjectivity or consciousness to explain the phenomena we will manage without it.

It is understandable, but it is no better an argument for all that (Bradley 1897, p. 18): 'It is doubtless scientific to disregard certain aspects when we work; but to urge that such aspects are not real, and that what we use without regard to them is an independent real thing – this is barbarous metaphysics.'[5]

Barbarous metaphysics, and barbarous psychology. Like Descartes, the impersonalist rejects the immediate impulse of sympathy for what is felt to be animal distress, in the name of a rational theory. The impersonalist has less excuse than Descartes, for it is an axiom of modern research that we are animals, evolved along with other animals, and our responses are adapted to the world we and our ancestors have inherited. Descartes could believe that human consciousness is detached from all things bodily, though he found no satisfactory way of expounding the obvious connections between Mind and Body. Modern impersonalists, who have mistaken methodology for ontology, are heirs of two quite different attitudes to humanity: the Rationalist and the Naturalist. If we are essentially Reason, then we may justly disregard the motions of our, or other, animal frames, but cannot hope to explain anything of our psychology by observations or experiments on animals. If we are essentially Animal (of a particular kind), we cannot so easily disregard our immediate responses or believe that our close kindred are unfeeling mechanisms. 'An epistemological lobotomy, which prevents an intelligent man from using the normal cognitive functions nature gave him, does indeed constitute an act of dehumanization.'[6]

I emphasise that our ability to recognise patterns of behaviour, to sympathise with other creatures, is indeed a cognitive function, part of the way we know the world. It is unfortunate that professional biologists and animal psychologists seem, on this point, to be several decades behind the philosophical times. Few philosophers would now describe 'mental states' as things uneasily inferred from purely impersonal descriptions, as though we could only *see* a creature twisting about, sweating, emitting high-pitched noises (and so on) and must thence *infer* that there is a mental cause of these motions, namely pain. Such an inference would be very weak indeed, for I have no reason to believe that such motions are associated with such mental states unless I can recognise the latter directly. I cannot infer the existence of fire from the sight of smoke unless fire and smoke are at least sometimes observed together. On such terms I can have no good reason to believe that any other creature is ever in what I call 'pain'. Nor are humans in better case because they (some of them) can say 'it hurts'. They could not have been taught the words, nor could I understand them, if they, if their parents, if we, could not recognise a pain state non-verbally expressed.

The attribution of mental qualities to a creature is not, in its normal form, an unreliable inference on the basis of securely established physical information. On the contrary, such attributions are the framework of all human endeavour and scientific research. If I did not believe that a fellow researcher *is* a fellow researcher, a being with cognitive capacities and ethical responsiveness, how could I take that scientist's reports as evidence (Ritchie 1964)? Of course, we are sometimes in error; of course, there might be creatures who always pretend (but not many); of course, there might be things that looked like creatures but are not (there are, called 'toys'). But these are particular problems that give us no good reason to doubt the general accuracy of our assessments and recognitions. In saying that a creature likes or dislikes, fears or loves, is envious or spiteful or sympathetic, we are not, in general, indulging an illicit animism, nor in 'mysticism' (as E. O. Wilson supposes: Wilson 1975, p. 176). We are recognising patterns of behaviour and may do so legitimately among adult humans, infants, and our non-human kin (Midgley 1978, pp. 344ff). It is of course the more difficult to do so the further removed, in genealogical terms, the creatures are.

Decent ethologists in fact know all this well enough: their practice is far better than their naively Cartesian theories would suggest. Thanks to the efforts of exact observers who have sought not to jump to conclusions too early, or too late, we have some detailed information about our kindred that does not support the view that animals are lawless, sexually rapacious, or murderously violent. Nor, of course, are they gentle, law-abiding, and supremely altruistic. But the post-Aristotelian, and Stoic, view that there are 'impulses to be noble' in animals (as in children) (Aristotle, *Magna Moralia*, 1206b.17) has received support. They are moved to act in an affectionate manner, to care for the small and defenceless, to avoid hurting familiars, to respect authority, to do their duty when they are themselves authorities, to honour sexual taboos, to fight for their young, and to feed their old. All this was indeed familiar to the ancients, some of whom concluded that Nature was a principle superior to the Stoics' vaunted Reason (Plutarch *Gryllus, or Beasts are Rational*, 991). Natural law is *quod natura omnia animalia docuit* (Justinian, *Institutiones*, I.8); it is therefore natural law at least for mammals (and others) that parents care for their children, that we be loyal to our clan-mates, respect status, acknowledge territorial claims, and the like. What is fascinating about the 'territorial instinct' is not that animals are possessive, but that other animals acknowledge their claims. Even butterflies, it appears, give the occupant of a patch of sunlight the moral edge over an intruder (Smith 1978, p. 144).

I do not imply that animals do not also cheat, kill, conspire, and desert. Jane van Lawick-Goodall's observations of the Gombe chimpanzees make it clear both that chimpanzees are social and responsive creatures, and that they can fail as blatantly as ourselves to be moved by distress to anything other than irritated neglect. It is worth remembering that chimpanzees are like humans also in this, that they are disgusted by obvious physical illness, and that they are ready to kill creatures, even of their own species, for their own purposes (Van Lawick-Goodall 1971).[7] We need not react against traditional views of animals by adopting romantic fantasies about 'the innocent lusts of the unfallen creatures'!

Stoic moral theory, whatever its failings, acknowledged that non-human creatures could be moved by considerations that also move good people. Human morality arose by reflection upon the ethical values I have mentioned, with a view to achieving the sort of universal, objective outlook that frowns upon personal attachment and non-rational sentiment. It is here, I believe, that they made their error. A morality that systematically denigrates and denies its own roots in ethical responsiveness is doomed. The clearest case of this is Monod's 'ethic of objectivity' (i.e. of impersonality). The primary command of that morality is 'thou shalt not "participate" in the world's workings'. Everything is to be seen without emotional affect, and the conclusion must be that of Epictetus, that we should not even identify with our own bodies. But in so detaching ourselves, we lose all basis upon which to argue scientifically, to pick out any particular aspect of the phenomena, to seek the truth. The end is emptiness (Monod 1972).[8]

A sound morality must be based upon, and not denigrate, the personal ties and attachments into which we are born. We may properly extend our respect for human creatures, as Stoics would have us do, from our immediate families to creatures of the same objective kind, but we cannot quite eliminate subjective discriminations without destroying the natural roots of our morality. We dare not wholly despise Nature in the name of 'Reason', for Reason (a compendium of natural faculties) is itself a product of Nature and draws its premises from the stock of natural sentiment (Lewis 1943).

NATURAL LAW

If these natural sentiments of affection, loyalty, and service are the necessary roots of morality, what are we to say about our relations with creatures not of our species? If a fully objective code of behaviour is not to be hoped for, are not zoophiles on the wrong track when they point to the objective similarity between creatures of another species and some of our fellow humans (infants or imbeciles or the aphasic)? Speciesists need not claim that all human beings are objectively different (save, of course, in species) from all non-human beings, but only that they are subjectively different: they matter more to *us*, not always to the universe. Stoics and utilitarians, of course, should not rely on this distinction: only objective value matters, value rationally acknowledged. My own naturalism cannot simply override actual feelings.

Again, if it is natural sentiment that lies at the root of morality, if natural law is *quod natura omnia animalia docuit*, how can I denounce the predatory aspects of nature? Is it not natural for creatures to prey on one another? How can we so self-righteously stand aside from the fray? A rationalist can reply with Plato (*Philebus*, 67b):

> Those who appeal to such evidence are not better than those who put their trust in the flight of birds. They imagine that the desires we observe in animals are better evidence than the reflections inspired by a thoughtful philosophy.

Or, as one of Aristophanes' heroes put it, to someone who claimed that it was only natural for him to beat his father, since cocks did it (*Clouds*, 1420f): 'Why don't you feed on dung, then, and sleep on a perch?'

The fact that chimpanzees grab young baboons to eat them no more justifies us in doing so than the fact that they neglect and repulse sick members of their own tribe justifies us in doing so. Their sentiments may not allow any weight to certain distresses; their behaviour may sometimes even run counter to their own natural sentiments – we are not the only animals sometimes to be torn between desire and proper feeling, or proper desire and misplaced feeling. What is natural is not simply what happens always, or for the most part. If it were, disease and error would be natural (Epictetus, *Discourses*, I. 11. 7). The form of life natural to a creature helps to define what happiness is for that creature's kind, what capacities are there to be filled, what occasions are needed for it wholly to be itself. This Aristotelian concept helps us to see what is wrong in imprisoning and frustrating, say, a veal calf or in declawing a cat: not that they suffer pain sensations,[9] but that their lives are systematically prevented from being full lives according to their kind. Disease and injury, though natural in the sense of being likely enough to happen, are precisely against the victim's nature. Similarly, not every sentiment is natural; some are pathological manifestations of glandular imbalance or social corruption. Sentiment is the root of morality, as sense experience is of science; neither sentiment nor sense experience can be wholly condemned without destroying the systems grown from them, but equally they are not unquestionable.

This is as much as to say that the natural world does display corruption when judged by informed sentiment. How exactly we are to tread the narrow track between Manichaean rejection of the natural world (and consequent

51

destruction of the ethical responsiveness that arises from that nature) and a pantheistic adoration of whatever happens (and consequent destruction of all moral discrimination) is a matter I have discussed elsewhere.[10] My suspicion is that only traditional theism can cope. But leaving that aside, it is surely proper to admire the beauty and order manifest in the world without incurring any obligation to copy predators or to refrain from change. What has been need not always be, even if we cannot now see any clear way wholly to eliminate past evils.

But the challenge still stands. Even if it is possible for people to respect, befriend, and care for creatures not of their own species, might this not be pathological? Is it not properly natural to be speciesist? A lion who really made no difference between his treatment of lions, lionesses, gazelles, and men with guns would not be a lion (nor long survive as a monster). Creatures are of the kind they are because they do, and their ancestors did, discriminate between species, between sexes, between ages, in just the ways they do. How can it not be the sentiment of a deeply disturbed human to seek an end to such discrimination?

Is it not natural, some would add, for human beings, evolved as social predators, to hunt? Are not our distinctive characteristics fitted precisely to such a predatory life? If they are, of course, we are doomed: for only a post-cataclysmic world could give our descendants any chance of returning to a hunter-gatherer economy. If we cannot be happy except as small bands of naked wanderers, ganging together to run down antelope, we are not going to be happy, no matter what ersatz substitutes we devise. Of course, we can learn from such societies, but we must also hope that, as it seems, we are a sufficiently adaptable species to find other ways of happiness.

Could these other ways be such as to satisfy a radical zoophile? The question is similar to one posed to radical feminists: how could we end discrimination between male and female without wholly destroying the social and biological bases of society? Science-fantasists may speculate about a time when people select, at will and temporarily, child-bearing or begetting modes, when the pronouns 'he' and 'she' are as obsolete as the pronouns betokening social status with which some languages are laced. A society that really did not discriminate between chimpanzees and human imbeciles would be even more bizarre.

But of course feminists need not believe that the wholly non-sexual society is desirable even if it is possible. The evils of sexism are that females are denied the opportunity to live authentic lives, that girls are conditioned to take a subordinate role, that males are isolated from their feelings and encouraged to behave in grossly competitive ways, that women (and men) are raped, beaten, and insulted. A non-sexist society is one in which people are not oppressed, exploited, and manipulated to fit sexual stereotypes. The evils of speciesism, similarly, are that creatures are robbed, assaulted, and killed, not simply that they are distinguished from members of our own species. It is right so to distinguish them, both objectively (for their species-specific qualities differ) and subjectively (for some species are more readily understood and liked by us). What is wrong is to use them with cruelty and disrespect.

It is natural to find sexual partners chiefly in the opposite sex of one's own species. In that sense, it is natural (and proper) to be both speciesist and sexist. But it is not natural to be concerned only for creatures who are members of one's own species (see Dawkins 1976, p. 11). The reason is simple: a species is a reproductively isolated population, such that its members rarely or never breed outside that population to produce fertile offspring. What is significant for neo-Darwinian evolution is not the species, but the gene lines tangled together in the gene pools. Characteristics are embedded in the genotype if they result, in a given community, in phenotypes that multiply, relative to competitors, the responsible genotype. This is how altruism, most probably, becomes a stable instinctual pattern: that those who benefit from altruistic acts generally carry the same genes as the altruist. It does not follow, as some careless writers have implied, that animal altruism is really selfishness, or even really a desire to multiply one's genes. The evolutionary explanation does not explain altruism away. Nor does it follow that only those who carry the altruist's genes are ever benefited: the altruist has no way of discovering who does and who does not. The altruist responds rather to the familiar cues of sight, smell, and evocative posture. Other creatures can 'exploit' this fact, as do cuckoos. Put it differently: altruists can be concerned for creatures not of their own species, only if they are familiar or sufficiently like what is familiar.

It is from these literally familiar roots that our concern for others may blossom. Stoics urged (as I pointed out in the previous chapter) that 'we should regard all men as our fellow countrymen and fellow citizens, and there should be one life and one order like that of a single flock on a common pasture feeding together under common law'.[11] Advocates of Earth's Household employ a parallel rhetoric. Just as a household may contain creatures of many species, each of whom evokes feelings of concern and affection (unless suppressed), so does Earth's Household contain many creatures with whom we can often find mutually helpful symbioses, against whom we must sometimes struggle, whom we need not hate or despise.

In the household of earth and heaven, Aristotle taught (*Metaphysics*, 1075a 19ff), the free men have more responsibilities than the children or slaves. The Stoics were doubtless right at least in this, that God has called us out to know the world in ways not open even to our nearest kin (as they, it may be, know the world in ways not open to us), and that we do in fact hold their lives and happiness in our hands. As later philosophers have taught, we are in the position of stewards, bound by duties experienced as feeling and expounded by reason (Darling 1970, p. 122) 'to serve the lesser creation, to keep our world clean and pass on to posterity a record of which we shall not feel shame'. Fraser Darling's words provide my peroration, but I will add one thing: our office as stewards, often enough, is not to reform and tame the world, but to allow our cousins their own ways forward.[12] Anarchism may not be the best political system for humans, but I suspect that it may be for the world at large.

I have wielded many mighty opposites in this paper: Pleasure and Virtue, Subjectivity and Objectivity, Nature and Reason. If they remain strong to move us, it is perhaps because all are necessary to the good life.

> Man is a lumpe where all beasts kneaded bee,
> Wisdom makes him an Arke where all agree.
> (Donne [1610]1929, p. xx)

Where exactly the wise man will put the Mean (Aristotle, *Nicomachean Ethics*, 1106b.35f),[13] I must leave others to decide.

6

HUME, ANIMALS AND THE OBJECTIVITY OF MORALS[1]

INTRODUCTION

One of David Hume's arguments against the belief that moral distinctions are matters of fact is that 'incest in the human species is criminal ... [but] the very same action, and the same relations in animals have not the smallest moral turpitude and deformity'.[2] If 'the guilt or moral deformity of [an] action' could be proved by 'demonstrative reasoning' from the mere relations of the objects under consideration (relations, that is, of 'resemblance, contrariety, degrees in quality, and proportions in quantity and number'), we should have to admit that a dog's copulation with his daughter was as much an evil as a human father's betrayal of his child's complaisance. To the imagined reply that a man may know that he is committing an evil, while dogs do not, Hume replies that the evil of incest cannot rest in our knowledge that it is evil (how could we then know that it was?). His point is not that we excuse dogs for copulating with their daughters on the grounds that they don't know what they are doing, but that there is nothing to blame them for. The evil of incest, accordingly, does not rest merely in the physical relations between the partners. It rests instead, so Hume goes on to claim in an outrageous *non sequitur*, merely in the speaker's attitude.

Hume's argument is open to rebuttal. Most commentators are so embarrassed that such a great philosopher should have thought so bad an argument 'entirely decisive' that they pass over it in silence. Is it really obvious that dogs and humans perform the 'very same act' when they copulate, given that they do so for different reasons, with different social consequences, with different attitudes to their partners and prospective offspring? If 'animal incest' and 'human incest' are acts of the same kind, then they are equally evil, or equally indifferent. To disapprove of the act when done by humans but not when done by dogs would be as silly as approving of assault when performed by whites but not when performed by blacks. Hume points to the inconsistency involved in believing (a) that canine inbreeding is the same act as human incest, (b) that canine inbreeding is not intrinsically evil, and (c) that human incest is intrinsically evil. But it

55

is not necessary to abandon the third of these beliefs, nor would it follow from such abandonment that nothing was intrinsically evil. Only one of the triad need be rejected, and the objectivity of morals can be preserved whichever choice is made.

'INCEST NOT EVIL'

The third belief has been rejected most consistently by the Cynics. Diogenes concluded that whatever animals did without sin, he too could do. Herodotus had noted that most nations had reckoned that humans might follow the animal example and copulate even in the gods' temples, or enter them after intercourse without washing first. Egyptians and Greeks, he held, were better advised.[3] Diogenes revived the argument. The 'natural life' led by animals could also be led by human animals, if they put aside their pride and unreasonable shame. 'When Oedipus had children by his mother, he should have concealed this or made it legal in Thebes. Domestic fowls do not object to such relationships, nor dogs, nor any ass'.[4] Incest (father-beating, cannibalism) is not evil 'by nature', but only 'by convention'.

Diogenes' conversion to the simple life came, according to Theophrastus, through watching a mouse 'running about, not looking for a place to lie down, not fearing the dark, not seeking any of the things that are reckoned dainties'.[5] What other animals did, human animals could do, by realising what they needed and how easy it was to get it if they were tough enough. Diogenes' animals, like those of most moralists, do what they like, and do not worry about their reputations, nor complain when the universe is not to their moral taste. 'Animals have little or no sense of virtue or vice; they quickly lose sight of the relations of blood; and are incapable of that of right and property.'[6] What Hume forgets is that this is precisely what has been recommended by those of Cynic descent. The good life has been understood as the life that animals lead, in obedience to their natural impulses.

> The soul of beasts has a greater natural capacity and perfection for the generation of virtue; for without command or instruction, unsown and unploughed as it were, it naturally brings forth and develops such virtue as is proper in each case.

It is their nature to flee subjection, and females are in no way inferior to males in spirit and valour.

> Beasts' life, for the most part, is controlled by the essential desires and pleasures. As for those that are non-essential, but merely natural, [they] resort to them without either irregularity or excess, [and] celebrate at the proper time a love without deceit or hire, [whereas] not even Nature with Law for her ally can keep within bounds the unchastened vice of [human] hearts.[7]

56

Animals, in short, have been held to be creatures that act in accordance with right reason, out of their undistorted affections. What is done 'naturally' has been held to be a pattern also for human behaviour. On this account Hume's argument must fail: if incest is not evil among animals it is not evil 'by nature'. It does not follow that there are no natural evils or natural goods.

The social aspects of animal life will concern me later. What is of interest here is that those who have followed in Diogenes' steps have shared with other moralists the notion that animals are essentially unsocial. When Aristotle asserted that an unsocial human being was either a beast or a god,[8] he did not intend to imply that all animals were unsocial, for he distinguishes 'beasts' precisely as unsocial, flesh-eating and aggressive animals, and acknowledges that some animals treat their offspring in 'more politic' a manner.[9] But though Aristotle understood that for many animal-kinds living together was more than 'pasturing in the same field',[10] as it was for cattle, there has been a tendency to assume that animals were individualists in a way that properly brought up people were not. Animals weren't flag-flappers, nor inclined to sell their self-reliance for security. Their children, once grown, were independent – so that father-beating, the conventional Greek's nightmare, was no special evil. Their virtue, natural virtue, lay in the value they placed upon their individual lives, the courage and temperance and prudence with which they made their own ways in the world. Human beings were unusual in that they needed friends if they were to live a worthwhile life.[11] Diogenes' mouse was happy in his solitude.

This vision is not without its value. Those moral philosophers who have characterised morality as a set of conventions founded upon social convenience could usefully be reminded that past philosophers have praised virtue as a necessary element of the worthwhile, self-sufficient life. The value that a creature puts upon its own life, its effort to maintain itself in its essential way of living, is what makes it admirable. 'Altruism', when that is construed as a readiness always to give way to others and prefer their plans to what would have been one's own, is an abdication of responsibility, a denial that one is oneself worth anything – and by implication a denial that any one individual is worth anything: only the collective counts. For the ethical egoist 'a person who has no respect for himself, who lacks courage, who neglects his life and values, who degrades himself or wastes himself on trivia may be morally condemned, although he has hurt or endangered no one but himself'.[12]

The virtue of an animal lies in his or her disposition and capacity to live his or her life. According to the tradition which I am now considering animals do, in general, maintain their ways. What they do is commendable. If they do not follow all the conventional rules of human society that is a reason for considering those rules to be merely conventional. Natural law is defined as *quod natura omnia animalia docuit* – what Nature has taught all animals.[13] If there is no sign that animals have all been taught a supposed law – as it might be, a law against incest – then incest, for example, is not a natural evil, not something that all creatures should avoid for their own lives' sake.

'INBREEDING AN EVIL'

But let me turn now to the next possible solution of Hume's puzzle, namely to abandon the second member of the inconsistent triad. Perhaps animal inbreeding is indeed an evil, and those that can justly prevent its occurrence ought to do so. Animals, perhaps, cannot prevent its happening (for they lack the knowledge and the power), but those who have charge of them ought maybe to exercise care on their behalf. Hume's argument can be phrased as follows: if we do not acknowledge any duty, however weak, to prevent animal inbreeding, even among animals in our charge, how can we claim that incest as such is an evil? The argument is paralleled by one familiar to vegetarians: if we have no duty to prevent predators killing their prey, how can we pretend that the killing of animals is an evil in which we should not ourselves indulge? We cannot claim that it is an evil only if the agents know it is an evil. Either it is an evil independently of their knowledge, or it is itself no evil at all.

The question of animal killing I considered in Chapter 3, and concluded that we have no general obligation to avert all evils. That we ought not to *do* evil is one thing; that we ought to *prevent* all evils, at whatever cost to the independence of our *protégés*, the stability of the ecosystem and the pursuit of our own just goals, is quite another. Predation may be an evil, even if it is one that we cannot hope to eliminate. We are familiar with the occasional moral duty to tolerate the existence of evils we ought not to encourage or engage in, but which we have neither power nor authority to halt. Correspondingly, even a moralist who did conclude that animal inbreeding was an evil would not be honour bound to engage in any ridiculous attempt to proscribe it, but it might be true that those animals clearly in our charge (domestic and farm animals) ought to be barred from incestuous relationships.

What would identify incest as an evil?

> Supposing that there is no presage of conscience whatever against such matches, yet the fact that progeny produced from such unions soon dwindle away and degenerate is as much a declaration of [God's] will against them as a presage of conscience before-hand would be.[14]

Leonard Williams has commented on

> the terrible pattern of deformities in the dog-world.... The small terrier is suffering from dislocation of the eye. The face and eyes of the St Bernard are dropping so low that often its eyelashes are turned

inwards. A number of dachshunds are becoming paralysed as a result of spinal trouble, and toy poodles are prone to a slipping kneecap. All this is due to unscrupulous inbreeding.[15]

The blame for this lies on the breeders, not the unfortunate dogs, but such results do suggest that inbreeding is indeed an evil. Recent evolutionary theory perhaps suggests that the original drawback of inbreeding may not be the production of deformity but the loss of genetic variation,[16] but once the pattern of outbreeding is established it would be dangerous not to continue with it.

What of Morris's second criterion for right action, the voice of conscience or immediate revulsion? That 'we' feel no such revulsion when considering the affairs of pedigree dogs is Hume's starting point. But our emotions are often not engaged by the doings of those whom we consider alien, or outside our present community: what are the sufferings of Egyptian slaves to us, or corrupt practices in Bangladesh, unless we force ourselves to recall what our attitude would be, were we the slaves or the oppressed? The sense of revulsion that constitutes one piece of evidence against a practice is what 'we' feel when 'we' are the ones involved or have managed to identify ourselves with those involved. So what 'we' feel about animal inbreeding should be what animals feel, or can be expected to feel: what 'we', the community of mammals as it exists for our sympathetic imagination, expectably feel.

In Hume's day it was taken for granted that animals would let nothing stand in the way of their desires. Their wants were simple – like the dog with one thought for each paw (Food, Food, Sex and Food) – and it was supposed that they could acknowledge no distinctions among the objects of greed and lust. This was not to say that animals do not have preferences, but that they do not seem to have taboos. What endeared them to one class of moralist was anathema to another. To live 'like an animal' was (and still is, in the mouths of judges) to live without any acknowledged restraints of decency, good manners or respect for persons.

Some of those who disapproved of animal behaviour would also frown at alien human customs. Samuel Johnson could not believe that 'savages', illiterate peoples, could have anything to teach him. 'Pity is not natural to man ... but acquired and improved by the cultivation of reason. Savages are always cruel.' 'Natural affection is nothing: but affection from principle and established duty is sometimes wonderfully strong.' [So savages have no more affection than do hens; nor do they marry.] 'A savage man and a savage woman meet by chance; and when the man sees another woman that pleases him better, he will leave the first.'[17]

Johnson's determined ignorance is now an embarrassment to his admirers (including myself). Why could he not have understood that other human tribes have their own arts and decencies? He spoke from within his tradition, as Aristotle did when he declared that the further barbarians were beast-like, in that they lived 'only by perception', without – he supposed – being able to give principled reasons for their actions, or even strictly to 'act' (to choose the right thing to do) at all.[18]

Moralists are now conscious that all human tribes have inherited cosmologies and political systems. We hope, at least, that there are no 'natural slaves', unable to internalise the law and acting out of immediate desire or fear.[19] But Johnson's attitude to animals, that they too are moved only by the prospect of immediate gratification, is still widely held. 'Anthropomorphism' is the deadly sin of supposing that animals have customs, friends, serious emotions or needs beyond 'the merely physical'. Most commentators now recognise that contempt for 'savages' serves ideological and commercial interests, providing an excuse for disrupting their life, turning them out of their homelands and denying that they have any need to be respected as fellow members of the kingdom of ends, of evaluative entities. That contempt for 'animals' serves similarly ideological ends is not so widely recognised. To behave 'like an animal' is to have dropped out, to have abandoned cultivated manners and an awareness of one's place in the social universe. To *be* an animal is to be mere material for the purposes of human beings, whether those purposes are humane or not.

This dogmatic rejection of what is supposed to be anthropomorphism is itself a reaction against the moralistic projection on to animals of our own cultural forms. Students of animal behaviour have preferred to suppose that animals are moved by much more local considerations, not by any sense of their place in any social universe. If their behaviour looks rational this is a product of 'the invisible hand'. The preference for relatively local, 'simple' explanations has been fruitful, even if no adequate account of what constitutes a 'simple' explanation has yet been given. If wood lice congregate in damp patches we need not suppose that they have some idea of what they are looking for, or an internal map of the neighbouring territory. It is enough that they move faster when it's dry, and slow down when it's damp. If salmon can find their way back to their natal stream, it may be that they are merely swimming up the olfactory gradient, swimming in the direction of the stronger scent. If hunting wasps construct nests and supply their future progeny with paralysed caterpillars, they can do so without any thought of those progeny, merely by following out the 'fixed action patterns' of their kind. They thereby give the impression of following a long-term plan – an impression that can readily be removed by interfering with the process – without any need to have that long-term result in mind or adapt their behaviour to achieve it.

The higher vertebrates and molluscs are not so readily interpreted as merely responding to immediate stimuli in accordance with fixed action patterns. But even if much of their lives *is* spent in acting out such relatively fixed patterns, we can reasonably enquire what the patterns are likely to be – and find that they are not so simple-minded as the traditional picture suggests. Animals that did not discriminate between sexual partners, that behaved like Johnson's 'savages', would often copulate with close relatives. Their offspring would be born at hazard and be cared for, if at all, solely by the mother. Even the admission of mother-love, incidentally, as an innate mechanism triggered by the sucking reflex or a gaping mouth so as to tie the mother's satisfactions to the satisfaction of her offspring, carries us beyond the simple model of animal egoism. There is good evolutionary reason either to produce so many offspring that a few survive no matter what, or else to produce a few offspring that are then well cared for. This evolutionary function will not usually be the goal even of human endeavour. What can be expected is that animals will generally have goals that serve this function. They will prefer sexual partners like, but not too like or too familiar with themselves; and they will (if they are higher vertebrates) care for their offspring. Since such care will require that they be able to provide for them, they will not, in general, do what produces offspring unless they have provision to support them. This is why many land birds form couples only when there is territorial space available, and may (in some species) be attached precisely to the space rather than to their individual partner. In those species the appearance of marital fidelity is an illusion: what generally keeps the two birds together is that each has an attachment to the territorial space. Those who are unable to make good their claim upon such a territory do not form couples, nor produce many offspring (except of course by 'cheating' – laying eggs in an established couple's nest, or seducing the female). In other species the problem is dealt with by enabling the birds to recognise each other as individuals, and binding them to marital fidelity. Barbary doves, for example, have been shown to be monogamous, to be faithful to their first partners even at unfamiliar nesting sites.[20]

These patterns of preference can thus be shown to make sense in terms of the needs of the offspring, and the nature of the animal's *Umwelt* (which is to say, the environment as it is for an animal of that kind, with those senses, capacities and preferences). We can be sure the characteristics of the animal kind in question will not be random assortments. Creatures that characteristically produce a few, slowly maturing offspring will not be indifferent to their offspring, nor mate promiscuously, nor be unable to distinguish individuals of their own kind.

Further predictions are possible. Members of the same species are natural rivals, for food and territory and mates. But it does not follow that arrogant individualists will be most successful in propagating their kind. Nature encountered her Hobbesian crisis long ago, and found ways of making peace prevail. Less mythologically: creatures that always fight to the finish, that will never accept defeat gracefully, that always kill or rob their rivals, may win an occasional battle, but must devote so much time to forcing their way on others that any submissive mutant will be able to leave more progeny. Therefore, goods will not usually be fought for directly; instead, creatures are likely to evolve 'contest-competition', so that they try out their strengths in a way that does not seriously damage anyone. Losers then accept their slot, and may even (in disaster areas) allow themselves to perish while the dominant few eat well. This last phenomenon need not be interpreted as conscious suicide for the good of the tribe. It is more likely to be a byproduct of the strategy of 'wait and see': better to wait for the dominant's leavings and hope for a return match later on than risk a real fight now. Conversely, it is usually better for the dominants to allow their subordinates lives of their own, sometimes even to assist them, and not to press home their attacks lest their victim turn upon them with 'the courage of despair' and cost them more than they care to pay (see Tinbergen 1968). The rules of 'war' were among the first to be noticed by ethologists: witness the 'merciful wolf', who spares his defeated rival when that rival rolls over and pretends to be a cub again. Lorenz's assumption[21] that the wolf is 'inhibited' from killing his rival (where a human victor would not be) is questionable on at least two counts. First, there is good reason to think that human beings too are well able to kill each other, but usually do not: their record does not seem much worse than the wolves'. Second, Lorenz gives no reason to describe the case as one of 'inhibition'. The wolf does not (generally) kill – but that is evidence that he does not (generally) *wish* to; perhaps he wishes only to establish his superior rank. The wolf need not be understood as a soul divided in the Platonic manner between Desire and Spirit. Similar apparent inhibitions obtain in the sexual area. Female chimpanzees resist the advances of their brothers, or of any too familiar males. When Lucy Temerlin, a chimpanzee reared with humans and without experience of her conspecifics, reached puberty she resisted the attentions of her human foster-brother and foster-father while avidly pursuing any other human males.[22] Here the reports do suggest more strongly that Lucy experienced considerable conflict between her desire and her aversion, a conflict that might, contentiously, be compared to those of moralising humanity.

For there to be a real analogy, such conflicts must be considered as something more than the merely contingent opposition of one appetite to another. When animals find themselves pulled in two directions at once, their behaviour is either a blend of the two opposed patterns, more or less ritualised, or else some apparently irrelevant 'displacement activity'. Courtship ceremonies have plausibly been interpreted as a way of resolving the tension between desire and fear. A moral conscience may be similarly displayed, but there are two features of it that are not so readily identifiable. The first is that the agents are averse not merely to the object that they desire, but *to their own desire* of it. They are displeased with themselves for being weak. For moral conscience to be operative, the agent must not merely feel but reflect on, or contemplate, his or her own emotion. The second (and connected) feature is that moral conscience reflects upon the actions and emotions of *others* as well as on one's own. To disapprove of oneself is also to disapprove of others similarly placed.

Indeed, the capacity to contemplate (and disapprove of) one's own emotions and intentions may fairly be regarded as secondary. I come to know of myself by knowing others who know me; I come to disapprove of myself by knowing of (and approving) others who might. So it is crucial to the existence of conscience (and self-consciousness in general) that there be social groups whose members attempt to regulate each other's behaviour. To do this they must be able to re-identify each other, to have some grasp of past history, to attend not merely to the relations between themselves and others but also to the relations between the others. Such behaviour is not always found where we might expect it. The cannibalistic pair of chimpanzees discovered in the Gombe, for example, were (understandably) feared and resented by their fellows, but there was apparently no attempt to ostracise or punish them.[23] Other breaches of tribal discipline perhaps earn greater disapproval, notably (in some species) the attempt to dispossess an established nesting couple, or a failure of parental duty. If vervet females can respond to their own cub's cry, and also look (pointedly) at the mother of another crying cub,[24] there is reason to think that they are operating such a social system, so that the roots of conscience are there.

Accordingly, there seems good reason to question the second member of Hume's inconsistent triad. Incest (for example) perhaps is an evil, even among animals, and shown to be so both by the generally obnoxious consequences of inbreeding, and by the fact that most females at least are somewhat averse to it (though whether they are averse to it in others, or actually disapprove of their own slight impulses towards it is another matter). To live like the animals may not be so revolting nor so revolutionary a policy as moralising judges and romantic drop-outs have supposed.

'INCEST NOT INBREEDING'

What of the first member of the triad? Is it really true that canine inbreeding is the same act as human incest merely because the external relations involved are the same? If we understand that 'the same act' has been committed when an old lady is pushed over (a) by a domestic dog (savagely), (b) by a hurrying child (carelessly), (c) by a mugger (brutally), (d) by a policeman (to get her out of the way), (e) by an avalanche (indifferently), then in that sense male dog and human father may perform the same act when they tup their daughters. But why should we accept such an external definition of action? Hume's other example betrays the confusion: a sapling whose growth strangles the parent tree, he claims, displays the same ingratitude that renders parricide so fearful a crime, but earns no moral obloquy. But it is obvious that the sapling (unless we are to suppose that it is a dryad), is not committing an act of ingratitude. The same moral act is not done merely when the immediate consequences are the same. Even a gander does not commit the same act, except in an etiolated sense, when he mates with the goose with whom he has conducted the triumph ceremony and when he mates, without ceremony, with another female.[25] It is not the same act, because it occupies a different role in the gander's life (and the goose's) – it does not lead on to marital or parental care. When we turn to the animal whose inner life we best appreciate, the human animal, it is clear that similar physical movements may have radically different meanings for the agents, and for any careful observer.

Accordingly, it should not so readily be assumed that the same act is done when canine and human males have sex with their daughters, sisters or mothers. Motive and meaning and social consequences may differ. Because morality is concerned with motives and meanings, we cannot equate 'incest' merely with 'inbreeding'. For a human being to commit incest of the commonest kind (a father's or step-father's seduction of his daughter) is to use another creature for his momentary pleasure, to rob a child of her childhood and to betray a spouse. Incest as it is defined in some societies resides precisely in a breach of those rules that define the roles and duties of social beings, and these may have very little to do with 'inbreeding' just as such. A man may commit incest in seducing his deceased wife's sister: dogs can do no such thing, even if they mate with sisters.

The evil of incest, in other words, may well lie in the motive, the lack of concern for existing obligations, and the breach of custom, not in the physical movements and their physical antecedents and consequences. Dogs, accordingly, do not commit incest, and it is pointless to suggest that we might disapprove of their committing incest. Nor is it true that 'the facts are analogous to human prostitution'[26] (except in the most superficial and uninteresting sense) if male humming birds allow access to selected flowers only to females who will mate with them. Similarly, when Jane van Lawick-Goodall sees a hyena killing a newly-born wildebeest, she feels sympathy and regret, but does not suppose that the hyena's act is an evil one.[27] The spider who eats her mate, and the mate who avoids being eaten by proffering a carefully wrapped fly, are doing no evil, though human couples who behaved like that would hardly escape comment.

On this account moral evil, and moral goodness, do not reside in the physical relations of the agents, but in their motives, their broken or unbroken obligations, the meaning attached to their acts in the social community of which they are parts. This is not to draw Hume's conclusion, that 'moral turpitude' lies only in the eye of the beholder: it is to accept that it lies in the motives and meanings (the subjective relationships) of the agents. If an incestuous father did not mean to break the law, and did not exalt his own momentary desire over the well-being of others, and did not isolate himself and his daughter from society, and did not take advantage of filial affection or infantile weakness, then perhaps his act was not *wickedly* incestuous. Correspondingly, so Hillel Steiner claims, 'we would not say that an elephant had acted rightly in kicking aside a heavy felled tree which was blocking the progress of an ambulance on a jungle road'.[28] She may do what she does out of immediate impulses of kindliness, or out of professional habit, but not out of any serious grasp of what she ought to do. Accordingly, her action is not strictly right action, for it is not fully and properly a moral act at all; it is not undertaken with a view to the right, any more than is the hyena's.

This is not to say that animals can do no good deeds, and no bad ones. They do not commit incest strictly so called, any more than they evade taxes, but some of their motives are commendable and some are not. Van Lawick-Goodall does not condemn the hyena: she feels very differently when confronted by chimpanzees who spurn and bully one of their own company who is partly paralysed.[29] Their behaviour evinces callousness and cruelty because they do know what they are doing. One chimpanzee, indeed, did overcome his own distaste to assist his sick companion. Even this is perhaps not true moral action, not a determination to do the right thing, but simply a kindliness. Nonetheless, that chimpanzee's heart was in the right place, and his acts (broadly so called) were commendable.

But what if there were rational creatures, capable of intending to do the right thing, who had natural motives of another kind than ours? Gilbert Harman proposes that alien intelligences who had no compunction about treating us as we treat other animals would be 'dreadful enemies to be repelled and even destroyed', but that we should not judge that 'they should not act as they do'.[30] That humankind ought not to be destroyed by 'supermantises', intelligent beings that reproduce like hunting wasps, would mean only that it would be (for us) a very terrible thing, a thing worth fearing; but no trace of 'moral turpitude and deformity' would attach to the acts or the events that brought it about (any more than to solar flares, or the black death). That the genuine actions of the supermantises are not morally evil, while similarly constituted acts of ours *would* be, rests on the very Humean ground that they lack certain fundamental sentiments: the acts are not the same, because they embody quite different meanings. The hyena is not being cruel, is not delighting in her sadistic control of her victim, and could not be expected to be moved by quasi-parental affection when the young wildebeest seeks parental care. She displays no moral turpitude, because her motives are to feed herself and her young, and she does not deliberately blind herself to the pain of her victims.

Supermantises, unlike hyenas or else unlike what we imagine hyenas are, are creatures with a vision of the world to which they can strive to accommodate their unruly emotions. Some of what they do must be accounted action in the strict sense: they do it as being the best thing they can imagine to do. Some of what they do may even issue from motives with which we could sympathise, were we not so deeply involved. Only a few supermantises, let us suppose, are so depraved as to *like* to see people squirm: most of them consider us only as nesting material. This is not to say, as we should for creatures of mammalian extraction, that they think of us as food for their young. Not being mammals, the supermantises have no need of parental affection: they enjoy laying eggs in suitable material, and have no special ties with the eventual product. For much of their history, indeed, they hardly noticed that there was a connection between ovipositing and the emergence of new supermantises. Nor do they feel the sort of concern for their prey that hunters and farmers must develop, lest they cull the creatures to extinction. The supermantises, let us suppose, are native to a planet so large that they have always been able to find new prey. The net result is that they enjoy messing up the world, and have never found any need to restrain themselves from that pleasure. Not being equipped to sympathise with the young or weak, there is nothing that they could mean by sparing us.

The moral of this story is that our community of moral agents is no larger than the mammalian order or, perhaps, the higher vertebrates. Only beings with experience of parental and filial affection can get outside themselves enough to take account of what other creatures value. Even they do so fleetingly, until they learn to take a more rational view. To understand an action as a moral evil it is necessary to see that it arises from *depraved* motives, a distortion of the meanings embodied in the social universe. For mammals in general, and human beings in particular, callousness and cruelty, disloyalty and selfishness, are depraved. For the supermantises it is sentimental kindliness that works against the emotions and purposes that they must have if there are going to be supermantises at all. On this account neither human beings nor supermantises can ask 'And who is right?'.

Hume's argument can now be restated. Insofar as human beings and supermantises are not doing the same thing, there is no contradiction in saying that human acts of murder are evil while supermantis acts of ovipositing are not – though they have identical results. In this sense, there seems no escape from species relativism. Moral evil is nothing but the projection of our deepest sentiments upon the acts we judge and nothing is 'really' evil, any more than anything is 'really' green or 'really' tasty. Acts are evil, leaves are green and caterpillars are tasty only relative to a given kind's perceptions, and nothing more can be said. If human and supermantis are to be judged by the same standards, those standards cannot rest upon species-relative sentiments. If human and supermantis are not subject to the same standards, because they never mean the same by what they do, morality is indeed subjective.

There are at least four responses to this argument: we may deny the possibility of supermantises; we may insist that rationality itself constitutes a common framework for moral discourse; we may argue that supermantises are not to be condemned because what they do is allowed by ordinary moral judgment; or we may agree that they are to be condemned, by reference to a higher good than species-survival.

First, are supermantises really possible? Conscience and self-consciousness take their beginnings from social life. If supermantises are so blind to the wills and needs of others, so little inclined to natural affection even for their own kind, it may seem doubtful that they could have evolved to a capacity for assessing their own actions in accordance with a vision of the world and their place in it. Creatures capable of reasoned choice must perhaps share with us, and with other mammals, the sentiments on which our ethical commitments are founded. If supermantises had the character I have described, they could not also be rational beings. Like hyenas and hunting wasps they do not strictly act at all, and it remains possible that (for example) deliberately hurting others is objectively evil, although super-mantises do no evil when they hurt others. Lacking ethical sentiment, they lack reason too.

This response is not entirely convincing. Even wild dogs display the most touching loyalty and affection toward their pack-mates (though this is not quite the loyalty we feel toward our kin), but regard all other animals as meat. Even lions, who are as mammalian as we, feel no compunctions about killing and eating lion cubs. The sentiments we share even with other mammals do not guarantee that, were they to become rational, they would share our moral views. Conversely, the only non-human animals that have a well-attested 'language' are bees: it does not seem impossible that there should be rational superbees, and their moral sentiments, while more agreeable than the supermantises', would probably not be ours. That there is some connection between social forms, sentiments and rationality is intuitively plausible, but in the absence of non-imaginary examples we cannot be sure what that connection is.

The second response is as follows: granted that we cannot be sure what sentiments a rational species would have to work with, we can at least insist that rationality itself is constituted by obedience to certain moral codes: to seek the truth, for example, and not to contradict oneself. If the supermantises can talk and organise their lives by joint discussion, there are at least some creatures (namely adult supermantises) whom each of them regards as something more than mere material. If they can talk to us as well, they must come to realise that we may also be contributors to the ongoing project of rational discourse, and are not to be treated merely as means to supermantis pleasure. All rational beings must, on pain of contradiction, treat all other rational beings as fellow members of the kingdom of ends.

These familiar Kantian arguments have some strength. But they do not constitute the whole of our morality. If the supermantises only parasitised terrestrial baboons we would still think that they were doing something evil. Even Kant had great difficulty in consistently excluding non-rational animals from the realm of moral objects. If we ought not to torment baboons so horribly, neither should supermantises (though their lack of immediate sentimental attachment may at first excuse them). The third available response is to say that neither we nor supermantises would be doing wrong, insofar as the primary moral duty of any creature is to preserve its kind. This second form of species-relativism does not deny that there are objective moral truths, but insists that the relevant truth is that we do right when we do what is best for our own kind. Supermantises are morally obliged to lay their eggs where they may: we are morally obliged to resist them.

Such species-relativism is objectivist in intention. Its oddity, like that of naive egoism, is that 'we' (the totality of moral agents) are morally obliged to struggle against each other. This need not be a contradiction, but its only plausibility rests upon a notion of the intrinsic value of the world maintained by such a struggle – which leads on to the fourth response. The supermantises, by hypothesis, intend the destruction of all things that they can; their self-perception is of creatures dedicated to the ruin of the world. Insofar as we, as moral agents and not merely as terrified victims, are opposed to them, it must be that we acknowledge the intrinsic value of the living world. Acting for the sake of the right is to act to preserve the living world itself, as a struggling community of many tribes and kinds. The supermantises may justly be condemned insofar as they are a general menace to the living world – as may we.

If we are to think that there is a moral system within which supermantises may be condemned, the likeliest truths of that system are that the living world be preserved, that moral agents should conceive themselves 'as members of a great City whose author and founder is God'[31] (i.e. Creative Value), and so move beyond natural affection and fear of natural consequences for themselves and their closer kindred.

> Throughout the whole system of the visible and natural world do you not perceive a mutual connection and correspondence of parts? And is it not from hence that you frame an idea of the perfection and order and beauty of nature? And have not the Stoics heretofore said this pattern of order was worthy the imitation of rational agents? Ought we not therefore to infer the same union, order and regularity in the moral world that we perceive in the natural? Should it not therefore seem to follow that man ought not to consider himself as an independent creature, whose happiness is not connected with that of other(s); but rather as the part of a whole, to the common good of which he ought to conspire and order his ways and actions suitably, if he would live according to nature.[32]

Berkeley, for reasons that are not wholly clear, did not draw the full conclusion, but only that rational creatures were made for each other. The stronger conclusion, that all kinds and examples of creatures are parts of the greater whole and that all rational beings should appreciate that whole, seems as firmly established as the weaker principle, that restricts the moral domain to those creatures that can talk and reason.

Even if we hold that moral acts are to be identified by their motives and meanings (so that what a dog does in copulating with his daughter is not what a human being does) we need not fall into species-relativism, the belief that the doings of a supermantis lie beyond our moral judgment. Insofar as such creatures constitute a deliberate danger to the whole web of life their mode of life is evil – as is ours.

CONCLUSION

Hume argued that moral distinctions were not matters of fact, on the ground that, if they were, the doings of animals would be as condemnable or commendable as ours. I have argued, on the contrary, that we may hold any of the following positions.

Even if we say that neither humans nor dogs do wrong in committing incest, it does not follow that there are no natural goods or natural evils. If we accept the tradition that follows the way of Nature, we will say that those creatures are commendable who are toughest and most self-reliant, who value themselves for what they are and cultivate such habits as will enable them to go on living.

Second, we may infer from the bad effects of inbreeding and the general disinclination at least of females to have sex with their close relatives, that incest (or inbreeding) is indeed a natural evil. On this account, that creature is commendable whose habits and emotions are of the type that creatures of that kind must generally have if the kind is to survive. The normal affections of an animal kind constitute the framework within which moral discussion must usually take place. A good mammal is one that cares for her young, gives deference where it is due, responds appropriately to her companions' signals of play, love, pride.

Finally, we may deny that non-rational animals ever strictly do what a rational animal does. Dogs do not *act*: they may be good dogs, but they are not (as it were) good-and-beautiful dogs,[33] creatures that act for the sake of doing what is right. Supermantises do act, but their vision of what it is right to do is hideously mistaken. They have failed, so the fantasy declares, to think past their own limitations and see that the world is more than their material. Accident has released them from the normal checks and balances that ensure that no creature, no creaturely kind, can quite devour the world. We recognise them as something more than dreadful enemies: they are our own distorted images. They behave as we do, and show their wickedness in disregarding the values that other creatures put upon their worlds.

The objectivity of morals can thus survive Hume's attack. But the actual nature of moral objectivity is another story.

7

ANIMALS, ECOSYSTEMS AND THE LIBERAL ETHIC[1]

THE PLACE OF 'RIGHTS'

The claim that animals, as well as people, 'have rights' may often mean only that their interests ought to be given some moral weight: they should not be treated 'cruelly' or 'inconsiderately'. The more demanding claim may also be made that animals should not be subjected to simple-mindedly utilitarian calculation: their choices, their liberty, should sometimes be respected even if this prevents the realisation of some notionally 'greater good'. Finally, talk of rights may have a clearly political context: if, and only if, animals have rights, governments are entitled to legislate on how they should be treated. If they do not, then any laws on the subject are merely moralistic, and as such to be regretted by any sincere liberal (Clark 1977, pp. 11ff). It is this last doctrine that I shall be investigating here, with particular attention to the writings of Regan and McCloskey. Only in this context, so it seems to me, does much hang upon the question of whether animals 'really' have rights: for those outside the liberal, or libertarian, tradition it is enough to know that we ought not to disregard the suffering of our fellow creatures, nor treat it merely 'aggregatively'.

Libertarian individualists share with old-fashioned liberals the conviction that government is best which governs least. This thesis may be founded on utilitarian calculation of the advantages of a free market economy (Mises 1949), on the egoistic theory that nothing can count as a reason for any moral agent's action but that agent's own good (Machan 1975), or on a brute intuition of the rights of rational individuals (McCloskey 1983). Their different backgrounds generate subtly different strategies, and there may be considerable disagreement even about ideals. Not all libertarians are absolute in their anti-statism: some may agree that the state, and its self-proclaimed right to tax and conscript unwilling citizens, are necessary evils in a dangerous world. Not all libertarians insist that citizens should never be taxed to provide welfare payments for the impoverished or sick: even on egoistic terms, it is in no one's interests to have hordes of starving and unhealthy beggars around one's land. Not all liberals, broadly so called, even

70

reject all moralistic legislation. Some will agree that some acts are so vile that they may rightly be forbidden by law even if they injure no one's rights: 'to tolerate infanticide, cruelty to animals, corruption of the young, duelling, drunken driving, is to condone certain immoralities', and there is an indefinable limit to such toleration (McCloskey 1983, p. 58). But all these concessions, and especially the last, are uneasy: 'a key aspect of liberalism...is the insistence that the individual has the moral right to act immorally, provided that he or she does not harm others' (McCloskey 1983, p. 57: he means only human, or even rational, others). It is this barrier between what may be 'morally' required, and what may (justly) be demanded by the law of the land, that both McCloskey and Regan variously acknowledge, and which gives their talk of rights its point.

It is an axiom of most modern political philosophy that states and governments can have no rights beyond those ceded to them by freely consenting individuals. What may a government justly demand of us? If there are any duties that anyone may justly demand that we fulfil, a government may do so too – and so may I. What I demand of others, as of right, I must be prepared to cede to them if the situation is reversed. Our mutual demands, moreover, must be capable of simultaneous fulfilment: if I demand something from you that you demand from me (both 'as of right') it can only be something that we can both enjoy. Otherwise each of us has a right to have what the other has a right to refuse – and so neither has any real right at all (leaving the notional 'rights', i.e. the mere liberties, of Hobbes's state of nature out of it). *Pace* McCloskey (ibid., p. 147), 'men's rights are always consistent and harmonious with each other and every other man's rights' (Spooner 1886, p. 21). 'Any alleged right of one man which necessitates the violation of the rights of another is not and cannot be a right' (Rand 1967, p. 325). Neither I nor a government can have a right to take what another has a right to refuse. It follows that if governments have no rights beyond those conceded to them by rational citizens (who would otherwise retain such rights for themselves), they can have no right to tax or conscript unwilling parties in the interests even of a majority, nor to impose upon some the moral ideals of others. The only rights I can have consistently with the rights of others are those of life, liberty and the pursuit of happiness: I do not have a right to make another citizen my slave.

Strict libertarians construe these rights as merely negative in their effect: my right to life imposes a duty on all moral agents to let me live, not to kill nor assault me, unless and until my mode of life constitutes a (deliberate?) threat to the rights of others. Welfare-liberals would add that the right may impose a positive duty on others to assist me to live, if they can justly do so: at the very least to assist me against assault (and deliberate fraud?) and to punish my assailants. That duty may not be so clearly assigned as the general, negative one: though someone ought to help, it may not be true of anyone in particular, nor of everyone taken singly, that he or she ought to help. It is true of everyone that they ought not to hinder, even if others do, but not that they ought to help, even if others do. There will, accordingly, be differences of emphasis between libertarian and welfare-liberal as to what the state has the right to do when it has the power. But even welfare-liberals may agree that the state (or anyone) only has a duty to help when it may do so justly, without infringing the rights of other individuals. I have no right to assistance at the cost of another's life and liberty, even if I ought, if justly possible, to be assisted – which is why it is not enough to point to the advantages to be gained, say, from destructive experimentation on innocent human victims to justify or excuse such action. The doctrine that is shared by libertarian and welfare-liberal is that it is one's rights that may justly be defended by vigilantes or a decent state: 'when we call anything a person's right, we mean that he has a valid claim on society to protect him in the possession of it' (Mill 1962, p. 309; see Regan 1983, p. 271).

There are, by contrast, many things which it would be good for me to have, whether because they would increase my enjoyments or spare me disappointments, or perfect my human or mammalian potential. Anyone who provided me with them would earn my gratitude. I would, *ceteris paribus*, be better off (even if not 'really better off') if I had a video-recorder, a larger computer, a holiday home in the Bahamas. A simple-minded utilitarian, elevated to the throne, would have to conclude that I ought in principle to have these things, if they can be obtained for me without 'undue' cost to the welfare of others. More realistic utilitarians, of course, would doubt that, in the present circumstances, giving such things to me (and those like me) would increase the total happiness as effectively and economically as feeding the hungry, clothing the naked and healing the sick. There would be earlier calls on the state's beneficence (funded, of course, by violent expropriation) than I, and what I had considered 'mine' would doubtless be merely a resource for others less well off (as long as such expropriations did not lead to a gradual decline of useful output). Welfare-liberals, even if they work from within a sophisticated utilitarianism, are likely to distinguish in practice between those goods to which anyone has a 'right', and those which it would merely be good for them to have: the desperately poor have a right to food (i.e. they ought to have it, even at some cost to me, and even if I resist expropriation); I have no right to a video-recorder. Libertarians, even if they begin from a hard-headed ethical egoism, may concede that there are cases of such acute and undeserved penury that the victims have a genuine right to the assistance of those who can assist. How could we have a right to withhold aid, if we thereby deny any effective exercise of another's right, and have ourselves enjoyed community support? Both sides would of course agree that pauperising the recipient of state (or any other) beneficence is a very bad idea: what is our duty is to assist each other to the point where we no longer need unusual assistance, and may pay our way as equals.

THE PLACE OF 'BEASTS'

Those moralists and statesmen who hope to engineer the greatest good of the greatest number, and who deny the existence of 'moral' or 'natural' rights, have always been vulnerable to the suggestion that they should include the welfare of non-human animals in their calculation. Even if it is not pleasure only that counts toward the greater good, but also virtue and intellectual achievement, utilitarians cannot simply leave non-human animals out of their calculation: their well-being counts toward net utility. At the same time it is implied that human as well as non-human animals might rightly be used and abused for that same greater good. There is nothing utterly and absolutely wrong, on this account, about cannibalism or destructive experimentation on human beings (say, on orphaned imbeciles, alcoholic paupers or criminal psychopaths) if great advantage (of the order accruing from experimentation on chimpanzees) were reasonably expected.

So welfare-enthusiasts may act more humanely toward the non-human than has been usual, and less respectfully to the human. They treat animals better, and humans worse, than tradition has demanded. Those moralists who have laid most stress on 'human rights' have accordingly been loath to admit 'animals' to the political arena. Even if they have interests, even if it would be morally praiseworthy in us to save or spare their lives, yet they can have no 'rights'. It cannot be the right of the state (or any other third party) to interfere in the liberty of citizens to do as they please with their own. Talk of 'animal rights' is perceived as a way of excusing the violation of human rights, and those who insist upon the latter sometimes seize upon strange allies in their rejection of the former. Rothbard, for example, praises Frey's attack on 'animal rights' (Rothbard 1982, pp. 155ff), without noticing that Frey himself is a utilitarian, and as adamantly opposed to human rights (Frey 1980). For libertarians, to say that animals have no rights is to say that all animal welfare laws are merely moralistic, and strictly incompatible with liberal principle.

It is as well to note one other area of dispute that has affected the argument. Environmentalism, especially in its 'deeper' forms (following Naess 1973), has directed our attention to the damage we have inflicted on the ecosystems within which all of us, human and non-human, live. We ought, so the argument goes, so act so as to preserve the splendid diversity of the living world, and restrain the operations of free market industrialism.

> The grand design of nature perceived broadly in four dimensions to include the forces that move the universe and created man, with special focus on evolution in our own biosphere, is something intrinsically good that it is right to preserve and enhance, and wrong to destroy and degrade.
>
> (Sperry 1983, p. 22; see Leopold 1966, p. 240)

Libertarians have suspected misanthropy and a concealed lust for power: 'the very same intellectuals who not so long ago were yearning for a technocratic dictatorship over all of our lives are now trying to deprive us of the vital fruits of technology itself' (Rothbard 1973, p. 257). These same deep environmentalists have also often been holists, arguing that ecosystems in general and the biosphere in particular were real entities of which we were parts:

> The problems we have to confront are increasingly the worldwide crises of a global organism: not pollution of a stream, but pollution of the atmosphere and of the ocean. Increasingly the death that occupies each human's imagination is not his own, but that of the entire life cycle of the planet earth, to which each of us is as but a cell to a body.
>
> (Stone 1974, p. 53)

Libertarians, as good individualists, think that they have heard such things before – from spokesmen of the total state. They may legitimately add that the record of bureaucratic socialism in these matters is not noticeably better than that of market capitalism, quite apart from its other disadvantages. Even sympathetic commentators suspect totalitarian implications in any doctrine that seems to elevate the good of the whole over the good of the suffering individuals who make up that whole (Attfield 1983). The notion that an ecosystem, or a species, is intrinsically valuable (apart from the enjoyments it provides to individuals) is one that zoophiles may dislike as much as libertarians (Regan 1983). Spinoza, whose thought has been an inspiration both to environmentalists and to libertarians, was fiercely non-zoophile (Spinoza 1982, 4.47s.1; see Chapter 8 of this volume). Deep environmentalists, libertarians and zoophiles, in short, are constantly at each other's throats. It is my object to suggest that they need not be. We can place the arguments of zoophiles and libertarians within the deep environmentalists' account of our situation, rather than remain content with bare intuitions about the intrinsic value of creatures that are 'subjects-of-a-life' (Regan 1983, pp. 243ff), or with indemonstrable assertions that 'the right-to-life is to be seen as self-evidently resting on man's nature as a person, that is, as a morally autonomous being' (McCloskey 1983, p. 72).

Not so long ago, the laws of the land allowed us to own other human beings. If we owned them, no third party might 'justly' intervene in our treatment of them, even if that treatment was iniquitous or imprudent. If we owned them, we might call upon the officers of the law to recapture them for us. Insofar as the state was called into existence (or defended in its existence) to defend the basic liberties of freemen, slaves (by definition) fell outside the law. Even when we had formally abandoned slavery, white explorers seem to have taken it for granted that any native peoples they came across were merely property. Many such explorers were devout and kindly persons, but it did not enter their scheme of things that natives could have serious plans or interests – or rights; what the white man wanted done was his right only, and he was ready to invoke armed intervention to enforce his will, or to evade the natives' attempt to punish or control him. Savages, when not enslaved, were patronised. The subtle historical processes that have led 'us' to renounce (and even to forget about) such attitudes lie beyond my brief. There are forms of libertarianism, resting merely upon immediate egoism, which would still not disallow such 'civilised' behaviour. What advantage do I get, in 'my' lifetime, from allowing my relations with Amazonian Indians to be governed by impartial law, and granting them property rights in their homeland which would interfere with my mining activities? Where we have the power to enforce our plans, there is no need to conciliate.

> Were there a species of creatures intermingled with men, which, though rational, were possessed of such inferior strength, both of body and mind, that they were incapable of all resistance, and could never, upon the highest provocation, make us feel the effects of their resentment; the necessary consequence, I think, is that we should be bound by the laws of humanity to give gentle usage to these creatures, but should not properly speaking lie under any restraint of justice with regard to them, nor could they possess any right or property, exclusive of such arbitrary lords. . . . The restraints of justice and property, being totally useless, would never have place in so unequal a confederacy.
> (Hume 1962, p. 190: *Enquiry Concerning Principles of Morals*, 3.1.152)

If we need to acknowledge the principles of justice only to avoid a Hobbesian free-for-all, neither savages nor (of course) animals need be given justice (though see Naess 1979). The liberty to do as we please with our own, and the corresponding agreement that some things *are* our 'own', is only granted by others if it would in the end be too troublesome to deny that liberty, too profitable to treat us as partners instead of slaves.

Even on these terms it may be open to environmentalists and zoophiles alike to argue that we, by hypothesis the lords and masters, would profit more from a relatively 'liberated' ecosphere. Mises' claim that animals are controlled only by fear, human beings by being offered the chance to achieve their own goals in cooperation with others (1949, pp. 624ff), is not entirely accurate. Domestic and farm animals are not best controlled with the whip and goad, but by giving them what they desire (even though they do not realise what the price may be). We are not at war with all animals, despite a long tradition to this effect (see Locke, *Treatises*1963, 2.16, pp. 319ff), even though we do sometimes have irreconcilable differences with some of them. Stable ecosystems are ones in which the chosen behaviour of indefinitely many organisms works together to preserve the whole, in a way which offers the greatest encouragement to admirers of 'the invisible hand'. Even egoists and utilitarians, in short, may come to understand that there are rules of mutual aid and non-interference which bring more profit in the end than simple-mindedly exploitative attitudes.

Alongside that egoistic argument for outlawing slavery, encouraging fraternity, is a more abstract one. I cannot claim, as of right, that some other be my unwilling slave, for I cannot discover any personal characteristic in virtue of which I would have that right which would not also guarantee an identical right for that other. 'Rights' that cannot be consistently enjoyed by all who can lay claim to them are no rights at all. I cannot, in reason, claim to own a being whose equal rights of ownership I have to concede in the act of claiming mine.

This abstract argument, of course, may be of less psychological force than arguments of egoistic prudence, or even sentimental fancy. But it does have some strength. Any creature that plans its life, even to a limited extent, thereby lays claim upon its own action, and on some part of the world. When we realise that this is what we are doing, that we are self-owners and sources of action, and that we would continue in being such even if we lost our current social status, or our health, or our intelligence, we must acknowledge that any right we have, any demand we make upon the world and our fellows to respect our claim must rest simply on the fact that we have made it. Freemen persist in their own freedom by acknowledging the equal claim of others (see 'Slaves and Citizens'). Their self-claimed rights and dignity are limited by the equal rights and dignity they must, in reason, concede to all who share their nature. For example:

> If the free will requires private property as a means of its realisation, all free wills require private property, and the system of private property must be such that all wills can find, and as far as possible do find such means.
>
> (Barker 1915, p. 55)

Their good, as freemen, is dependent on maintaining the framework of mutually acknowledged rights and dignity that precedes any particular legal institution. It also depends on the continued well-being of the biosphere, and therefore on the relatively unhampered life of other creatures (see 'Gaia and the Forms of Life').

This is at least a better attempt at rational argument than is a blank appeal to intuition (though this is not to say that it is bound to convince all parties), or the blank assertion that God has given us the Earth and all inferior creatures (as Locke, *Treatises* 1963, 2.26, p. 328). The intention of its authors may often have been to delimit the class of right-holders as human, or as rational beings: 'morally autonomous beings', in McCloskey's phrase. It is this 'natural' or 'moral' law which requires that no one lord it over other human beings, no one determine for them what their lives are to be. Creatures without such wills present no necessary obstacle to rational action: we do not unjustly deny them their rightful claims ('rightful' by the standard that makes our claims right), because they make no claims. This, presumably, might serve as an argument for McCloskey's assertion that 'moral self-direction and self-determination ... is basic to the possibility of possessing a right' (McCloskey 1983, p. 66), and that what 'cannot be possessed of moral rights ... may legitimately be used as resources by man for food and other products' (ibid., p. 40, re whales; see also p. 140). It certainly does not follow, of course, that creatures who themselves present no obstacle, as of right, to our use may legitimately be used: there might be no offence *in justice* in our using them – it might still be an offence by 'the laws of humanity'. As so often, the liberal's insistence that people have a right to act 'immorally' turns out to rest on the tacit assumption that the behaviour in question is not even immoral. What should follow, for a libertarian, is that third parties have no right to come between whalers and their prey, or farmers and their veal-calves, since none of us have a right to impose our 'merely' moral standards on other autonomous agents. We have, of course, no obligation to like or help or communicate with those who behave themselves unseemly, and the state certainly has no right to fund such projects with our money.

Older zoophiles have sometimes ended there, with the plea that even if animals are not owed justice, they are owed charity. Even if there are acknowledged rights of property in non-human creatures, we may still urge owners to treat them well – and this plea, if successful, would radically alter what we do to them at present. Regan's plea, and that of other modern zoophiles, has been instead that we do owe them justice, and this for two reasons which this argument does not meet. First, it is implausible to claim that the only evil done in imprisoning, tormenting and killing even a rational agent is that we thereby interfere with his or her moral choices: much of the evil is simply that we do what he or she does not want done. That evil is also done if our victims are non-rational, not morally autonomous. What difference does it really make whether or not they have or could have a principled objection to our behaviour? If they have no will in the matter I do not violate their will, but I clearly violate their wishes.

Second, what ground have we got to make so radical a distinction between wishes and the will, between the desires and projects of a non-human or sub-normal human and the principled will of a rational agent? Why should it be supposed that I make my claims upon the world as a carefully moral being, in some way that a non-rational being could not manage? 'A cat who is being hurt will struggle, scratch and try to bite. Why is not this a claiming of its rights?' (Sprigge 1984, p. 442). Why isn't a blackbird claiming his rights when he proclaims his territorial possession? What is lacking in too much discussion of these questions is any serious attention to what 'animals' are like, and what evidence there is for the vast difference in nature that humanists like McCloskey must conceive. It is quite inadequate to appeal to current English linguistic usage, as if that settled the question. If it is wrong (not merely imprudent) to batter human infants this may be partly because it seems likely to interfere with their future projects, but it is chiefly wrong because they do not like it, nor would like its further consequences if they knew of them. The same wrong is done in battering baboons: who could imagine that baboons don't mind?

It follows, if the abstract argument for natural human rights must be extended to allow similar rights to other agents (even if not strictly 'moral' agents), that our property rights in non-human animals must often be suspect. A right that licenses the violation of a right is no right at all, and 'self-owning' is a category more widely extended than we had thought. A being 'owns itself' if its behaviour is the product of its own desires and beliefs, if it can locate itself within the physical and social world, and alter its behaviour to take account of other creatures' lives and policies.[2] This, I take it, is Regan's concept of what it is to be 'the subject of a life', not merely living (1983, p. 243). Such self-owners are, in the relevant sense, equals, and a just, liberal society cannot allow them to be owned by others, even if it allows them to be employed on terms not strictly of their making.

THE PLACE OF HISTORY

Although the ethics of self-ownership, extended to non-human creatures of the appropriate kind, has considerable strength, it cannot stand alone. The effort to convict sinners of self-contradiction, of affirming what they simultaneously deny, will fail if the sinner falls back on mere self-assertion, the Hobbesian 'right of nature' to do as much as he or she can to maintain his or her own existence and delights. Anyone else has as much right, true, but such rights impose no duties either of a negative or a positive kind. If these were the only 'natural rights', it would indeed be rational to establish Leviathan with fire and the sword, as our only escape from a chaos of warring interests – and what laws there were then would depend on the mere will of the sovereign, whether that was Asoka, Genghis Khan, the British Parliament, or, as libertarians would wish, the whole community. Even if we do concede the abstract argument for non-Hobbesian natural rights, what rights can all self-owners have, once the class is extended to include blackbirds and foxes? It has been assumed, for better or worse, that such extension amounts to assigning to all higher vertebrates and cephalopods (at least) the very rights that humans have claimed for themselves. It is then mockingly deduced, or uncomfortably accepted, that moral agents ought to protect blackbirds against foxes, even if not worms against blackbirds (McCloskey 1983, p. 122). It is not enough to reply (as Regan 1983, p. 357; cf. Chapters 3 and 6 of this volume) that foxes commit no injustice because they do not know that they are doing wrong: if their victims genuinely have rights, and the same rights that humans are presumed to have, then they have a claim on us to be protected in their enjoyment of those rights. If a criminal psychopath attacks my neighbour, and I do nothing to assist her when I could, it is I (not the psychopath) who have violated her right of defence. If wild animals have no such general right to assistance, do we, as self-owners, have quite the rights we hoped?

It seems better to abandon abstract argument, in favour of historical. It is not now, and never has been, true that owners have been allowed, let alone assisted, to do just as they pleased with what they 'owned'. 'Ownership' itself, far from being a merely solipsistic category (so that in the absence of other self-owners I might lay claim upon the world), is a social concept – or a cluster of concepts (acknowledged rights of use, exchange or rental; duties of service and protection). The self-owning individual is a relatively late social invention (see MacIntyre 1981, p. 212), and takes its beginning from the complex of rights and duties assigned by public sentiment. We have to do with historical claims and protections, not with the pre-social rights of self-owners: rights established not by abstract argument, but by the slow discovery of a mutually acceptable forbearance and cooperation – a process, incidentally, that there is no sound reason to limit to human intercourse. There are some ways of treating animals which almost everyone would agree amounted to forfeiture of any claim to 'own' the animal, and juries might well refuse to convict someone who rescued the unfortunate beast whatever the law said and however feeble their grasp of general principles of justice. If McCloskey were right, Dr Taub's hideously injured and neglected monkeys should not have been rescued and ought indeed to have been returned to their 'owner', but no one but a ninny (or a very frightened researcher) could think themselves obliged to defend Dr Taub's 'property rights' in those monkeys (see Pacheco 1985).

> You bought the animal with your money, it is true, and he is your property. You could not purchase the right to use him with cruelty and injustice. Of whom could you purchase such a right? Who could make such a conveyance?
>
> (Lawrence 1796, Nicholson 1879, p. 92)

In fact, of course, Dr Taub bought the monkeys with tax-payers' money.

The first begetters of libertarian doctrine did not appeal to absolute rights of self-ownership (restricted by the equal rights of others). Private property was defended as the likeliest way of enabling a society of freemen to subsist in mutual harmony, and cultivate their virtues: if we each had some portion of the land to tend we would be less likely to fall prey to tyrants. But we did not own the land itself: only the lawfully acquired fruits, and we owned these only for their lawful use. 'Nothing was made by God for Man to spoil or destroy' (Locke, *Treatises* 1963, 2.31, p. 332; see Hargrove 1980). Individual liberty rested on the value God placed in every soul, as a unique expression of His glory, such that any despotism, however benevolent in purpose, must issue in a decline of valuable diversity. Each of us has a profound and vital interest in the virtue of our fellow citizens, and in the continued viability of the ecosystems within which we live.

Leopold's vision has been the inspiration of much recent environment-alism:

> We abuse land because we regard it as a commodity belonging to us. When we see land as a community to which we belong, we may begin to use it with love and respect.... That land is a community is a basic concept of ecology, but that land is to be loved and respected is an extension of ethics.
>
> (Leopold 1968, p. viii)

This can be used to ground both libertarian and zoophile intuitions in a necessary moral synthesis. Our moralising predecessors defended their moral views in the context of the moral universe they inherited or posited. Where modern moralists think that the universe which would be maintained by the rules they advocate is to be justified solely by its value to 'us' (whoever 'we' may be), the ancients thought it obvious that it was the whole world which was to be admired:

> It is a visible living creature, it contains all creatures that are visible and is itself an image of the intelligible; and it has thus become a visible god, supreme in greatness and excellence, beauty and perfection, a single, uniquely created heaven.
>
> (Plato, *Timaeus* 92d)

Our individual selves, so far from being thought absolute self-owners, were considered elements and partners in the whole universe, even by those of a liberal persuasion. Universal 'self-ownership', which is to say the duty and prerogative of each element of the universe to maintain its own integrity as a part of that diverse and lovely whole, is not an abstract, logical requirement, but an aspect of the way the 'visible god' works. When Berkeley, for example, set himself to show the value of righteousness, he appealed to our understanding of ourselves as 'member[s] of a great City, whose author and founder is God' (Berkeley 1948: Alciphron 3.10, 3.129). He was Cartesian enough to forget, sometimes, that there were other spirits than the merely human whose welfare might be considered, but his intention here was clear. We should not be misled by the word 'city': what Berkeley meant was the whole created universe (see my various papers on Berkeley). It would be absurd, said Aristotle, to suppose that human beings were the most important things in the world (*Nicomachean Ethics* 6.1141a.20f). The value which Aristotle urged us to 'contemplate and serve' (Aristotle, *Eudemian Ethics* 8, 1249b.20) was the same god which the universe reflected in its continuing activity: the honour due to us as rational beings rested on the value of the universe we understand. It is because the cosmos is worth knowing and preserving that those who can know and preserve it deserve their status: we are the servants, the 'shepherds of being' (see Sprigge 1984, p. 456, after Heidegger). 'Could [the poet] say of Athens, dear city of Cecrops, and will you not say [of the cosmos], dear city of God?' (Aurelius, *Meditation* 4.19). The cosmic whole was maintained in being, at the behest of God, through the integrity and mutual cooperation of its elements. That world, in Philo of Alexandria's graphic phrase (1930: *Quod Deus Immutabilis* 176, vol. 3, pp. 97, 489), was a sort of cosmic democracy – not a mob rule, but a genuinely liberal society, where none are allowed to lord it over others, but must all take their place and their turn.

Accordingly, the view which Regan dubs 'environmental fascism' (Regan 1983, p. 362), that 'the integrity, stability and beauty of the biotic community' is the proper criterion of right action (Leopold 1968, p. 217) is nothing like as novel as Leopold and others supposed (nor is it fascist). When traditional moralists are told that certain Amerindians 'conceive of themselves as belonging to the land, in the way that flora and fauna belong to it, [and] cultivate the land by the grace of the immanent spirits, but cannot dispose of it, and cannot conceive of doing so' (Lee 1959, p. 169), we are inclined to murmur 'how else should any one think?' What sane intelligence supposes that he or she owns the land, or that all moral agents should bow down before his or her own inherent and absolute value? What sane community of merely human individuals? We may 'own' the fruits of the land, but we cannot justly dispose of the land itself (as Jefferson well knew).

The main theoretical objections usually made to deep environmentalism are as follows. First, it denies to individuals any absolute or inherent value. Second, it allows inherent value to things other than the merely sentient, whereas it has been a moral commonplace for most of this century that states of mind and experience are all that can be 'really' good or bad. Third,

> the practical implications ... are reminiscent of the morally objection-
> able views and attitudes of primitive moralities. To treat a person, a
> dog, a fly, a flea, an ant, a malaria organism, a tree, a thistle, a stone, a
> grain of sand, a pool of water, an ocean, as equals, as ends in
> themselves, would be to act in a grossly immoral and insensitive way.
> (McCloskey 1983, p. 56)

Intuitionism, as a meta-moral theory, unfortunately leads to the substitution of abuse for argument (see MacIntyre 1981, pp. 16ff). Insofar as the doctrine under discussion precisely denies that any of these individuals can justly or reasonably be considered ends-in-themselves, the attack is sophistical, but a more helpful version may be found.

The objections to 'very deep environmentalism', then, come from individualists, 'mentalists' and non-egalitarians. What all these lack is the patience to consider what the real political implications of a reasonable holism are. The simple answer to individualism is that there are no individuals. There are, to be sure, people, frogs and beech trees, breaths of wind and drops of acid rain, but none of these countable entities are self-sufficient, with essences and welfares atomically distinct from those of others. The doctrine which Regan (1985, p. 152) finds unaccountable, that I am something conceived four thousand million years ago or more, that 'we are the rocks dancing' is the merest scientific realism. Only if there is a distinct spiritual being descended upon this portion of the immortal substance of the universe (*From Athens to Jerusalem*, pp. 175ff) is there any sense in taking me seriously as a separate thing, and if there is such a spiritual eye that too cannot be conceived solipsistically. Once again, there is no point in appealing to current English usage to settle this metaphysical dispute. My being and my welfare cannot be disentangled from the being and welfare of the created universe. The living world (which is itself an element or function of the cosmic whole) is like 'the federation or community of interdependent organs and tissues that go to make up [a physician's] patient' (Gregg 1955; see Lovelock 1991). Claiming a spurious advantage for individuals at the price of damage to the whole is simply silly. 'If men spit upon the ground they spit upon themselves. Man did not weave the web of life, he is merely a strand of it. Whatever he does to the web he does to himself' (Seattle 1854).[3]

The answer to 'mentalism' is more complex. Both Regan and McCloskey agree that the 'inherent' value of their self-owners does not rest upon the 'intrinsic' value of the experiences they happen to have: humans are not worth more to the casuist if they happen to be happy – that indeed is the crucial difference between utilitarian and strongly libertarian theories. Neither can consistently deny – and Regan does not try to – that such inherent value may reside in non-sentient things. What neither admits is that the structure of valuable experience is, traditionally, precisely founded on the value of the thing experienced. It is because mountains, lakes, forests, ecosystems are worth appreciating that our appreciation of them is worth taking seriously. Their value does not reside in the pleasure they give us (or anyone else). The pleasure is a noble one because the whole of which they are a part is noble. What both Regan and McCloskey also neglect is to make clear what that whole is: not the universe as it is posited by merely physical theory, a realm of colourless abstractions, but the world as it is upheld in consciousness, perhaps for ever, perhaps only for a moment. 'We as consciousness are to be thought of as existing for the sake of the objects which need us in order to exist rather than its being the objects which exist for our sake' (Sprigge 1984, p. 455).

The non-egalitarian objection, insisting that entities of our class be valued more highly than entities of any other, at whatever cost to the health of the whole world-system, might be left to die of its own arrogance. But the confusion it represents deserves to be countered. The holistic strategy is to live according to such rules, and in the exercise of such virtues, as are needed for the continued existence, health and beauty of this Great City. 'The patriot aims at his private good in the public. The knave makes the public subservient to his private interest. The former considers himself as part of the whole, the latter considers himself as the whole' (Berkeley 1948, vol. 6, p. 254). It does not follow that such holists will consider it correct, on all normal occasions, to sacrifice children to the fever bacillus, nor that they will surrender their autonomy to a totalitarian government. What they will hope for is a state of health that can incorporate even such bacilli as we now equate – wrongly – with diseases; what they will prefer (when that cannot be attained) is the least destructive strategy to maintain their own being, and that of their kind. If the whole is sustained by the mutual interaction and simple integrity of the parts, the holist's task will often be simply to act as one thing among many, in accordance with the virtues necessary to our particular age and kind. Any moralists who seek to live out their understanding of themselves as a part of some whole invisible to their peers (as it might be, the human species in a profoundly nationalistic age), will be charged with treachery and savage indifference to national disgrace or misery. Such moralists will not deny the force of national feeling, nor urge us to abandon all such local ties (which serve well enough to give us a local habitation and a name) – until they are plainly destructive of the wider value, and of our ties to other creatures also of our kind. Honest cosmopolitans will recognise as wicked any sneering suggestions that they are savages (because they do not treat the 'lower orders' as the proper sacrifice in any clash of interests). 'He who boasts of the dignity of his nature, and the advantages of his station, and thence infers his right of oppression of his inferiors, exhibits his folly as well as his malice' (Primatt 1839, p. 22).

CONCLUSION

The rights that all self-owners have simply as such cannot include any right of immunity to disease, predation or famine. No such right can be justly defended for all self-owners, since the terrestrial economy is organised around the fact of predation. None of us can be treated absolutely and only as 'ends-in-themselves', never to be material for another's purposes. Of all of us it is literally true that we are food. If blackbirds have no right not to be eaten by foxes (and people, correspondingly, no duty to protect them), since such a general right would deny the right of life to foxes, but blackbirds have all the 'natural' rights that all self-owners have, it follows that we too have no right not to be eaten. The only 'right to life' that all self-owners might be allowed, just as such, is the right to live as the creature one is, under the same law as all others. Foxes do no wrong in catching what they can: they would be doing wrong if they prevented the creatures whom they prey upon from enjoying their allotted portion in the sun, if they imprisoned, frustrated and denied them justice. Foxes, obviously, are not at fault.

The libertarian thesis, applied to the terrestrial biosphere, requires that no one do more than enjoy a due share of the fruits of the earth, that forward-looking agents plan their agricultural economy with a view to allowing the diversity of creatures some share of happiness according to their kind. It does not require that everyone abstain from killing and eating animals, if that is how the human creatures that there are can live. Some people may so abstain, because they see no need to live off their non-human kindred, but this (on liberal views) must be their choice, not their duty. Libertarians, by the same token, will not see any general duty to assist people against aggressors. Even aggression, it turns out, is not necessarily unjust, a violation of right, though enslavement is. Even if some acts of aggression are unjust, there is no general duty to defend the victims. Any duty that such libertarians acknowledge to assist the prey will rest upon their sense of solidarity, not on abstract rights of self-ownership.

This radically anarchic view of human and extra-human intercourse, in which all creatures have the right to live, but not to live for ever, is probably one of the roots of ordinary libertarian theory. To be a freeman is to be, in imagination, a wild animal, not a domesticated one. But the discussion can be edged a little further. If the libertarian ethic is to be founded in our perception of the diverse and lovely universe of which we are parts, the cosmic democracy, it is necessary to add that wild animals are not generally individualists. They exist, as we exist, within circles and networks of loyalty and mutual dependence. There is, as Berkeley said, a principle of mutual attraction that draws us together 'in communities, clubs, families, friendship, and all the various species of society' (Berkeley 1948, vol.7, p. 26). Those societies often enough include creatures of more than one species, and it is these little families (however ill they are organised) that constitute the roots of our present concern for the non-human creation. Modern zoophiles, knowing well that dogmatic humanists will readily charge them with pet-loving sentimentality, have been chary of founding their case on such domestic affections, and have preferred utilitarian calculation or abstract notions of egalitarian justice. But it is because we have experienced the possibilities of interspecific affection and communication that we can envisage a new, radical possibility. We can moderate the merely libertarian ethic by the ethic of solidarity: both depend upon our vision of the moral universe, both are necessary.

> We should propose to our selves nobler views, such as to recreate and exalt the mind, with a prospect of the beauty, order, extent, and variety of natural things: hence, by proper inferences, to enlarge our notions of the grandeur, wisdom,and beneficence of the Creator, and lastly to make the several parts of the Creation, so far as in us lies, subservient to the ends they were designed for, God's glory, and the sustentation and comfort of ourselves and fellow-creatures.
>
> (Berkeley 1948, vol.2, p. 89: 'Principles', 109)

This would be a 'fascist' vision only if it implied that there was some elite group entitled to inflict upon an ignorant world the legislation they thought justified, at whatever cost to the ideals and lives of their victims. There is no such implication: on the contrary, it is just those elite groups which most offend against the rules of liberal solidarity.

The 'natural' rights of self-owners are more limited than human rights are generally supposed to be. By 'the law of nature' none of us may justly demand more than our 'fair share of life and liberty'. But it may also be compatible with justice, even required by a more elevated sense of 'justice', that we should give each other more than we have a right to demand: we may construct 'laws of the nations', and tacitly agree to assist those who are in need, so long as we may justly do so. These mutually helpful associations create new, non-natural rights: the cats who share my household have no 'right', in the abstract, to my special care and attention, but once received into the household and contributing their particular value to it, they do have such a right. If I began to starve or to ignore them, I should offend against justice. These historical claims and tacit agreements may be tested against our perception of what rational agents would agree to if they had enough information. The 'social contract', so called, is a device whereby we can make sure that all parties to a reciprocal arrangement are profiting from the deal, by extending the childhood technique for sharing cakes out fairly: the one who cuts the cake does not know what piece he or she will get. It does not matter, for the purposes of this model, that the participants are not in fact rational and well-informed: it is enough that they might be, and that some results are better for them than others (see Elliot 1984).

Historical rights, as defined by the law of nations, and not the law of nature, are what animals, and humans, chiefly need. The abstract rights of self-owners are insufficient to ground a humane order, and themselves take their real strength from a form of society that has been historically developed. The rights of 'British beasts', for example (see Chapter 3), are more extensive than the natural rights of animals, and rest for their force upon emotions of solidarity, as well as considerations of contractual justice. Such solidarity may take in more than domesticated animals: our gradual discovery of the terrestrial biosphere, our increasing capacity to sympathise with the great whales and all that move in the waters, with all the myriad organisms that carry on their lives without any thought of us, may well enable us to accord 'rights' even to creatures who have not made even the most notional of contracts with us. If 'we' are illumined by this vision of the living world, we may request a like forebearance and enthusiasm from our fellow citizens. Those who show that they cannot conceive of the world in its richness, cannot sympathise with their fellow creatures, may seem to us to be menaces. It is, correspondingly, our 'natural right' as self-owners so to organise society to introduce that vision to all with whom we must associate. But at this point the liberal ethic finally collapses: if we have a right to encourage such visionary solidarity in our fellow citizens, ignoring any claims they make to have their 'private lives' immune to public judgment, it no longer matters whether animals 'have rights', as distinct from merely being 'morally considerable'. There is no natural right to found one's life upon the thesis that one is alone in the world, or that the world is devoid of value till one has assigned such value: those are the thoughts of knaves. There is, accordingly, no natural, indefeasible right to treat non-humans in the manner even of a decent farmer or experimenter (let alone Dr Taub), nor any wrong in requiring people to acknowledge and act upon their solidarity with the rest of creation.

I have argued (1) that it is chiefly within the context of liberal or libertarian political theory that the question of 'animal rights' has any real significance; (2) that such liberal theory, though it may find support in abstract argument, gains its real plausibility from the vision of cosmic democracy; (3) that such a vision, as it has taken shape in the historical development of public consciousness, also grounds duties that go beyond the rights of self-ownership associated with libertarianism. Decent treatment of non-human animals, accordingly, should rest upon that vision, not on abstract self-ownership, and the question of their 'natural rights' loses its significance. The rights all self-owners have are insufficient for a humane order, and are themselves better supported, as historical rights, by a sense of social solidarity, and admiration for the visible god.

8

THE DESCRIPTION AND EVALUATION OF ANIMAL EMOTION[1]

What follows is my imagined conversation with two authors, a philosopher and a psychologist. The philosopher, Benedict Spinoza, is one I respect; the psychologist, Howard Liddell, sometime professor of psychobiology at Cornell University, writes like a humane and intelligent man. I emphasise this point, that I have no grudge against either, because I am going to criticise their moral views. It is my experience that people who hold to some version of the 'boo-hurray' theory of ethics – which is to say, a good many scientists – always take moral criticism to be a form of personal insult: I do not, and it is not.

'ANIMALS ARE NOT HUMAN'

First the philosopher:

> The emotions of animals that are called irrational differ from the emotions of men as much as their nature differs from human nature. Horse and man are indeed carried away by lust to procreate, but the former by equine lust, the latter by human lust. So too the lusts and appetites of insects, fishes and birds are bound to be of different kinds.[2]

Spinoza's reason for thinking this is not the banal fact that equine lust typically has horses for its objects, and human lust has people, nor yet that rather different behaviour is required of lustful fish, insects and humans – though these points are important – but rather that both lusts are bound up with each creature's basic endeavour to maintain and improve its own life. To lust as a horse is to want to be, as a horse; nor do such creatures have any option in the matter, nor capacity to consider their own lusts, and correct or cultivate them. The joy of one kind is different from the joy of another, because kinds are essentially distinct. This is not the place to comment on Spinoza's species-essentialism, a doctrine he took over from the medieval tradition, but not from Aristotle, whom modern taxonomists usually blame for it.[3]

Virtue is human power, which is defined solely by man's essence; that is, it is defined solely by the *conatus* whereby man endeavours to persist in his own being. Therefore the more every man endeavours and is able to preserve his own being, the more he is endowed with virtue.[4]

The principle of seeking our own advantage teaches us to be in close relationship with men, not with beasts or things whose nature is different from human nature, and that we have the same right over them as they over us. Indeed, since every individual's right is defined by his virtue or power, man's right over beasts is far greater than their rights over men. I do not deny that beasts feel; I am denying that we are on that account debarred from paying heed to our own advantage and from making use of them as we please and dealing with them as best suits us, seeing that they do not agree with us in nature and their emotions are different in nature from human emotions.[5]

Hating humans is never good, but Spinoza expressly allows that we may hate all others: that is, desire their destruction.[6]

Spinoza's argument is, as always, a subtle one, and I am not sure that I have entirely understood it. It is an additional irony that his general outlook and philosophy seem to support recent environmentalist and 'deep ecology' movements. It is Spinoza's eventual conclusion, after all, that our highest good lies in contemplation of the whole, and understanding our place in it. 'Things are not more or less perfect to the extent that they please or offend human senses, serve or oppose human interests.'[7] At the same time, he rules out any obligation to consider the needs or interests of non-human creatures. Indeed, 'the requirement to refrain from slaughtering beasts (or doing them any other hurt or harm) is founded on groundless superstition and womanish compassion rather than on sound reason'.[8] The very fall of Adam, on Spinoza's account, came

> when he came to believe that the beasts were like himself (and) straightway began to imitate their emotions and to lose his freedom, which the Patriarchs later regained under the guidance of the spirit of Christ, that is, the idea of God, on which alone it depends that a man should be free and should desire for mankind the good that he desires for himself.[9]

There seem to be two arguments advanced for excluding non-humans from rational consideration, the Hobbesian and the moralistic. The Hobbesian first: if any of us are to achieve our individual advantage we need a civil association of the like-minded, an assurance that others will not aim to overmaster us, and a constant challenge and example to our intellectual powers. We do not need to consider, and ought not to consider, any of the feelings or emotions or life-projects of other creatures, since they can be no general threat to us (of a kind that can be obviated by a compact of mutual forbearance and assistance), and cannot share in the general good of humankind (namely, the increase of knowledge and sound learning). We are still in a Hobbesian state of nature with all other creatures.

Second, the moralistic: Spinoza explicitly dissociates himself from the Cartesian view that animals do not have feelings but that if they did we should be bound to take account of them. He acknowledges – indeed he insists – that

> in the animal world we find much that far surpasses human sagacity and that sleepwalkers do many things in their sleep that they would not dare when awake – clear evidence that the body, solely from the laws of its own nature, can do many things at which its mind is amazed.[10]

But he did not conclude that it was 'unnecessary' to postulate a mental aspect to what went on physically: extension and thought, and the laws of extension and thought, were two aspects of the one infinite universe. Physical and mental explanation were not mutually exclusive. If we are at once mental and physical beings, there is no good reason to deny that animals too are subjects of experience, in their degree: what physical difference is there to go along with so vast a mental gap?

It is worth digressing for a moment to emphasise this point. A surprising number of people still seem to think that offering an explanation in terms of intentions or feelings or the like is somehow incompatible with an explanation in terms of physiological condition, as if intentions occupied space to the exclusion of nerve fibres. That something is happening at the neurophysiological level as I write this essay is obvious. We might even have a usable theory which would reveal that what went on was all that physically could go on (though I doubt it). This would not show that I had no intentions or feelings in the matter. There are many levels of true description, from the chemical to the political, and which of these – if any – offers a truer explanation is not something that could be settled by experiment. Intentions and feelings may be non-spatial (that is, spiritual) items associated with physical states (a dualistic doctrine that some commentators now pretend appeals only to the senile, although no non-question-begging argument has been produced against it). They may be characteristic properties of states which are neither simply physical nor simply mental, or even the very same states of matter that the neurophysiologist describes, though experienced from another point of view. Whatever the nature of such intentions and feelings may be, there is at least no reason to think that what has a physical explanation or description cannot also have a mental one. It follows that you cannot prove that an animal is not conscious merely by saying that its motions are in accordance with biochemical laws. Nor can you suppose that animals are like us physically, but that there is no need to think them (broadly) like us mentally, without admitting merely magical conjunctions into the universe: 'it just happens that consciousness has lighted on us, but not on creatures obedient to the same physical laws'. The onus, as Spinoza saw, has to be on those who wish to deny all feeling to the non-rational in the face of outward similarity.

But though animals, on Spinoza's account, can feel, and though we might speak of many emotions that they shared with us, those emotions were of another kind than ours, and could not rationally matter to us. This is what I have called the moralistic argument. He may have been influenced by a point that he adduces elsewhere, which is also used as the basis of the atrocious argument used by David Hume (which I discussed in Chapter 6):

> Every one looks with admiration upon traits in animals which he would execrate and regard with aversion if displayed by men, such as the wars of bees and the jealousy of doves. For while these are forbidden to men, we regard the animals as all the more perfect because they are thus endowed.[11]

The animals behave in ways that can be described by using moral terms, 'war', 'slavery', 'harem', 'incest' and the like, but they do not display any vice in so doing. What they do is not the same as what we might wickedly do, nor are animal 'acts of virtue', loyal and affectionate behaviour to 'spouse' or 'child', acts in the same sense as ours. Hume argued that since animals did the same things as we did, but without condemnation, moral evaluation must be solely in the eye of the beholder. Spinoza, more plausibly, would deny that they did the same things at all, as not having the same things in mind, nor capable of the same reasonings. Sociobiologists who think it obvious that a sultan's harem is the same sort of thing as a walrus's,[12] or that the human ban on 'incest' is of a piece with the disinclination of female chimpanzees to mate with too-familiar males, should take Spinoza's warning seriously. It is not merely a verbal point, but a correct observation that for example humans commit incest by mating with step-children or deceased wives' sisters or clan-members, and that female aversion to too-familiar males has precisely nothing to do with maintaining the ban.

A further digression: there is a point, for Spinoza, when we shall have to agree that everything is as perfect as it can be, just as it is, and that our attitude to animals, appreciating them as what they are, without condemning them for what they cannot help and which is no imperfection in them, should also be our attitude to human 'malefactors'. These latter will still suffer for their 'crimes', but the rational man acknowledges

> that a horse is excusable for being a horse, and not a man; nevertheless he needs must be a horse, and not a man. He who goes mad from the bite of a dog is to be excused; still, it is right that he should die of suffocation. Finally, he who cannot control his desires and keep them in check through fear of the law, although he is to be excused for his

weakness, nevertheless cannot enjoy tranquillity of mind, and the knowledge and love of God, but of necessity be lost.[13]

The man who lives not by reason but in obedience to passion lives as if he were an 'animal', or nearly so. Though animals cannot be blamed – or even intelligibly pitied – for so doing, humans have a higher capacity for reordering their lives by a calculation of their global advantage, and sharing in political and theoretical debate. To think immediate sense-experience – to which level animals are confined – is important, is to lose sight of a higher perfection. Animals can neither be condemned nor morally admired, and their concerns ought not to concern us. 'Sexuality', Kant remarked for similar reasons, 'exposes us to the danger of equality with the beasts'.[14]

ANIMALS ARE RATHER LIKE HUMANS

Let us turn from Spinoza, plausibly called the first 'modern' philosopher, so many of whose ideas have conditioned the thought and practice of people who think themselves severely 'practical', to Howard Liddell, the experimental psychologist:

> There is no doubt from our observation of hundreds of sheep and goats that the mildest electrical stimulation of the skin of the limbs is interpreted as gravely threatening. Such a minimal startle stimulus to the forelimb of the untrained animal leads to vehement aggression or attempts to escape through leaping or struggling if this is physically possible.[15]

> Pavlov's classical conditioning procedure leads, if long enough continued, to emotional bankruptcy and chronically disabling behaviors in the experimental animal. We have succeeded in precipitating such chronic emotional disorders (or experimental neuroses) in sheep, goats, pigs and dogs.[16]

On one occasion, Liddell reports, the goat-keeper was startled and upset by the sudden 'anxious apprehension' displayed by a particular goat who had hitherto been fond of him. The goat, he knew, 'was not mistreated by punishment or rough handling' in the laboratory: what he did not know was that the goat was being systematically stressed by repeated electrical shocks, and 'had begun to carry its troubles back to the barn'.[17] Liddell did not beat his animals, and seems concerned to make it clear that the shocks were, in themselves, mild ones. Presumably he thought it wrong to inflict particularly severe pains on animals, at least when lesser pains would serve, though the only reason I can see for thinking it wrong to do so is that the animals would have been made miserable – as they were, on his own admission, by what Liddell did do to them. By his own account, the sheer monotony of the experiment 'imposed almost intolerable discomfort' *on the experimenters*, a fact he mentions to help explain why the animals came out of it so badly disturbed.[18] His techniques could be guaranteed to produce experimental neurosis. In one set of experiments individual lambs were taken from their mothers (leaving the other twin of each pair as a control), and subjected to the usual stresses. Predictably, the deprived lambs coped less well with those stresses than the controls, became lethargic, unsociable, incompetent and died young.

Liddell makes the usual, ritual acknowledgement that there is no scientific demonstration that, say, a dog shares any of our feelings or thoughts,[19] though he adds that a psychiatrist has similar problems with the behaviour of acute psychotics. Neither animal psychologist nor psychiatrist can expect rational, verbal answers to their questions. But his insistence on making sure that the stimuli are, in themselves, mild ones, and his claim that the neuroses are similar in outward manifestation and inner cause (he instances 'self-imposed restraint'), suggests that he has no real doubts that animals can feel. He also insists that it is 'obvious that words such as loneliness, companionship and gregariousness when used to characterize animal behavior are evaluative rather than descriptive. They are used to avoid circumlocution'.[20] The use of 'evaluative' here leaves me very uncertain of his meaning, and I can offer only the following four possibilities. There may well be others.

First, he may mean that such terms reach beyond what can be immediately sensed and described, that they name theoretical entities which may serve to explain the immediate empirical data. Notoriously, what counts as empirical or theoretical is highly context-relative. That this book is a material object is, in ordinary conversation, a datum, hardly worth mentioning unless there is a chance that it is a hologram; in other contexts, it is a theoretical interpretation of immediate sense-data. Even the most hard-nosed of animal psychologists had better sometimes be prepared to notice that an animal is very angry, very miserable, or very affectionate, even if these assertions can be understood as going beyond the immediately accessible data. We do that all the time. That an animal genuinely confronts us as a subject of experience, that we are present to it in something like the way that it is present to us, is something that does not logically follow from any lower level of description, any more than the thesis that this book genuinely confronts us as a physical object strictly follows from any report of sense-data. We may nonetheless rely upon it. My own suspicion, incidentally, is that 'loneliness' and the rest will turn out to name internal complexes that might also be studied, under different and more esoteric names, by psychologists: 'loneliness' is that complex induced in sociable animals (including us) by prolonged dissociation from companions (on which more below).

Second, he may mean to say that what identifies the animal's emotional condition as 'lonely', 'gregarious' and the rest is that it bears the same relation to the rest of the animal's life and its society as loneliness does to ours. What is at issue is analogy, not homology, similarity of function not similarity of internal structure and ancestry. So Konrad Lorenz wrote:

> Psychologists have protested that it is misleading to use terms such as falling in love, marrying or being jealous when speaking of animals.... [But] since we know that the behaviour of geese and men cannot possibly be homologous – the last common ancestors of birds and mammals were extremely primitive reptiles with minute brains and certainly incapable of any complicated social behaviour – and since we know that the improbability of coincidental similarity can only be expressed in astronomical numbers, we know for certain that it was more or less identical survival value which caused jealousy behaviour to evolve in birds as well as in man.... These terms refer to functionally determined concepts, just as do the terms 'legs', 'wings', 'eyes', and the names used for other bodily structures that have evolved independently in different phyla.[21]

This functional interpretation of 'emotion-words' and the like has a long and respectable history, and does eliminate the pseudo-problem that, if such words had only introspectible feelings as their referents, no one would ever know if we were using the words in the same sense as each other, or as our own past selves. Pure functionalism, of course, with its implication that there are no such introspectible realities at all, has its own problems. But the general thesis, that such terms apply not solely in virtue of undiscoverable similarities between occult mental processes but in virtue of functional analogies between public, and social, activities, is a good one.

Third, Liddell may intend to say that understanding an animal, or even a person, involves an exercise of imaginative sympathy over and above mere reportage, or theory about causes or functions. To speak of loneliness is to evaluate the situation in which the animal finds itself, from that animal's imagined viewpoint. This is undoubtedly a dangerous exercise, and a good Spinozist should have no difficulty pointing out that it is very difficult to divest ourselves of our human nature so as to 'see things' as the animal does. What right have we to assume that the animal even perceives things, as such, at all, or has anything remotely resembling our long-term plans? The proof, perhaps, lies in seeing how well experienced and imaginative people do manage to cope with animals. It is no surprise that we are quite good at it, since our species has for millennia gained many of its advantages through being able to predict the behaviour of prey and domestic animals.[22]

Finally, Liddell may mean – and it is useful to me to assume that he did – that imputing loneliness is to make a value-judgment, to say that this is a condition to be pitied, as being one that we should hate to be in ourselves. In referring to the animal's condition only in suitably sterile ways we would be standing back from sympathetic involvement, possible agreement with the animal's view. In doing so, we are not – as psychologists sometimes seem to think – refraining from making a judgment, and concentrating on the 'facts': we are actually endorsing a particular evaluation, that the animal's condition is not a thing that rational people would worry about. We can neutralise that endorsement, but if we don't, it stands, and no one listening to us will be in much doubt of our moral view.

ETHICAL EVALUATION IS NOT IRRATIONAL

The act of evaluating is not essentially irrational, and people can often be shown that the particular evaluations they had made were in one way or another misplaced: they were inconsistent, ill informed, partial, or arbitrary. A good deal of harm has been done in this area by mistaken use of the notion of the 'naturalistic fallacy', which has been taken to mean that there can never be good reason for any evaluation, which must therefore be 'personal' and 'arbitrary'. This was, emphatically, not G. E. Moore's meaning.[23] It is one thing to agree that there are no logically self-evident principles from which we can demonstrate, by strict deduction, particular moral truths. It is quite another to deduce from this truism the particular moral judgment that one ought never to rely upon sound reasoning in the pursuit of ethical decision. We have long ago given up the fantasy of founding all science upon logically self-evident principles. Why should we be so scared of non-demonstrative but reasonably persuasive argument in ethics and politics?

Do we ever have information to be sure (within the limits set by general epistemological scepticism) that an animal's emotional condition is one to be pitied? 'Pity', said Spinoza, 'is pain accompanied by the idea of ill that has happened to another whom we think of as like ourselves.'[24] It follows from his general system that 'the man who lives by the dictates of reason endeavours, as far as he can, not to be touched by pity',[25] though pity is a necessity in those not moved by reason, by the calculation of their own advantage as members of civil and intellectual society. Spinoza may have intended to imply that there were three levels of benevolent action: those moved by reason act to promote the advantage of humankind; those moved by proper pity, founded on a correct assessment that the sufferer is like themselves, that they might be in as bad a state, act emotionally, to help a fellow-human; those moved by 'womanish compassion' weep at an animal's distress, making themselves of one kind with the animal and projecting their sentimental fantasy on to the animal.

The question whether it is right to pity an emotionally disturbed animal, and correspondingly wrong to create that disturbance, rests on the prior question, is such a one really like us? Presumably a sexually repressed, lethargic, obsessively ritualising animal is only badly off in so far as there is some other state it might be in which is a less impeded, more assisted manifestation of its nature. There is an observable difference between a lamb that frisks away from and back toward its mother, acting out the pattern of its growing life, and a lamb that lies still, cowers in dark corners, cannot cope with additional stress, and so on,[26] even though both behaviours are responses to the environment, and both are, in a sense, 'in a lamb's nature', there to be evoked. In refusing to give any weight to our sympathy with the neurotic lamb, our delight in the happy lamb, Spinoza implicitly relied on the following theses: (a) that the rational man should delight in what must be, should see the neurotic lamb as a perfect expression of nature's workings at that point (as was Belsen); (b) that any impulses we have to such sympathy are not to be delighted in, but rather repressed. But these theses are in conflict. If we ought to appreciate things just as they are, we ought to acknowledge our own natural sympathies, evoked by the same sort of cues that evoke pity for human distress. If, on the other hand, it is possible for us to be depraved, relative to that species-nature which allows us higher joys and perfections, it is also possible for animals to miss out on the fulfilment of their species-natures, what is possible for them as what they are. If we ought to be moved by the thought of our defect, why not by the thought of theirs? If they were genuinely of a wholly alien kind, we could indeed have no clue to how they might be well or badly off. We do have such clues, and they are not aliens. Nor is it, in the long run, at all likely that we would be better human beings if we excised our impulses of pity, our appreciation of the things they appreciate.

Let us suppose that Spinoza was right to take his stand on egoistic principle, though there is no final argument to prove that egoism is more rational than any other project. The good, for each of us, is what we must have for our true advantage. It is to my advantage to live in peace with my neighbours and join with them in political and intellectual endeavour. But why is it not also to my advantage to waken in myself (or not to repress) a feeling for the manifold, partial lives that go to make up the whole sweep of the living universe? 'Concern for the well-being and health of animals cannot be dismissed as sentimentality: indeed, it may often makes sound practical and economic sense' (Dawkins 1981) – though it is a fallacy to imply that it would be irrational to take the health and well-being of animals as one's end if this did (or to the extent that it does) conflict with other goals. Economics is not the science of what we *should* desire, but the art of putting a price on what we *do* desire. Other advantages aside, is it really so obvious that human beings who treat all other creatures as their enemies or slaves live happy lives? If we can so readily and effectively read the feelings of our domestic and farmyard kin – a skill which has obvious evolutionary advantages – is it not best to agree that they do, after all, feel very much as we would feel if we lived under their disabilities? What the sheep goes through as she waits, in harness and monotony, for yet another shock, is not beyond conjecture, and the refusal to pity this condition is not obviously correct.

95

It is not my intention to leave you with the thought that we ought always to act out of pity. Spinoza was right so far: those who act out of immediate emotions, of pity or anger or affection, may fail to see the wider context in which acting so is not going to do any good. The virtuous person indeed acts out of his or her considered judgment of what should be done, for the advantage of all, and in obedience to such rules as prevent us straying too far. But pity and affection, shared jokes and shared miseries are part of the apparatus that brings us information about the world we live in, and the sort of things that surround us. Simply to redescribe what we would otherwise and honestly see as misery so that it no longer matters to us is not the mark of reason, but of self-deceiving emotion, an attempt to make things be what we would wish, by magic, without the trouble and expense of making real changes. Magic changes what we see, but not what it is (Sartre 1962). Spinoza's challenge can be turned round: it is the person who refuses to see his or her own kinship with the beasts, and who denies that such miseries matter, who is denying reason. The world was not made exclusively for us, and our true good lies in enjoying and caring for the good in all things.

9

UTILITY, RIGHTS AND THE DOMESTIC VIRTUES[1]

CALCULATIONS OF UTILITY

Those who know Raymond Frey and myself only through our writings usually suppose that we must be on very bad terms, and were doubtless expecting a very acrimonious debate to open the Wolfson Lecture Series in Oxford in the autumn of 1986. In fact we are friends and sometime colleagues. It is clear that we disagree on many issues, not least the treatment of animals, but we don't necessarily disagree for the reasons and in the ways that others sometimes suppose. We are both opposed to irrationalism, to the fashionable doctrine that there can be no moral or other arguments worth considering. We are both opposed to the related dogma of amoralism, the idea that no moral conclusions are worth taking seriously, whether because there are no 'moral facts' or because no one ever 'really' acts morally or for moral reasons. There are people who habitually condemn what they describe as 'moralising', without ever noticing that precisely by condemning such behaviour, they are themselves engaged in the practice they condemn. Those same people generally have very definite (and plainly moral) views about a wide variety of dubious practices: rape or child-abuse or racial discrimination. Both of us believe that it is important to make our decisions after due consideration of the relevant evidence and of the principles by which we act. Both of us accept that there are some things that we would not be prepared to countenance and some implications of proposed moral principles that amount to a practical refutation of those principles: no one should be allowed to excuse him- or herself from the duty of moral thought by pleading that he or she was only following orders or the existing guidelines. Neither of us, even if we occasionally indulge our more rhetorical selves, as I have just done, thinks it appropriate merely to abuse our opponents – though both of us, faced by recalcitrant immoralists, have been reduced on occasion to reminding people of what the Nazis and their fellow-travellers did, and on what pretexts!

In all this I have said no more than that Frey and I are both philosophers, professionally and personally inclined to use and to criticise arguments, and to follow those arguments where they lead, even if that is to unfashionable places. Frey may well be more extreme than I, despite his reputation in certain quarters as a stout defender of common sense against 'foolish animal liberationists'. For the odd thing is, as I shall emphasise in a moment, that Frey is regularly welcomed as an opponent of 'animal rights' by people (e.g. Rothbard 1982, pp. 155 ff) who have failed to notice that he is also opposed to *human* rights and that he is in fact as much an anti-speciesist as I am (and maybe more so). Confronted by invasive experiments on, say, chimpanzees and mentally defective human beings, Frey would use very much the same calculations as Peter Singer and conclude that one set of experiments was justified only if the other set was also. He has no different moral principles to use about 'animals' than about 'humans' and would allow such invasive experiments on the humans if there were good reason to think that a net general advantage could be gained by them. Where I might acknowledge the very real inhibitions and historical precedents that prevent most of us from being happy with such experimental use of humans, Frey would think us wrong to treat them any differently from chimpanzees – and experiment on them both. Whereas I wish chimpanzees (and other creatures) to be treated in something like the way that we presently treat humans, Frey wishes humans to be treated in something like the way we presently treat animals. Neither of us thinks that radically different rules apply to creatures of different species, except insofar as their differences mean that what is an injury in the one case is not an injury at all in another (cows, for example, are not injured by being confined within the county of Devon: Singer 1985, p. 6).

That we are both philosophers means that we both recognise the virtues of abstract argument, divorced from the day to day pressures that bear upon those who must make quick decisions (although we also both recognise that there are such pressures and that it is often up to the daily practitioner of an art to take responsibility for those decisions: how, for example, to deploy scarce medical resources). It also means that we make it our business to connect pieces of information from many different fields, to notice that what is said in one region of the world of letters must have repercussions for what is said elsewhere. Neither of us can quite manage, as a general rule, to isolate the results of evolutionary theory so that 'non-humans' are reckoned to be members of one and the same evolutionary system as humans and at the same time of such a radically different kind that radically different morals apply to them. What it is wrong to do to a recently discovered human tribe may also be wrong to do to a non-human troop. If we justify the use of chimpanzees as experimental subjects (because it gives 'us' an advantage or increases 'our' knowledge), we should notice what we are saying about invasive treatment of Amazonian tribes and be ready to point to some credible and morally relevant difference between the cases if we wish to use different rules. It is certainly not enough to repeat that they are different *species*: a species is not a collection of individuals with the same ethically relevant nature, but a set of interbreeding populations. Nothing requires a member of one species to resemble all its conspecifics in one particular way, or more than it resembles any of another species.

So how do Frey and I differ, and how is it reasonable to differ about the treatment of our non-human kin? It is perhaps best to approach that question by asking first how other spokesmen for 'animal rights', broadly so called, might express their differences. How do Peter Singer or Tom Regan stand against Frey? As I have already suggested, Singer and Frey are both utilitarians, both anti-speciesists. Both believe that that action is correct which, in the circumstances, is likeliest to lead to the largest net satisfaction of preferences among those affected by the act. Both agree that animal pains and pleasures count toward this calculation, as Bentham and J. S. Mill proposed long ago. Classical utilitarians were not speciesist, nor did they suppose that just any human pleasure was worth any amount of animal pain. The gradual legislative process that outlawed cruel treatment of domestic and other animals owed a lot to utilitarian calculation and the associated rejection of traditional discriminations. Frey and Singer are agreed in this. For that matter they are also agreed in thinking that most non-humans have so little grasp of the future and of their own selfhood that they are not injured by being deprived of a 'naturally long life'. So long as other chickens, just as 'happy' as the last, are brought into being, there is no wrong done, in Singer's terms, by killing some. All utilitarians tend to have some difficulty with the injury supposedly done by killing: there is an injury only if someone's preferences are thereby denied or their states of mind rendered more disagreeable. Those who don't know about their coming death and have no long-term projects are not injured by it. As good utilitarians, neither Frey nor Singer believes in 'rights': if there is a particular action that would, all things considered, lead to a 'better' outcome, no one has a right to veto it. I cannot claim that there is anything which is 'my' property alone, such that I may justly refuse its help to others. If everyone would, all things considered, be better off if what is called 'my' property, 'my' life, 'my' body, 'my' purposes were otherwise deployed, then I may justly be forced to do my utilitarian duty. So also may animals. The only question is whether some particular practice does in fact provide a net utilitarian advantage. Frey believes that most of our present practices (but not all) do; Singer thinks that many (but not all) do not. In the last resort the difference is not one of principle but of present calculation: how much worse is the present situation than some ideal result, and how difficult, how costly, would it be to get nearer the ideal? I can see no morally neutral way of settling this dispute.

That, of course, is the problem.[2] Utilitarian calculation was originally offered as a simple, morally neutral way of deciding what was the 'better' outcome, morally neutral in the sense that anyone could agree upon the result, whatever their personal moral (or other) preferences. It seems an obvious thought: that change is to be preferred that leaves someone better off and no one worse off, that satisfies someone's desires without causing any positive distress. Where that ideal is unobtainable, we had better vote on it, taking due account of the strength of feeling in those affected. How else would we decide whether to have Rum Raisin or Chocolate Chip ice cream than by asking what is wanted, with what strength? The trouble is, once we are past such simple and genuinely neutral calculations, the result is impossible to calculate. We have no way of deciding who is how much happier as a result of what action, over the long run. We have no way of doing so partly, and crucially, because how happy they will be depends in part on their own original moral assessments. If a good many people are made unhappy by, or strongly disapprove of, bear-baiting, for example, or beating donkeys to death, then it may be a utilitarian goal to end such practices. If they are not too bothered by the sight or thought of donkeys dying in pain, there may be a utilitarian advantage in allowing owners thus to let off steam. Whether to ban the practice depends covertly on the prior judgments of those involved. If people think it wrong enough, utilitarians will seek to ban it; if they don't, they won't – but this obviously does not help at all in deciding whether or not to disapprove of it in the first place.

On the surface, Singer and Frey differ simply in their calculations of the utilitarian greater good, but the fact is that neither of them can satisfactorily perform such a calculation, least of all without reference to a prior, non-utilitarian assessment of what is to be done. I may as well admit that in my judgment Frey has the technical victory here: even if some other farming practices than the present ones were, all told, a better option, there is precious little reason to think that any single act of mine would lead to the amelioration of those present practices. So I can have no utilitarianly-grounded obligation to give up eating flesh, to campaign against what ideally would be reckoned an inferior result, or to castigate those who make a different calculation. Where I differ from Frey is that this very point seems to me a refutation of utilitarianism, for it applies to every other area of life. Nothing I can ever hope to do will have, in the long run, much effect on the general welfare, and no moral dilemma is easily resolvable in terms of the net welfare consequent upon each of the alternative actions. Utilitarianism is therefore, in my judgment, a wholly empty programme. People who think they are utilitarians have actually chosen their particular futures on quite different grounds.[3]

ANIMAL RIGHTS

So how would Tom Regan disagree with Frey? Regan has often expressed some irritation, reasonably enough, that the slogan 'animal rights' is commonly attributed to Singer (Regan 1986, pp. 94ff). Singer, as I have just pointed out, has no more time for 'natural rights' than Frey, and the arguments, such as they are, for agreeing that 'animals' have such rights are not Singer's at all but Regan's or Henry Salt's (Salt 1980, Regan 1983). It is Regan who thinks that all those animals who may reasonably be considered 'subjects-of-a-life' have just the same 'natural rights' as, we suppose, all humans have: we hold this truth to be self-evident, that all subjects-of-a-life are created equal, and have equal rights to life, liberty and the pursuit of happiness. Each such subject has the right to veto certain practices upon its person or property, whatever the supposed advantages to others. Each such subject has just the same rights, in nature, as all others, and no state authority, conversely, has any right to violate those rights. Even if great advantages could indeed be won by experimenting upon some such subject without his or her consent, this should not be done, because we could not will that every such subject should thus be at the disposal of all others. To be a subject-of-a-life is to be an end in oneself, just as Kant supposed. Kant's error was in thinking that only human subjects were ends in themselves. There is no discoverable difference between all humans and all non-humans that would license different moral treatment. Regan, in brief, is opposed to both Frey and Singer: where both those latter wish humans to be treated more or less as we now treat animals (with an eye to aggregated utility), Regan wishes animals (some animals) to be treated more as we now treat humans.

Human rights are usually invoked to bar the sort of simple-mindedly utilitarian calculation that denies any property in their own life, body and possessions to any individuals and also to define the proper limits of governmental interference. Rights are those claims and entitlements that the law may properly be invoked to protect. Good liberals do not suppose that governments have any right to control their subjects' lives absolutely or to interfere between a person and his or her 'private morals'. What we do on 'our own time', with our 'own' bodies and possessions, is 'our business', unless and until we violate the rights (and not simply damage the interests or offend the moral sensibility) of another. Right-wing liberals even deny any governmental right to redistribute income or secure the welfare of the needy; left-wing or 'welfare' liberals prefer to think that we have welfare rights (of recipience) as well as liberty rights (of action) – so that the 'right to work' means something quite different in right- and left-wing propaganda. Both sides agree that governments ought not to legislate simply for the general welfare, however defined, but to protect the rights of subjects. Those rights are not simply created by governmental action; we do not readily agree that regimes that regularly 'violate human rights' are really doing no such thing but simply failing to create such rights. Any particular government does wrong if it legislates against the lives and liberties of its subjects or fails to legislate in their favour.

This is why animal welfare legislation was opposed in the nineteenth century even by good liberals who had no personal interest in maltreating animals; since only humans had rights in this strong sense, the law had no business defending a donkey against its owner or a badger against anyone who could catch it. We might disapprove, as we also disapprove of lying, drunkenness, infidelity, deliberate stupidity, or a failure to look after the fabric of one's house. But unless such vices issue in particular acts that violate the rightful expectations of others they are not our business. So those who managed to get animal welfare legislation on the books did so in the full consciousness that they were endorsing the state's right to legislate on 'moral' matters (and did not need any longer to speak of rights at all). Others solved the crux by insisting that animals (or some animals) had rights for just the same reasons that humans did (see Nicholson 1879, p.16, and Chapter 7 of this volume).

This second path is made more attractive by the argument from 'marginal cases' – a title that I confess I think is misleading and even offensive. Kant identified the ground of 'rights' as our respect for the rational in all its embodiments, and social contract theorists suggested that rights were what any self-seeking rational individuals would insist upon writing into the social contract. Both accounts leave infants, imbeciles, lunatics, and the senile on the fringes. None of these can be said to be actually (even if potentially) rational, and none of them needs to be taken account of by self-seeking rational individualists. If only rational beings have rights, because only such rational beings have any prospect of ever forcing their claims upon us, then such 'marginal humans' have no rights. If 'we' treat them fairly well, it is only because we have certain sentimental attachments of a kind that 'we' seek to enforce on others even if such legislation is not strictly in accord with liberal principle. We might similarly force people to keep certain standards of animal care, but not because we think that either animals or imbeciles have rights in their own right. A government that failed to protect them would be within its rights; a government that did too much to protect them would not be.

Some philosophers have been ready to accept *at least in principle* (that saving phrase) that there would indeed be no absolute wrong done in breeding babies for the luxury restaurant market or experimenting invasively on imbeciles: after all, they wouldn't exist at all if we didn't plan to use them like that, and anyway they are not intelligent enough to understand and object to what we're doing.... Our not doing this rests only on the moral outrage and personal discomfort such a practice would generate here-now. Those who think that such practices would be wrong, such as to be resisted by any competent agent, even if no one (or no one else) was much offended by them, have to agree that something of the same wrong would be done (is done) in invasive experimentation on chimpanzees or breeding farm animals for food. The wrong is simply that we thereby do things that deny to our victims the life that they might otherwise lead, do things to them that cause them distress and pain, treat them as if they were our property and not their own. If human imbeciles ought so far as is possible to be allowed or assisted to live their own lives, why should not non-human creatures be allowed or assisted so to do? It is not only rationality that deserves respect but the individual dignity of each subject-of-a-life.

There are, of course, difficulties with this doctrine. Animal-loving utilitarians were concerned about the pains and pleasures of their clients and were simultaneously prepared to legislate to protect them and to treat them aggregatively, for the common good. Rights theorists think that more matters than mere pain and pleasure. We ought to act according to maxims that we can conceive to be universal law. Rights are those claims and entitlements that can be conceived to be preserved without contradiction: every human's rights are compatible with every other human's rights, even if our interests aren't. So an animal's rights, supposing that it is granted that he has at least as many as a human imbecile, will include more than a right to a trouble-free life and a painless death; nothing that can live its life without violating the equal rights of others ought to be prevented from doing so, and imprisonment, castration, slavery and death are all *prima facie* wrongs even if no 'pain' is suffered. On the other hand we are no closer to seeing what exactly the real rights of all subjects-of-a-life might be; it will not do to suppose that they all have just those rights that are popularly supposed to be human rights, because we have yet to see whether such human rights can be granted to all such creatures.

This latter point is one that I have argued at length in earlier chapters; it seems to be impossible to suppose that literally all such subjects-of-a-life have just those rights against arbitrary arrest, killing, even misuse that human beings have been supposed to have. A right is a claim that ought to be defended by governmental (or any other) action. Whose claim is to be defended as between worm and blackbird, blackbird and cat, wildebeest and lion, whale and Inuit? To protect one creature is to make life impossibly difficult for another; if their rights are equal, none has an unlimited right to life, and none can claim to be injured (in the sense that his rights are violated) if he is killed. The rights that all subjects-of-a-life could have seem to be the very minimal ones of extreme right-wing liberalism, namely the right to live as long as one can manage, without any corresponding right of assistance from others. Prey animals have a right to evade pursuers, and predators have a right to catch them; neither does any wrong, and neither does any rational law-enforcement agency in the vicinity if it simply ignores the problem. Our right as mere subjects-of-a-life consists merely in the right to live under the Law of the Jungle and, at best, not to have one's options radically and deliberately confined. The law that should be enforced would be something like the supposed 'balance of nature' (though one might reasonably have doubts even about that).

There are other difficulties with Regan's argument, notably that there is some conceptual problem with the very notion of a 'subject' distinct from the experiences that it has or (on other views) that compose it. Regan needs some such idea of a subject that is more than a mere stream of sensations and perceptions but does little to clarify it.[4] Nor is it easy to insist that what matters about a creature (so far as its moral status is concerned) is its essential nature rather than the web of relationships and approved meanings in which it has its being; it may be true that chimpanzees and imbeciles have very similar mental capacities (though it is actually an error to suppose that chimpanzees are mentally defective), but their meanings in (human) society are not the same. We need more argument than Regan gives to insist upon the 'real' as against the 'social' nature of a creature as what defines its moral status.[5] As it happens, I agree with Regan's account, so far as it goes, and regret the tendency in some recent philosophical writing to eliminate the notion of the Self. Without the Self we have no final defence against an aggregative and totalitarian utilitarianism a lot more simple-minded than Frey's.

Regan believes that all animals who can plausibly be said to live their lives, to be something more than a mindless aggregate of sensations and perceptions, ought to be treated as ends in themselves, not subjected to conditions that they would not choose for themselves with a view to their own goals in life. This is not because they 'have rights' in some metaphysical sense, as if the rights they had were the reasons that they ought not to be treated disrespectfully. To say that they have rights is simply to say that they ought to be treated thus and so, not to give a reason for this rule. The reason they should be so treated, and the law invoked to defend them in the peaceful enjoyment of the same liberties as ourselves, is that they do not differ from 'us' in morally relevant ways. I may be a better mathematician than Clever Hans (because he wasn't a mathematician at all), but being bad at mathematics is not normally a good reason to deny one civil rights! The creatures we live with, oppress and often admire have their own purposes and lifestyles that deserve as much consideration from us as we deserve from others. As far as our relation with 'tame animals' goes, I am in complete agreement with Regan: I too believe that we treat such creatures wrongly when we systematically deny to them the sort of respect and care that we are so eager to have lavished on ourselves. Where I differ from him is in doubting the fundamental postulate of 'liberalism', as I have defined it, namely that there is a difference in principle between what is and what is not one's 'own' business. Rights play no large part in my political philosophy, and I do not care to express my own concern for animals in terms of their putative 'natural rights', especially as the only rights that literally all such animals could have are not very significant. I have no right not to be eaten by a crocodile, and neither does anything else, simply in the abstract, and a sheep has no right not to be eaten by me; I do sometimes have a civil right against the river police that they should make the river as safe as possible, and others than I have thought it a poor reward for the giver of wool and cheese to be killed and eaten when we have no need of flesh foods. What concerns me most are not abstract natural rights but concrete historical ones. The rights of British beasts are more important for their lives and liberties than the 'natural rights' of all creatures under heaven. Those latter rights, against each other or against Heaven, can only be for a relatively stable and unpoisoned biosphere within which they can get on with their living (and their dying). That does not promise any individual security, though it is not quite irrelevant to the moral questions about our present dealings with the non-human. I should add that I do not share Regan's apparent conviction that our only important duties in these matters rest upon the sort of rights that he imputes to subjects-of-a-life.

THE GREAT CITY

So what is my quarrel with Frey or with the mass of traditionally-minded people? Most people, no doubt, still believe that there is a radical difference of natural kind between humans and all other creatures, and even sometimes speak (in the face of all the biochemical and behavioural evidence) as if chimpanzees were more like earthworms than they are like humans; our predecessors have openly, and our contemporaries covertly, insisted that humankind is a different kingdom from animals and from plants alike, with a radically different sort of soul. Those who have held this theory have been able to add that even 'defective' members of our species are proper humans 'underneath', that all apparent resemblances between our species and any other are merely illusory, and that humankind is patently superior to both other kingdoms. Everything in the world is 'for our sake', and we do no wrong in making use of it.

This was never, I must insist, a Christian dogma; it was a doctrine, welcome enough to ordinary human sensibility, formulated by Greek philosophers and adopted by some Christian thinkers as a way of insisting on their distance from Manichean doctrines about the world and our place in it. It was thought to be dangerous to suppose that we were 'like animals' because 'behaving like animals' was equated (wrongly) with selfish and materialistic concerns (see Chapters 5 and 6). It was thought to be dangerous to advocate abstention from flesh foods and the like because this was taken to imply that the world of nature was evil, not such as to be decreed by a benevolent creator. There was even a certain strength in this: perhaps it is indeed because we are unlike other animals that we can give them more consideration than they could normally give others, and perhaps it would be wrong to insist too strongly that the world as it is is evil (for the reasons mentioned above: we cannot even begin to establish laws for the lion and the ox, the blackbird and the worm and the cat). For better or worse we are stuck with the world and with our particular problems.

That humankind is a different kingdom is now unbelievable for most of us; the capacities and interests that we have are recognisably those of a terrestrial mammal from primate stock, with special (and related) gifts for grammatically structured language, cooperative and empathetic identification. Those specifically human capacities are very widely spread in our biological species, but 'a species' is not a natural kind, and we have no a priori reason to suppose that all our conspecifics are thus characteristically 'human' or that no other creatures have any trace of those specific traits. The very philosophers of Greece who identified the adult rational human being as the primary moral object also acknowledged that our moral sensibility develops from the familial and friendly concerns of other animals. We are moral because we are mammalian, long before we are also rational enough to reconsider our roots.

So where do our moral loyalties lie? Primarily with our children, our clan-mates and our domestic companions. We begin to be moral beings not by rational intuition of the form of rational humanity, as though adult rational humans were the paradigmatic moral objects, but by local and familial concern for our children, our friends, our domestics. The idea that rational adults are the primary rights-holders and children and other dependents are 'only' sentimentally protected is absurd; it is they who are most protected by law and public opinion and parental sentiment in every human community (see my 'Children and the Mammalian Order' 1989). The first charge upon our moral account is to care for those in our care, to be loyal to those with whom we have bonds of affection and familiarity. Only a doctrinaire humanism can ignore the obvious fact that among those domestic ties are ties of friendship and family loyalty to animals not of our species. We have carried to an extreme what is always an animal possibility: to adopt, affiliate, domesticate creatures who are not members of that group of interbreeding populations of which we are members. Historically and philosophically children and dogs have rights before any notionally human stranger does. Certainly, improved knowledge of that human stranger, or the class of such strangers, enables us to imagine a friendlier relationship developing, and accords them rights of a similar sort – but that does not put them above the creatures of our immediate household. It is because we have experience of getting on with creatures of a seemingly disparate kind that we can get on even with human strangers; treating them 'like animals' is not always a bad idea.

My first principle, then, is simply to insist on the primacy of the historically founded household and tribal group, a community of many ages, sexes and species. Dogs, horses, cats and cattle are members of one and the same society with us – granted that they have not 'chosen' to be so, and may have radically different concepts of what society it is that they share in, but that is true of us as well. That is why I do not share the view of some animal liberationists that domestication is of its nature tyrannical and that all domestic 'pets' should be released to make their own ways in the world. That would, in my view, be as pointless and as cruel as it would be to throw out your children or refrain from disciplining and educating them on the specious ground that they have not 'chosen' to be born into our particular family and culture. I do not think it an infringement of liberty to educate and give moral training to a child or to a 'pet'. What is offensive is to deny to them the right to participate in the social order on such terms as allow them to form friendships and follow vocations in ways suitable to their age and kind. The ideal for which liberals are groping is not that of independent action without any obligation of care or cooperation, but the open fraternity of mutually respectful well-wishers.

My first point, that is, is that 'animals' are not all outside the community of which we are a part. The self-styled animal-lover who prefers to have a dog killed rather than trained to live peacefully and usefully in society, or take the trouble of finding the dog a temporary home while he or she goes on holiday (see Hearne 1987) betrays a fundamental loyalty, reveals a thoroughly mean spirit. That cannot possibly be a matter of indifference to the rest of us; we cannot afford to have such selfish, stupid and disloyal folk imagining that they are all OK. We acknowledge as much by rearing our children to be 'kind to animals' and to fulfil their obligations to them. We often misjudge kindness and misidentify our obligations, but our main problem is, as it has been for most human communities, that we thereby establish habits of care and concern for animals that we then make it our business to extirpate or neutralise in other areas (Diamond 1979).

The confusion goes back a long way: hunting tribes who genuinely 'must' kill animals for food and clothing must also establish a rapport with the creatures that they hunt. They may even introduce some of those prey animals into their households as honoured guests and friends and certainly feel respect for the wild things. Their projections and empathetic identification with the animals they hunt creates a Lord of the Animals who must then be propitiated. The animals must be seen to 'consent' to their deaths and must be compensated for their troubles.

One of the roots of religion is blood-guiltiness, the need to balance empathetic identification, aesthetic admiration and the needs of the tribe. Once animals are 'domesticated' (which is to say, affiliated) and their treatment gradually veers away from anything that they might be presumed to have bargained for, it becomes necessary for our peace of mind to suppose that the gods have 'given them to us' (though even at this stage there are usually conditions on the gift, as that we must not eat the blood, which is the life). In the final and fatal confusion of modern atheistic humanism, the notion that the animals are 'ours' to do with as we please is maintained even in the absence of a worthy giver. It is at this point that people, and especially those initiated into the scientific community, begin to talk patent and anti-evolutionary nonsense to the effect that 'animals' are unconscious. Descartes himself advanced as a reason for believing this that if it were false, we should have to agree that many of our practices were cruel and unjustified, and therefore change them (Rosenfield 1941).

The excuses and rationalisations that we have offered for regarding what we do to 'animals' as beyond serious moral consideration are wearing thin. Those who work cooperatively with domestic animals are well aware that they occupy the same 'moral universe' as ourselves, though with differing capacities and obligations. The corruption of modern farming and experimental practice (as well as the corruptions often evident in the treatment of 'pets') at least have the merit of alerting us to the moral problem we face, of forming and consolidating a genuine community of many ages, sexes and species. As we turn aside from our mistaken concentration on the rational adult as the paradigmatic moral object and the norm of our species life, we can begin to see that it is not impossible also to make room for those 'marginal' cases that I mentioned before. Children, imbeciles, lunatics and the senile are not marginal to society, any more than domestic animals. Society does not exist to serve the purposes of self-seeking rational adult individuals but to maintain the households within which we all grow up.

It is that set of households, that continuing city with its historically formulated rights and obligations, that gives us the best model for the world at large. For it is no part of my principles that moral obligation stops at the threshold of actually cooperating cities. We live within the wider world; our generation is better able to appreciate than almost any other since pagan times that the dynamic order of the cosmos, especially as it is represented here-now in the terrestrial biosphere, is the earthly home of all value, that its survival is of desperate concern to every living creature, and that insofar as (some) humans are able to reach beyond their parochial boundaries to contemplate and admire and serve the cosmos we do indeed show our special contribution to that same cosmos. The final context of our worldly activity is not our immediate household or nation state, nor yet the socio-political nexus of suffering humanity, but the whole earth. It is of that 'Great City, whose author and founder is God', so Berkeley said (1948, 3, p. 129), that we should think ourselves citizens. That principle of mutual attraction which draws us 'together in communities, clubs, families, friendships and all the various species of society' (ibid., 7, p. 226), leads on to a loving appreciation of the whole earth and the spirit that guides its doings. 'The poet says, dear city of Cecrops, and will you not say, dear City of Zeus?' (Aurelius 4. 23). We must act by such rules as are necessary for the continued health and being of the terrestrial biosphere. In saying this I do not, as some have supposed, make a radical break with tradition. On the contrary, the very founders of liberalism based their political philosophy precisely on a recognition of that cosmic viewpoint and the splendour and moral demandingness of the living world. Individual right, Kipling's 'leave to live by no man's leave underneath the Law', and private property were

UTILITY, RIGHTS AND THE DOMESTIC VIRTUES

defended as the likeliest way of enabling a society of freemen to subsist in mutual harmony and cultivate their virtues: if we each had some portion of the land to tend, we would be less likely to fall prey to tyrants, and the land itself would prosper. What we owned, however, was not the land itself but the lawfully acquired fruits, and we owned these only for their lawful use. 'Nothing was made by God for Man to spoil or destroy' (Locke, *Treatises* 1963, 2.31, p. 332). Individual liberty rested on the value God placed in every soul as a unique expression of His glory, such that any despotism, however benevolent in purpose, must issue in a decline of valuable diversity. Each of us has a profound and vital interest in the virtue of our fellow citizens and in the continued viability of the ecosystems within which we live.

Aldo Leopold's vision has been the inspiration of much recent environmentalism:

> We abuse land because we regard it as a commodity belonging to us. When we see land as a community to which we belong, we may begin to use it with love and respect. . . . That land is a community is the basic concept of ecology, but that land is to be loved and respected is an extension of ethics.
>
> (Leopold 1968, p. viii)

It was precisely because the whole world was worth admiring that our human capacity to admire it was also admirable. Ecology, considered not as a supposedly value-neutral science but as the study of earth's household, is founded on just the loving appreciation and would-be civil companionship that the ancients endorsed. The moral sensibility born in our household and cities must be extended to the whole earth, and we must ask ourselves how the one Creator would require us to act for the benefit of His creation.

> A wise man . . . does not look upon himself as a whole, separated and detached from every other part of nature, to be taken care of by itself and for itself. He regards himself in the light in which he imagines the great genius of human nature, and of the world regards him. He enters, if I may say so, into the sentiments of that divine Being, and considers himself as an atom, a particle, of an immense and infinite system, which must and ought to be disposed of, according to the conveniency of the whole.
>
> (Smith 1976, VII 2.1.20: p. 276)

Frey has often retorted to me that my appeal to the One Creator, to God, can have no significance for an atheist like himself. I am not sure that this need be entirely true; the appeal, in one sense, is simply to ask by what rules the biosphere could be conceived to be run, what could intelligibly or usefully be demanded of us all. It seems fairly clear that current policies in farming, deforestation, industrial pollution and the like cannot long continue, and that we would be well advised to ask what sustainable practices are available to us. These will not guarantee rights to life, liberty and the pursuit of happiness in anything like the traditional sense to 'all creatures in the world', but I have already said that I expect no such rights. Nor does my appeal rest of necessity upon any realistic belief in a transcendent deity. That the cosmos as a whole, and especially the terrestrial biosphere here-now, is admirable, is the global context of all our admirations, is expressed by reference to the divine underlying structure of that cosmos. I do not thereby commit myself to any view about the nature of any concern felt by 'the cosmos as a whole' for my life or for any human or other life. Sperry's claim that

> the grand design of nature perceived broadly in four dimensions to include the forces that move the universe and created man, with special focus on evolution in our biosphere, is something intrinsically good that it is right to preserve and enhance and wrong to destroy and degrade.
>
> (Sperry 1983: 22)

does not consciously rest, as far as I can see, on any kind of orthodox metaphysical theism, though he thereby expresses part of what Kohak does in more traditional terms:

> Are we a higher species? A disinterested observer, coolly examining the evidence and assessing humanity's impact upon the globe, would not be likely to come to that conclusion. . . . At best, we are one species among others. But then, what justifies the totally disproportionate cost of our presence? Ask it for once without presupposing the answer of the egotism of our species, as God might ask it about his creatures: why should a dog or a guinea pig die an agonizing death in a laboratory experiment so that some human need not suffer just such a fate?
>
> (Kohak 1984, p. 92)

But I may as well come clean. I do indeed believe that there is a God, and that it is our failure to acknowledge that God which is at the root of our confusion and degradation in epistemology as well as in morals. I can well understand that people who believe the world to be the product of blind and indifferent powers should think that it can be given value only by our wishes, though I do not understand how anyone can take his or her own particular wishes very seriously when it is clear that he or she could have had quite different ones and not made any error. 'What beauty can be found', Berkeley's Euphranor enquires in criticism of the high-minded atheist, 'in a moral system, formed, connected and governed by chance, fate or any other blind unthinking principle?' (Berkeley 1948, 3, p. 128). But perhaps if we have no alternative, we shall simply have to put up with that. What I do not understand is how anyone who supposes that the Origin is blind, lazy and inane can think that it is at all likely that we hairless primates on a heap of rubble should be able to find out how the world works. The one hypothesis on which this would be at all probable is that the world has been set up for us to understand and enjoy (or we have been set up to understand and enjoy it). Only if the pattern of things is a pattern imprinted in our hearts – as of course the founding fathers of modern science, like Galileo, actually believed – can we rationally expect to find that pattern. And in thus discovering how the world is intended we also find how we are intended to be. If our special human gift is to contemplate and serve the cosmos, if we are, in Heidegger's phrase, 'servants of being', it behoves us to attend more carefully than we yet have to the other creatures that share the world with us, among whom we live both at a domestic and at a more cosmic level.

In brief, we ought to change our present ways not simply because the present ones involve too many creatures in pain and distress we do not need to cause (though that is true enough) nor because all creatures with lives to live ought to be permitted or even helped to live them (though that too is broadly true) but because the households in which we first learn ethical behaviour already include non-humans whom we ignore and abuse because we allow ourselves to be influenced by theories and excuses that we know full well are false and because the whole earth that it is our duty and our joy to serve requires that all kinds and conditions of living creature have their own lives and territories. You may, if you choose, regard my references to God as myth-making of the unserious kind in which some commentators have sometimes thought that Plato used to indulge. But in the interest of a rousing conclusion, I reaffirm that I mean just what I say. Those who muzzle the ox that treads out the corn, plough up the wilderness, hunt species to extinction and consume the lives of those whom God has given to us to care for should stand in fear of the judgment.

> Then shall the land enjoy her sabbaths, as long as it lieth desolate, and ye be in your enemies' land; even then shall the land rest and enjoy her sabbaths. As long as it lieth desolate it shall rest, because it did not rest in your sabbaths when ye dwelt upon it.
>
> (*Leviticus* 26. 34ff)

10

ETHICAL PROBLEMS IN ANIMAL WELFARE[1]

WHAT PHILOSOPHERS CAN'T DO

I take it that no one who is still reading this book believes that philosophical enquiry is sheerly irrelevant to the problems that we face. Such enquiry, after all, is only an attempt to think through those problems without taking too much for granted. People who won't do this are usually, though they fail to realise it, acting out the theories of some earlier philosopher: the sort of self-styled 'practical person' who is ignorant of the principles upon which he or she acts and careless of the long-term consequences of what he or she does.

> The need for philosophy is just the ultimate form of the need for knowledge.... The only choice we have is between a conscious metaphysics and an unconscious one, between hypotheses which we have examined and whose limitations we know, and hypotheses which rule us from behind, as pure prejudices do.[2]

No one thinks it improper or pointless to treat issues 'philosophically' when the alternative is to treat them dogmatically, conceitedly, over-emotionally, or without serious effort to consider other arguments and points of view. But experience suggests at least two other misunderstandings of the philosophic life which may cause trouble.

First, philosophers, and especially moral philosophers, are sometimes thought to be expert moral casuists, with straightforward and rationally grounded solutions only needing to be propounded to be believed. That is how we conceive of experts in the physical sciences and in the law, even if they do not in fact always have simple answers to give us. When it becomes clear that philosophers disagree among themselves about even the simplest and clearest matters, it may seem pointless to invoke their aid. If there are no agreed solutions, and not even agreed methods, what sort of expertise have we?

Second, philosophers as individuals are popularly held to have 'philosophies', systems, favourite opinions carefully rehearsed and ordered. Societies inviting me to speak have sometimes, I suspect, been faintly disappointed, or even annoyed, that I did not come across as a whole-hearted advocate of whatever philosophic creed it was that they had identified me with.

So it turns out that philosophers don't only disagree with each other: they may well disagree with themselves:

> Just as parents have affection for the offspring of their bodies, so also is the mind naturally attached to its own reasonings. And just as to their parents who are emotionally attached the children appeal as the fairest and handsomest of all even though they might be the most hideous of all, so it is with the foolish mind. . . . However this is not the case with the wise man and his reasonings. Rather, when it seems convincing that they are true and correct, then especially does he distrust his own judgment but makes use of other wise men as judges of his own reasonings, and from them believes assurance.[3]

Philosophers, no more than poets, 'believe' in what they say: we are not citizens of any single community of ideas; our philosophy rests rather on our wish to go a little further, trusting not in any single doctrine but in the mere capacity of rational imagination not to let us down.

In brief: if the presence of philosophers is valuable, it is not because we are likely to offer unanimous or clear solutions to practical or theoretical puzzles, and certainly not ones that all our absent colleagues would agree upon, nor yet because you can always count on a philosopher for a rousing piece of rhetoric in defence of your favoured programme. Our value is not that we have answers, but that we have questions, and some knowledge of the puzzles created by attempted answers of the past.

In saying all this I may, of course, have given rise to yet a third misunderstanding, namely that philosophers are professional sceptics of the tedious kind who ask questions but will not stay for an answer. That too is not quite right: few of us believe that there is any hope of founding all our serious beliefs on logically incontrovertible principle. There will always be room for debate, and rational disagreement. It does not follow that we can do without beliefs, or that we need to be much shaken by the mere fact that we could logically think the opposite of what we rationally do.

ABSTRACT PROBLEMS: CONCRETE CASES

So what are the problems of animal welfare? When Socrates asked his friends such questions as 'what is Justice, Courage, Happiness?', their usual reply was to give instances of just or courageous actions, or happy people. That was not, he said, what he was after. If you give me a list of courageous actions, or of occasions when 'animal welfare' was preserved or defended, it is usually possible to devise some superficially similar occasion which you would not be easily persuaded was of the same kind. What Socrates wanted to be told was what that kind was, what is it that an act must be to be truly courageous, what must be preserved if 'animal welfare' is to be preserved? Is courage so defined always a good thing? Suppose we decide that courage is the disposition to carry on doing what one had decided to do despite the personal danger: we might well wish that some people were less 'courageous', for their own and everyone else's good. A little cowardice should be admired. Justice itself, if it requires us to tell no lies and to repay our debts, might involve us in doing what is obviously the wrong thing (returning the Gestapo agent's gun and telling him where to find his prey). So my problem is not solved by a list of 'animal welfare organisations', nor stories about abandoned dogs, or terrified cattle or dying seals. What I want to know is: what counts as 'animal welfare', and how far does it count as something that is worth defending, preserving or increasing? These problems are abstract ones, and may seem cold and irrelevant to the genuine heartfelt concerns of veterinarians, or RSPCA officers, or animal lovers or conservationists. But those same 'heartfelt concerns' may conflict, and the 'welfare' that each tribe seeks to preserve may not be what others had in mind any more than 'liberty' or 'democracy' mean quite the same thing to Western liberals, or communists, or Khomeyni.

SO WHAT COUNTS AS ANIMAL WELFARE?

So what is animal welfare? Broadly, it must be that state or condition or habitual activity in which animals are 'well-off': but what does that amount to? A condition without positive pain, whatever that is? But would a creature in a coma be well-off? Or a creature unable to feel pain, and so in constant danger from sharp edges, fires and rotten food? Presumably not – unless the alternative, in that particular case, were even worse. So a concern for animal welfare is not identical with a wish to prevent animal pain – or else animal welfarists would be wholly dedicated to a policy of genocide. If pain were the only thing that mattered, all deaths, and not just some, would be a merciful release.

So shall we add that animal pleasures count? An animal is well-off not only if it is spared the major pains of life, but if it can and does enjoy its major or minor pleasures. So animals that are well-fed, well-housed and well-tended are well-off, even if they are soon going to be killed, or even if they have no chance to do the things peculiar to their kind which they would do if 'free'.

Human beings so treated are not regarded as well-off, even if they are better off in some prisons than others. Prisons are recognised as punitive, because they deprive the prisoner of 'freedom', and particularly freedom to engage in ordinary human actions: playing, courting, parenting, investigating other possibilities, etc. A Prisoners' Aid Society might aim to make them 'better off', but would not think them 'well-off': they are in a state where they have reason to want change. Our human welfare is not well served by keeping us in jail (unless, which seems unlikely, the experience reforms us).

These activities count as part of human well-being because they matter to human beings and we would count ourselves as badly off if we had no chance to engage in them. So shall we identify animal welfare as that condition in which animals can do what matters to them – not only eat, drink and sleep, but also have dust-baths, groom each other, gallop over the grass and sing? Would such extras matter if a prisoner had been reared as a 'happy slave', ignorant of human possibility or of the outside world? Would such a prisoner be well-off because he or she did not know what they were missing, or even felt no lack? We sense that there are worthwhile human activities that can be engaged in only as free men (whatever freedom is), such that to be denied them is a loss even if the victims do not know what they are missing, or if they are missing anything at all.

Does the same thing apply, analogously, to animals? Is a 'stall-fed ox', brought out to be masturbated for a farmer's gain, 'well-off'? He hasn't been killed, or maimed, or 'badly treated' (in the sense of being burned, beaten, castrated, starved or even 'spoken harshly to'). Perhaps he has never, since his calfhood, seen a cow, and certainly has never served a herd in the way his wild ancestors and cousins do. But is he living a life well-lived according to his kind, doing what admirable and enviable creatures of that kind would do? Could one not suspect or feel that the more he seems contented with his lot, the more distant he is from his species-good? Rabbits kept in rabbit hutches for so long that they have no concept of escape even when they have the chance to, may be, in one sense, well-off; in another, they are 'deleporised', dead rabbits before their body dies.

Finally, does animal welfare include life itself? Suppose a deer, or baboon, or seal that has lived 'freely' and in good fortune for its life so far, and has years to live if all goes 'well', is killed 'untimely'? We reckon humans who die young, who don't fulfil their promise, are to be pitied even if they never knew their end. Even if they have lived happy lives, perhaps, we think them injured by their early deaths. We grieve for octogenarians, no doubt, but who would think them badly-off because they're dead? Not all deaths are an equal evil, whether because death may be slow, agonising and untimely – or may not, or because not all those who die are equally to be missed. So clearly we have less reason to protect some animals against imaginable deaths than others. The death of diseased seals is something that counts against the welfare of the seals in a way that the death of ageing seals, or even healthy seals by normal hazards of the sea (the price they pay for liberty) is not.

What counts as an animal's being 'well-off', though difficult to specify in any particular case, is not all that obscure. We know what sort of things count as good for creatures of this kind or that. Maybe there is a case to argue about domestic dogs: are they well-off in principle, supposing them to be well-fed, well-cared for, well-befriended, without any wish to leave? Or is there a case for saying that they are as slavish, as far from canine well-being, as any 'mindless', unrebellious slave?

Perhaps Rover would be no better off if sent to join a feral pack of dogs? Rover, of course, would soon be dead, but is it obvious that dogs should be domestic? Are household pets a different case to zoo or laboratory animals: sometimes well-cared for, in a sense, yet unable ever to lead the lives their species would lead, and for that very reason not 'well-off?

WHY DOES IT MATTER?

Animal welfare organisations are presumably formed by people who suppose that animal welfare does 'matter', absolutely, and they think themselves entitled to bring it to other people's attention. It matters that 'animals' be well-off – though perhaps that category of 'animals' needs more careful scrutiny. If there are no 'beetle welfare societies' as such, this may be because no one much supposes that beetles are ever well-off or badly off, or because we think that beetles will be well enough off anyway (and will probably be the only non-microscopic creatures to survive the nuclear winter), or because the well-being of beetles, slugs, mosquitoes and water boatmen (not to mention rats, sharks and vultures) does not engage our sympathy even when they are doing 'us' no particular harm. Notoriously, cuddly and photogenic creatures, preferably ones that are not competitors, get more attention than creepy, slimy, ugly, or just boring ones.

Sometimes a concern for animal welfare is simply a concern that natural beauty, somewhat parochially defined, be preserved. We object to dying seals in much the same spirit as we object to dying elms: that there be healthy, glossy, jolly-looking seals around our coasts matters to 'us', who don't have to bother about our fishing nets – just as it matters that there be healthy, long-established elms around our countryside. If seals or elms became too inconvenient or expensive, we would transfer our affections and our cash. It is because we want a 'beautiful' landscape that we want healthy animals across it: we feed squirrels (with a particular nostalgic affection for *red* squirrels, and not grey) and poison rats, unless we realise that squirrels are just fluffier than rodents, and do damage to our trees. To maintain that lovely landscape we are prepared to cull the animals who live in it, without regard for their individual welfare, and not always very much even for the welfare of the mass of creatures of that kind. Conservationists, game-wardens and cattle-farmers have a lot in common, even if the end product they are seeking differs.

I do not mean to denigrate these motives, nor to deny the good that proper conservation does: people who attend to the whole ecosystem we inhabit would think twice before introducing sheep to eat up men and countryside together. A sound conservation policy seeks to maintain a sustainable ecology, a world within which creatures of many kinds find a place, even though many of them, individually, will not do well – a point I shall return to. These aesthetic, discriminatory or conservational motives for wishing animals well, largely because a world of 'well-off' animals, or one in which the 'ill-off' are out of sight, is nicer for 'us' to live in, are not usually 'moral' reasons.

I have a 'moral' reason for my action if it is done for the sake of someone's good, not only mine, and irrespective of any special, accidental ties between me and the beneficiary. If I help my aged aunt because (a) she means to leave me money or (b) she looks so sweet when (fairly) well, that is no moral action. If I help her because I like her, and therefore like her to be well because she likes herself to be well, many moralists would say that was also no true moral action. Most of us would disagree.

We owe loyal affection to those close to us in ways not easily captured by moralising dicta. Such moralists have tended to suggest that any help I give my aunt is only moral if I would, for just the same reason, help any old lady, or any human being in distress, or any creatures similarly situated. That is why good realists sneer a little at 'British sentiment' as being hypocritical: why do we despise Koreans for killing dogs to eat, while munching lamb chops? What difference is there between eating dogs and eating sheep? It cannot be simply that sheep do not enter our society as 'pets': often enough they did – witness the poor man's lamb in the prophet Nathan's parable.

By way of riposte to the realists: what non-sentimental reasons are offered for the differences between roast pig and roast baby? In the last half century good liberals have done their best to show that any concern for human embryos, or even for human babies, is a sentimental attachment not to be enforced on others. If it is all right to procreate embryos for experimental purposes, or to provide spare organs for the needy, it does not seem entirely easy to insist that cannibalism is intolerable. And now you know why philosophers are unpopular!

There are perhaps two ways to go from here. The first is to admit that many of our actions rest on sentiment, on personal and unreflective attachments. We mind about those close to us, about those like us, about those who embody qualities our evolutionary and historical past have taught us to admire and love. People who entirely lack such sentiments are not rational sages, but psychopaths. To ask such questions as 'Why should we mind what happens to our future selves, parents, spouses, children, friends and fellow professionals, family pets or farmyard cattle?' is very odd. Of course we mind about such things: maybe there are, somewhere in outer space, such creatures as the supermantis, who have no special friends, nor any soft affections. To a supermantis, any other supermantis of the requisite class and station serves as well: any concern for other things' well-being is so alien a thought as never to occur at all. Such creatures would probably have no conception of themselves as individuals, nor any way of thinking even about their own interior states. If they are 'rational' it is not as we are. For us to be like that would not be wicked, but insane.

Moral discourse is not divorced from sentiments like this, and there is no reason to be ashamed of them. Animal welfare, as far as it is a goal for us, will be the welfare of those creatures with whom we share our lives, toward whom we feel affection, with whose troubles we can sympathise. It is worth remembering that our natural sympathies, affections and understandings do not extend only or even chiefly to members of our own species. We are motivated to mind about our fellow human beings as much as we are motivated to mind about our fellow mammals or higher vertebrates, and may mind more about the latter because we know more about them. There is a real sense in which the average human male can sympathise more easily with a randy bull than with a fellow (female) human being with period pains. 'I know just how you feel', addressed by a would-be sympathetic male to such a female, is neither true nor helpful. For similar reason, I know more about what our domestic cats require from life than I know about Brazilian Indians.

But there is a second response available. Sentiment is not enough. Once we have begun to enter into the feelings and purposes of another so as to be concerned for his or her well-being, not as an adjunct to oneself, but in his or her own being, we can hardly avoid the questions posed by those who are, in relevant ways, like our friend. Precisely because I mind about what happens to my wife irrespective of any further consequence for my present self, the fact that she is my wife becomes at least in part irrelevant. It may be what first caught my attention, but what I am attending to is something that would not be essentially different if she were not (or even never had been) my wife. If I don't want my wife to be mugged, raped, robbed, defrauded, debauched or killed because all these things would injure her (not merely me), how can I be indifferent to the mugging, raping, robbing and so on of other people who might easily have been my friend? If I show that I would not mind such crimes at all, my claim to mind about her is suspect: apparently I only mind because such acts reflect on me, or damage what I think is mine. Similarly, if I genuinely care what happens to other members of my species, how can I not mind at all what happens to other creatures of like kind, but not of my own species? In the days when species were considered natural kinds, distinguished by having specific, radically different natures, I might have held that much of what can happen to a human being can no more happen to a dog or a chimp than to a stone, or to the number seven bus. If species are instead mere sets of interbreeding populations, and our natures are not wholly different from theirs, then we are stuck with minding about creatures other than just those immediately close to us, simply because they are susceptible to the same injuries. Minding about animal welfare is a function partly of sentimental attachment, partly of rational discovery that 'they' are a lot more like 'us' than we thought, and that to mind about 'us' commits us to minding also about 'them' on pain of being hypocrites.

But the question still remains: how much do they matter, and how do we deal with them? A proper concern for human welfare, after all, does not require us to make beings as 'well-off' as they as individuals could be. I acknowledge no duty nor desire to provide everyone in the world, or everyone in Britain, with a video recorder, Jacuzzi, free access to the international computer network and a holiday home, nor even a duty to ensure that everyone could have as many of the world's goodies as they happen to desire, or even a 'fair share' of those goodies. Would a fair share be an equal one, or a share commensurate with need, or one commensurate with merit, or one obtained without violence, fraud or other wickedness? How could I possibly make it a goal of mine to ensure such (quite different) ideals were realised?

Simone Weil insisted on eating only what would be available to prisoners of the Reich: that, I suspect, is in some sense also our fair share, what we would be assigned if every living human were assigned an equal share of all the goods there are. But most of us suspect that this was almost suicide, or martyrdom: suicide would usually be wrong, and martyrdom is not obligatory.

I have no obligation, least of all in law, to care equally for every human being. Even those of us who attempt to do without personal friends and special clients only pay equal attention to the people who they meet, the down-and-outs who turn up on the doorstep. We don't deny our aid to them merely because on a 'fair share' basis they aren't entitled to more than we could give to everyone. Robbers may have a special obligation to assist those whom they have beggared. The rest of us may feel in some sense obliged to help, but how much we help, and when, is our decision, and the beneficiary has no case against us.

Analogously, we have no necessary obligation to assist 'animals' with whom we have no direct contact. We may do them good (say, by rescuing them from flood or fire), but only *have* to do so if we have caused the flood or fire. Wild or distant animals have no right of support, unless it is our fault that they are beggared, but animals within our household, or wider society, may have that right. Pet owners who neglect their animals are in breach of an implicit contract, and of the law. We respect the claims of 'owners' on condition that they care for the animals in their charge, and if they neglect those duties we may (and must) condemn them, and take on the burden of care ourselves. Veterinary practitioners are obviously at the workface here: what duties do they have to patients and to clients and to the wider community? If the patient's welfare must be paramount, as the Royal College says (without defining what that welfare is), how do vets deal with clients who will not or cannot care for the patient as the veterinary practitioner would wish? When do they have recourse to law? Only some

119

animals, in other words, like some human beings, have positive rights of assistance against us when the assistance is required only to remedy natural failings. Enforcement of the duties of animal-ownership is another matter, as is recompense for past injustice.

Such positive welfare rights, and rights of defence against particular injustices, are not the only sort of rights there are. Negative rights of liberty are much more widespread. I may have no duty to feed, clothe or even protect a Philippine tribesman. In international law I have no right, let alone a duty, even to protect such tribesmen against genocide if the only way to protect them is to invade the Philippines. But although I have no positive duties here, I plainly have many negative ones – notably not to rob, maim or kill. Positive duties to strangers are rarely assignable, enforceable or significant. Negative duties are quite easy. If someone else is already looking after Jo, I have no need to. If someone else is doing her negative duty by Jo (not to molest her), my duty not to molest Jo remains the same. Analogously, I may rightly be forbidden to molest, maim or kill an animal whom I have no special duty to care for. I may be required to assist some animals against such molestation. I am required to care for some animals with whom I have some special tie.

And what about Rover? Obviously I have an enforceable duty to look after him and attend to his well-being. If I abandon him, my claims of ownership will lapse just as my parental rights will lapse if I abuse them. But how do I attend to his well-being? Should I release him on a startled world? The argument reflects the ancient dispute over civilisation: is civilisation a good thing or not? Are we distorting our children's happy natures by bringing them up in chains, or are we enabling them to achieve such goals as would be quite impossible for solitary savages or feral apes? My suspicion is that those who think dogs, real dogs, are better off without us share those false perceptions of society that have dominated recent history. If the social order is only a human one, and includes only such obligations as individuals have freely incurred, then dogs and children alike need liberation, and social order collapses. If on the other hand the social order is a historical community of many races, ages, sexes and species, such that we come to life by learning obligations that we freely choose, there is a strong case for acknowledging dogs, horses, cats and sheep and other commensal species as part of a civilised order that is open to improvement.

What obligations of care and courtesy do we owe animals? The ones that must be paid them if the social order is to be one worth living: they have a claim on us for services rendered throughout history, and still offer us the chance of forming new friendly relations that will be their own reward.

So perhaps you can count on a philosopher for a rousing piece of rhetoric after all.

11

THE REALITY OF SHARED EMOTION[1]

As is probably already clear, I am at once a realist and something other than a materialist. I hold to what Lovejoy called

> the primary and most universal faith of man, his inexpugnable realism, his twofold belief that he is on the one hand in the midst of realities which are not himself nor mere obsequious shadows of himself, a world which transcends the narrow confines of his own transient being; and on the other hand that he can himself somehow read beyond those confines and bring those external existences within the compass of his own life yet without annulment of their transcendence.
>
> (Lovejoy 1930, p. 14)

Rorty, citing this passage, declares that Aristotle, Aquinas, Dewey and Austin would (like Rorty himself) reckon this realism artificial and far-fetched (Rorty 1979, p. 2). If they would there is at least one 'fact of the matter' which transcends the narrow confines at any rate of my own 'transient being', for I am certain that it is Rorty's own anti-realism that Aristotle and Aquinas, at any rate, would have thought absurd. Crudely, realists believe that a given statement p is correct if it is true, if 'things are as they are said to be'; anti-realists believe that such a statement is true (or 'true') if it is correct to describe things so (where 'correct' means only that we have what we think are good reasons to offer such a statement as one to be endorsed). Once it was 'right' to say that there were witches, although it is now right to say that there were not: 'truth' can only be context- and theory-relative.

As a realist, and as one who takes seriously the problem of how it could happen that creatures like us could ever hope to gain knowledge of a genuinely extrinsic reality (noted in an earlier chapter),[2] I find myself at odds with two movements of thought which seem to dominate the philosophical, literary or scientific establishment. On the one hand, I am merely irritated by those who claim that 'there is nothing outside the text', that 'true' means only 'what we find it seriously appropriate to say', that we can only 'turn out to have been mistaken' in the sense that some newly

121

preferred language has replaced the old. On the other hand, I simply cannot absorb or comprehend the apparent thesis of the eliminative materialists, that they are not in fact attempting to persuade others that they should not believe that there are any beliefs. Of R. W. Gerard's thesis that 'ideas don't move muscles' Walshe (1968, p. 293) commented, 'if it was not an idea that motivated him so to employ his relevant musculature to utter this opinion, what can it have been?' If we can no more determine which beliefs we ought to hold than which deities we ought to propitiate (Stich 1983, p. 2, because, so Stich supposes, there are really neither deities nor beliefs), it is simply ridiculous to suggest that we might be (as Stich), or actually are (as the Churchlands), under any rational obligation to believe in eliminative materialism. The Churchlands reply (P. S. Churchland 1984, P. M. Churchland 1986) that this is like an imaginable claim that the denial of 'vital spirit' is pragmatically self-refuting, since the unbeliever would be implying that he or she was, as lacking such spirits, dead. The reply is ineffective: even if vital spirits did exist we would have an available language to describe the other possible grounds or conditions of being alive. 'If eliminative materialism is true then meaningfulness must have some different source' than the Gricean (P. M. Churchland 1984, p. 48), and no such analysis is even on the horizon. If it were it would have to meet so many of the existing requirements on what it is to intend, mean, believe, reason and so forth as to amount to just those things.

Paradoxically, anti-realists and eliminative materialists end up doing, and saying, very similar things (indeed some of them are the same people). Either there is nothing 'outside the text', or else what is outside the text is something that all of us must, and do, ignore. Materialists are as optimistic as ever theologians have been that some day we shall be able to see 'not as in a glass, darkly, but face to face', that we might achieve the status of Rorty's imagined Antipodeans and cease to think that anything is happening here-now but the concatenated firing of nerve fibres (Rorty 1979). But in the meantime authors struggle to get their typescripts in on time, argue with reviewers and fiercely resent criticism, or, as they suppose, misquotation.

> We may if we like by our reasonings, unwind things back to that black and jointless continuity of space and moving clouds of swarming atoms which science calls the only real world. But all the while the world *we* feel and live in will be that which our ancestors, and we, by slowly cumulating strokes of choice, have extricated out of this, like sculptors.
>
> (James 1890, p. 288)

The ancient division between what is true 'by nature' and what is true 'by convention' still remains, even if anti-realists deny that anything ever could be true by nature, and eliminative materialists posit a 'truth by nature' which we must, perforce, ignore.

As a realist, of course, my sympathies are often with the materialists.

Anti-realists have no real recourse against moral or metaphysical opponents but to say that 'we' don't talk like that. As Nieli points out, ardent Wittgensteinians for example simply have to accept that within the Nazi form of life Jews were seriously, and for that form of life appropriately, called parasites and poisoned humanity (Nieli 1987, p. 241). Patricia Churchland makes a similar complaint against those who would deny her the right to correct or eliminate 'accepted' ways of speaking: without such a right how could we escape the conventional reality of witches, spirits, alchemical powers and so on? Instrumentalism is often a last ditch attempt to avoid the pain of radical correction, the realisation that we were simply wrong, that our language was not 'cutting the world at its joints'. But the Churchlands' appeal to our common memory and judgment that we have managed to escape the nets of language, and corrected our moral errors, sits very ill with their version of materialism. Their hope that the spread of neurological information (which they equate a little too readily with the acquisition of up-to-the-minute metaphors and vaguely neurological reference) will lead to a more 'humane' society is not merely wildly optimistic, but self-contradictory. 'If we had to renounce folk psychology we should probably have to reject the notion of personhood and moral agency as well. But to do this is to plunge into the abyss' (Stich 1983, p. 242). 'Ethical considerations preclude free experimentation on human beings, of course' (P. M. Churchland 1984, p. 97), but Churchland does not say what those considerations are. Either they rest upon a respect for human beings as rational agencies, or (less plausibly) on disinclination to cause them pain, or (less plausibly still) on sentimental attachment to the human form. But no one is a rational agent as we have hitherto 'understood' the concept; the sheer subjective nastiness of pain is no part of a rigorously eliminative metaphysics; and sentimental attachments are exactly the kind of things that a clearer view of reality must break. The Churchlands are victims of the common illusion that we can retain the moral or political 'advantages' of a system while systematically eliminating the knowledge claims on which, historically and logically, it is founded. We have good historical reason to suspect that if we train ourselves to see 'living' or 'human' things as 'matter in motion', we shall treat them as such. I share Patricia Churchland's belief that we are well rid of a belief in witches, and though I doubt that alchemy was a 'terrible theory' (because I doubt that it was ever meant to be about merely chemical realities) I agree with Paul Churchland that at least some theories constitute 'an outrage against reason and truth' (see Stich 1983, p. 245). But that is because I believe that we are rational and responsible agents, with real duties of compassion, justice, honesty and scientific rigour.

Anti-realism and eliminative materialism are alike not merely in the weakness of their response to moral danger. What they share is a rejection of the merely and experientially given. If there were a real 'given', anti-realism would have a definite limit: some things simply could not be magicked away. In the words of my friend and colleague Howard Robinson, if anti-realism is correct 'what is to stop us eliminating death, poverty and unhappiness by conceptual revisions?' (Robinson 1982, p. 82) From the correct and commonsensical observation that our experience is often importantly structured, and hence restructurable, by particular personal and historical modalities, some have concluded either that everything is, or else that what is not is unimportant and unspeakable. The nastiness of pain is either something directly and ineluctably given, and eliminative materialism is false, or else a gloss that is somehow and perhaps 'inappropriately' put upon an event better described in neurophysiological terms. If Rorty's Antipodeans mean anything important by saying 'it's just awful' of their C-fibres' firing, they are not eliminative materialists, but merely speakers of a language heavily contaminated by neurophysiological jargon. Replacing 'Zeus' by 'Whirligig' (in Greek, 'Dine', which has a punning relation to 'Zeus'), is no change (see Aristophanes, *Clouds*). 'They have just the same range of experience, but describe and report upon it in different ways' (Wilkes 1978, p. 102). Wilkes 1988, p. 244ff seems to doubt that there is any such real thing, while still insisting, against the Churchlands, that ordinary language has its uses.

Eliminative materialists insist, and anti-realists deny, that there is a world distinct from our imaginings or utterances about it. The issue is further confused by a tendency on the part of anti-realists to appropriate the term 'real' for their own use, and then claim to be 'real realists'. 'Reality' turns out to be the set of generally approved sentences, or the ideal limit of a process of 'scientific enquiry' defined not by its tendency to approximate an extrinsic truth, but by its obedience to local norms of openness, repeatability, consistency and the like. I shall have more to say later about the ways that an appropriate 'we' is selected, and what rules of scientific etiquette are currently proposed. Eliminative materialists similarly confuse the issue by appropriating such terms as 'pain', 'feeling', 'thought': on the one hand these no more denote natural kinds than 'weed' or 'fish' or 'phlogiston'; on the other hand, they can sometimes be made to stand in for whatever neural or biochemical type-state turns out to be causally implicated in whatever type of behaviour turns out to be the reality behind folk-psychological discriminations. The problem is, of course, that there is probably no single type of neural or biochemical state, nor any single type of behaviour that plausibly maps our usual, untutored judgments. It would really be better to abandon all efforts to retain the old discriminations, or the terms used for them. At the same time it is sometimes useful to denounce dualists: in order to do so the eliminative materialist retains the option of insisting that a being with the appropriate biochemical state and correspondent 'behaviour' is simply bound to be in such and such a mental state. 'Sensory qualia are . . . an inevitable concomitant of any system with the kind of functional organization at issue' (P. M. Churchland 1984, p. 41): 'sensory qualia', that is, in the only sense available to the eliminative materialist, namely the neural states associated with actually picking out such-and-such things in the world. Just as anti-realists distinguish real and unreal (within their textual framework) and claim that they are not rejecting any 'real' thing, so eliminative materialists find occasional use for 'folk-psychological terms', materially defined, and claim that they thereby accept all that could possibly exist of what their opponents imagine that they deny.

In these manoeuvrings anti-realists and eliminative materialists seek to avoid the supposed horrors of scepticism. A rational realist like myself, believing that there is a reality more than 'an obsequious shadow' of my thoughts and preferences, must acknowledge at least the theoretical possibility of a serious and enduring gap between the truth and our thoughts about the truth. It might be true – though I do not for a moment suppose it is – that what I call my wife is only a careful automaton, or that the whole world of my experience be only 'a dream and a delirium'. Anti-realists eliminate the gap by denying that there is or could be a truth thus disjoined from what 'we' say. Eliminative materialists eliminate it by denying that there is or could be anything but a 'physical' reality: I have no 'thoughts' about my wife, and she has none about me. Both camps are fond of enquiring what difference it could make as long as the same story is told, the same physical realities monitored. That they think it could make none casts the gravest doubts on their being what I would naturally believe them to be: namely, conscious and rational agents. My response, that my wife is a genuine, old-fashioned person, and that this world, even if a dream, is embedded in a wider reality to which I can wake up, does not rest on 'intuition', 'gut-feeling' or slavish obedience to social norms. What it does rest on I shall tell you in a moment. What I must first point out is that anti-realists and eliminative materialists alike, in their haste to avoid the threat of scepticism, have actually succumbed to it. Scepticism, historically, is the determination to act in obedience to the experienced compulsions of nature, custom, desire and the rules of such crafts as we elect to practise 'so as not to be wholly inactive' (Sextus Empiricus 1933, p. 17). It is they, and not the realist, who have succumbed to the fear of uncertainty by giving up the impulse or obligation to match their theories to the world beyond. They both entertain a fantasy of 'direct awareness', embodied either in the thesis that our awareness constitutes all there is of reality, or in the apparently opposed, but really equivalent thesis, that physical reality is all there is of awareness.

THEORY AND PRACTICE

My quarrel with modernity, so to speak, obviously does not end there, but this is not the time or the place to consider and reconsider theoretical responses from sophisticated anti-realists or materialists. I have written at such length in order to make room for my own rock-bottom methodological assumptions, which are, I assure you, straightforwardly commonsensical – but what philosopher does not think that of his or her own assumptions? The primary context of all our enquiries is the folk-psychological realm of perceptions, reports, beliefs, intentions, judgments of truth or relevance of evidence. That realm, structured through gesture, language and production, readily tries out and even absorbs all manner of theoretical insights (or errors), but it does not embody any single theory which can sensibly be described as out-moded or unhelpful, any more than the collection of nails, screws, bolts, screwdrivers, chisels, hammers, drills that have accumulated in my toolbox embody 'a theory' of what to do about the house, or how to do it. The only toolbox that might embody such a theory would be one purchased new, and never actually used! Psychological discoveries, for example, of the ways we cope with cognitive dissonance or of our curious and unreasoned belief in the 'just world hypothesis', can readily be incorporated into our toolkit. So can neurological discovery or, more often, journalistic report of neurological hypothesis. I certainly agree that such new discoveries or hypotheses cannot be outlawed because they conflict with 'ordinary' ways of speaking: 'the abuse of accepted modes of speech is often an essential feature of real scientific progress' (P. M. Churchland 1984, p. 41). 'Language is the depository of past discoveries, but it is also a hypnotic, blinding the mind to its own concealed, redundant and often erroneous assumptions' (Whyte, cited by Plutchik 1980, p. 79). But it does not follow that we should all abandon our accumulated and familiar toolkits and start to use the latest 'complete and scientifically engineered toolkit' instead. People who believe in brand new, complete and easily usable toolkits, whether these are abstract or concrete, are mildly amusing as home handymen, irritating as advertisers and academic theoreticians and terrifying as political reformers.

Tools which serve well enough, in experienced hands, for many purposes are often to be preferred to tools designed for exactly defined ends. The largely inarticulate craftsman, operating by know-how and immediate judgment, is almost always to be preferred to the theoretician who will not concede the rightness of a particular practice or description unless some mechanical rule can be stated for adopting that practice or description. Theoreticians have something to offer (what philosopher could safely deny it?), but they should be humble before their inarticulate betters, and eye their own tendency to eliminate the vague, the arbitrary or ad hoc with some suspicion.

The relevance of these remarks in praise of vagueness and complexity? Eliminative materialists dismiss what they regard as 'folk-psychological theory' because it is difficult, or even impossible, to give context-independent definitions of such crucial terms as 'belief', 'intention', 'emotion', 'thought' or 'consciousness'. 'Belief-ascriptions', so Stich suggests, 'are similarity claims' (Stich 1983, p. 106), and what counts as relevantly similar depends on the speaker's current purposes: what is, conversationally, implied by the thesis that 'someone believes something', depends on the conversation. Stich concludes, perhaps a little gloomily, that 'is a belief that *p*' does not express or correspond to a genuine property (ibid., p. 225). It does not do so partly because there is no one answer, context-independent, to a question about 'Fido's' or 'Tabby's' beliefs, and partly because there are many cases in human affairs where verbal and non-verbal systems seem to be disconnected. 'Subjects' verbal reporting systems have no access to the processes actually underlying their non-verbal behavioral changes' (Stich 1983, p. 233): and what else is new?

One response to the vagueness and multiple usefulness of supposedly 'folk' terms is to suggest that there are certain 'central' and 'literal' meanings. 'The attribution of anger to infrahuman animals is largely metaphorical' (Averill 1982, p. 282), apparently because the attribution of anger to adult humans is part of a complex social, and even legal, activity. Other commentators see no reason to deny that, for example, chimpanzees show the 'full picture of human anger in its three main forms: anger (i.e. aggressive action), sulking, and the temper tantrum' (Hebb 1972, p. 202). According to Searle, though I am not sure that he would in fact extend this remark to cover attributions of anger, 'only someone in the grip of a philosophical theory would deny that small babies can literally be said to want milk and that dogs want to be let out or believe that their master is at the door' (Searle 1983, p. 5), even though the baby has no conception of milk as such, and dogs no grasp of the indefinitely many logical implications of the proposition that so and so is at the door.

The puzzles about clear or literal attribution of 'psychological states' may lead commentators to replace such attributions by merely neurological modalities, whether or not those are held to be 'more or less' what psychological attribution had been after. If an emotion or a belief is simply whatever it is that generally produces such and such identifiable motions, and it turns out that there is indeed some identifiable, single cause to match each separate common term, then we can go on using such attributions with a renewed conviction.

> Anyone would surely judge (Harlow's monkeys) as looking severely depressed and regressed (in a clinical sense). The parallel behaviours observed in children and in monkeys exposed to somewhat similar deprivations strongly suggests that the same emotional system, grief or depression, has been activated.
>
> (Plutchik 1980, p. 107)

Even if a somewhat different physical structure or process is involved (and there seems no reason, a priori, to suppose this here), we need not shrink from labelling it 'depression' any more than we refuse to call a cephalopod's light-receptors 'eyes' merely because they have a different evolutionary ancestry from vertebrate 'eyes' (Lorenz 1981, p. 90). Similarly, the wings of bird, bat and butterfly.

There are of course important questions here: do such terms as 'anger', 'grief', 'love' identify, even in a majority of cases, functionally identifiable causal conditions that precede the emergence of the human species and culture? Or are they in some real sense 'culture specific', either because the attribution of such emotions is to be understood as offering a legal or moral excuse or justification for action, or because we have actually acquired more complex causal systems than our kin, systems which depend for their effect on our multiple reflected awareness of possible action? Whatever is true of anger, it does seem possible that 'romantic love' is a cultural invention, and not genuinely the 'same' as sexual or affective impulse. 'It is no more reasonable', for that matter, 'to suggest that an animal is "defending his territory" than it is to believe that the intruder is defending his God-given right to territorial expansion' (Moyer 1987, p. 13). Such 'invented' syndromes build upon the biological, but cannot be equated with any discoverable biochemical or neural condition shared with our relatives. It does not follow except for eliminative materialists, that they are unreal. Tables, chairs and lecture-halls are real even if they do not appear, as such, in any scientific theory. Even if 'being in a temper' is as much a social construct or socially defined role as 'being possessed by the Voodoo *Loa* Erzulie' (see Deren 1975, p. 289; Clark *The Mysteries of Religion*, 1986, 214ff) it may have as real and definite effects as 'being married' or 'being minister of state'.

Some have suggested that our socially constructed emotional rules vary so greatly as to have created radically different emotional universes. There is no straightforward one-to-one translation between the English vocabulary of anger and the Japanese vocabulary of *ikari* (Averill 1982, p. 67ff; see also Hayward 1987, p. 88, re 'wabi') or so we are told. If that is so then it may seem a waste of time to locate emotion-specific physical syndromes or functionally equivalent systems in non-human creatures: as time-wasting as to locate natural names by tracing the etymologies of different human languages to the sort of grunts, bays and giggles that a pre-human, pre-vocal species might have made. Explaining anger (or *ikari*) as 'really' being a certain biochemical syndrome that can also be discovered in the non-human is like explaining the ancient Greek practice of erecting ithyphallic herms by their front doors by mentioning the practice attested in non-human primates of using the erect penis as a threat or dominance signal. The woman who is my spouse is not my spouse as being the subject of any physical property, and animals do not even have 'common-law spouses'. The analogies between matrimony and the 'life-long fidelity' of cranes are the stuff of moral fables, but not of natural history.

UNDERSTANDING FROM INSIDE

But it is time to change course. What, after all, is the ground for our distinction between literal and metaphorical usage, between history and fable? And is it really true that the range of emotion available to Japanese and Westerner and ancient Greek, not to mention chimpanzee, baboon and elephant are quite so various? Of course, different theories have emerged out of our experience: the distinction that Onians identified between *thumos* and *phrenes* (Onians 1951, p. 44ff) is not one that quite lines up with our own distinctions of heart, mind and soul. Equally obviously some ancient theories have so structured our imaginations that people go on complacently re-inventing them: Maclean's tripartite brain, divided between the reptilian, old mammalian and new mammalian, each with its clearly identified structure and function, is, as Reynolds has pointed out, something that sounds right to us precisely because it embodies Plato's tripartite soul (Reynolds 1981, p. 35; see also Reynolds 1987). And that, quite probably, sounded right because it embodied a very ancient Indo-European conception of the proper order of society. But the stories that are told with the aid of these terms are not stories about alien beings. We understand Achilles and Odysseus and King David. Lady Murasaki and Jane Austen were sisters under the skin. Harré's claim (Harré 1984, p. 128) that 'accidie' and melancholy are 'extinct' or 'obsolete' emotions, only vaguely discerned by an occasional depressed scholar nowadays, is likewise, to me, simply unbelievable: what Evagrius called 'the noon-day demon' is alive and well even if we call it something different. And if, as the Churchlands insist, our folk-psychological understanding is no advance on that of Sophocles, this may be because he understood us very well. There is clearly some strong psychological pressure that compels some imaginative psychohistorians to pretend that there are alien intelligences in our history, or across our borders: nothing else could easily explain the pleasure with which Julian Jaynes' fantasies (Jaynes 1976) are greeted by biologists and philosophers without any historical sense. But the truth is that our ancestors were quite human, and those of our contemporaries who are not, as we say, 'civilised' or 'Western' are human too. 'The Orient has helped to define Europe (or the West) as its contrasting image, idea, personality, experience' (Said 1979, p. 2) but *that* Orient is a Western fable: people who live 'there' turn out to be like us. There are no one-to-one translations of 'anger' or '*ikari*'. But who ever supposed that any languages could be translated just like that (except perhaps very naive computer programmers)? What we have no single word for, we can still say. What we cannot say at all we can often still communicate.

Language and, more generally, custom teach us how to cope with life, and with emotions. Some of that teaching, and its associated concepts, may well be inaccurate or unhelpful – I doubt, for example, that 'psychopathy' or 'schizophrenia' are well-formed syndromes. Over much of the world what they teach is that it is through speech and reasoned discourse that we can tame those passions that would otherwise drag us back to the 'animal'. Men are judged – and I do, deliberately, say 'men' by their capacity to control and ride and rise about 'emotion'. Spinoza (1677 (1982), p. 193) interpreted the story of Adam's fall as one consequent on his 'coming to imitate animal emotions and lose his freedom' (see Chapter 8 of this volume). It is therefore rather strange to learn that non-humans, and human infants too, are only 'metaphorically' emotional. 'What is the natural expression of an intention? Look at a cat when it stalks a bird, or a beast when it wants to escape' (Wittgenstein 1958, p. 165). If the non-metaphorical sense of a term is that which it has first, then animals are paradigmatically 'emotional'.

> When do we act like sheep? When we act for the sake of the belly, or of our sex-organs, or at random, or in a filthy fashion, or without due consideration. When we act pugnaciously and injuriously and angrily and rudely, to what level have we degenerated? To the level of wild beasts, solitary carnivores.
>
> (Epictetus 1946, 2.9.2; see also Anonymous (*Philokalia*) 1979, vol. 1, p. 49, contrasting self-esteem and envy with anger and desire, which are held to be common to us and to non-rational animals)

I do not mean to imply that non-humans merited such scorn, but that the animals with whom we have shared our lives, or at least the land, for millennia, have all been appreciated to be emotional beings, governed by much the same syndromes as ourselves, though without the chance of understanding. We are all mammals, vertebrates, together. The attempt to think all this away leaves us less well-informed: witness the effort to exclude 'anthropomorphic' language in describing chimpanzees, outlined by Hebb. 'All that resulted', he says, 'were an endless series of specific acts in which no order or meaning could be found' (Hebb 1946, p. 88; see Gordon 1989, p. 1ff).

That a cat whose fur has been ruffled for just that bit too long by the child of the house is 'going to get cross' is as non-metaphorical a claim as any.

> After a few trials with the 'bad' trainer (who took the titbits she had discovered for himself) she (which is to say, a female chimpanzee) stopped pointing (out the hidden food) and began throwing objects at him.
>
> (Plutchik 1980, p. 108, after Premack)

> Cats that have had all the brain removed above the level of the midbrain, except for the endocrine tissue of the hypothalamus, which is left neurally disconnected...can walk if stimulated... *and show behavioral components of fear and rage.*
>
> (Reynolds 1981, p. 62, my italics)

And should they not? W. B. Cannon, by the way, called this response 'sham rage' (Cannon, cited by Plutchik 1980, p. 13), but I am at a loss to see what pretence could be in question. In brief, whatever anger is, or 'anger' is intended to denote, it must be something that such animals display. This is one reason that Stich offers for denying that 'anger' and the like could name a truly mentalistic entity. On the one hand the attribution of any particular belief or intention to the non-human is irreducibly vague or context-dependent. 'We cannot say whether animals think or not, or what kinds of thought they think, because we have no clear use of the word "thought" in connection with creatures that never speak' (Findlay 1963, p. 21). On the other hand 'there is reason to suppose that the cognitive processes operative in ourselves are not fundamentally different from those in young children and non-linguistic animals' (Stich 1983, p. 214). If what moves the cat or the chimpanzee is recognisably what may move us, and rightly has the name 'anger', but cat and chimpanzee have no definite beliefs, then 'anger' does not name anything involving such a definite belief.

And this is perhaps compatible with introspective psychology. Observing in ourselves tensed muscles, flushed face, pounding heart, clenched or bared teeth we conclude that we are angry, and then that we have reason to be, that we have been wronged. Experiments reveal, and I cannot see why Stich or the Churchlands think that the revelation is surprising, or that it constitutes a problem for 'folk psychology', that we can be tricked into not 'acting angrily' when we feel what we might have called 'anger'. Those who know (or believe) that they have taken drugs to produce such physiological effects are less irritable than those who know (or believe) that they have taken depressant drugs.

The discovery is a lot older than behavioural psychology, a fact concealed from those who leap over the centuries and never bother to read works from other traditions. Consider the advice of the Byzantine theologian Evagrius, that we should recognise the images and feelings engendered in us by the different demons who encamp around our soul: knowing that the image of past unpleasantness, the physiological unrest, the suggestion that particular muscles are ready to contract, are all external, till we consent to them, it is (a little) easier not to be deceived.

> A man who possesses spiritual knowledge has said that [the illusion of God's glory in a form pleasing to the senses] results from the passion of self-esteem and from the demon's touch on a certain area of the brain.
> (*Philokalia* 1979, vol. 1, p. 64)

Or consider the Buddhist strategy, of letting such sensations, perceptions, thoughts, arise and fall, without attachment, without 'living through' them.

Have I surrendered to eliminative materialism? Do our words for such emotions really name such physically describable syndromes as we share with, at least, our fellow vertebrates? I have no particular objection. But I emphasise that it is a grotesque and well-known fallacy to confuse cognition and the thing cognised: were it not, idealism would have been established long ago (Findlay 1963, p. 1). Our experience of the physical syndrome which is, typically, anger is not itself that syndrome. Materialistic theory does not solve this crux by postulating other physical states that somehow replicate the first (without repeating it): experience remains an act, or passion, of another sort. It comes in two forms, or has two modalities: we 'enjoy' and 'contemplate'.

In living through, or 'enjoying', anger, lust, greed, our attention is focused on an object structured by the demands of the emotion we live through. Which is why, once again, it has been thought that animals are especially 'emotional': 'Buytendijk considers it doubtful that animals perceive "things" [that is, stable and enduring substances] or that buzzing bees and howling dogs experience any feelings or pain *in the way humans do*' (Speigelberg 1972, p. 290, my italics) a witness to the staying power of very ancient images. Buytendijk's judgment rests on little more than personal intuition. One of W. B. Yeats' friends meditated on the subject of 'what it is like to be a canary', and concluded that the canary's world contained colour but no outline: doubtless, Yeats remarked sceptically, he had made an error in his contemplative technique (Yeats 1961, p. 411). Tinbergen's insistence that we should not project our feelings and emotions onto animals applies here too – we should not too readily think of 'animals' as 'unthinking' or 'blindsighted' either – but the story is plausible enough. Most animals seem not to live in a world of independent, causally related objects, but of signs and pathways, opportunities and perils. The sense, elicited through curious or playful behaviour, of a world that stays the same, with definite furniture and re-identifiable companions, is a gradual creation which may at least provide the model for noticing and naming those very emotional syndromes which had hitherto ruled us. Seeing a rounded object emerge from the mists we turn our attention on our own emotions, and objectify them so as to be free of them. 'In daily life we have created an emotional entity that we call anger. We have done so by giving it a name in noun form' (Schafer 1976, p. 281).

Or else, having once seen them, we endorse them once again, and act in deeper consciousness, out of principle. 'Righteous indignation' is the thing we build up out of anger when we can persuade ourselves that it is not our anger only, that it is not I but Justice that must be appeased. Most of us have seen enough of the effects of that to be a little nervous, but mere disengagement from all emotional affect is unlikely to be less dangerous.

For the discovery of a world that remains the same for just anyone, unstructured by any aim or impulse of our own, can leave us adrift.

There is no such thing as personification, only depersonification.... The question, how did man ever come to God is senseless; there is only the question, how did man ever come away from God?
(Otto 1962, p. 261, cited by Hillman 1975, p. 17)

'God' here stands not for a transcendent Lord, but for a lived reality structured through and through by personal meanings, a reality of threats and promises and − we say − 'projections'. That we begin, historically and individually, from a lived reality which − once we have, partly, left it − looks animistic, value-laden, is, by the way, one reason why I agree with Wilkes that Aristotle did not make the later distinction between material and mental realities (though he did distinguish form and matter, as well as soul and body), but disagree with her that he was therefore a happy materialist. What gets invented over the years is not the mental realm, but the material. But that is another story.

The gradual education of our sense and sensibilities often seems to involve the withdrawal of projections, leaving the 'real object' as something in its own right, not a vehicle for our misplaced empathy or moralising judgment. Things aren't as much like 'us' as we first thought. Washburn's level-headed and unjustly neglected study of 'the animal mind' raises the serious question, 'what is it like to be a wasp?'.

> Anger, in our own experience, is largely composed of quickened heart beat, of altered breathing, of muscular tension, of increased blood pressure in the head and face. The circulation of a wasp is fundamentally different from that of any vertebrate. The wasp does not breathe through lungs, it wears its skeleton on the outside, and it has the muscles attached to the inside of the skeleton. What is anger like in the wasp's consciousness? We can form no adequate idea of it.
>
> (Washburn 1917, p. 3ff)

And even if the wasp could speak we could not understand her. The withdrawal of our failed projections, and the concomitant 'objectification' of the things left behind in the 'melancholy long withdrawing roar' of animistic sympathy, should often be an acceptance of ignorance. The impulse to avoid that pain by saying that what we don't know is not knowledge, that our inability to prove one thing is a proof of its opposite, that what 'we' no longer 'identify' with may properly be treated as 'mere things', may often be very powerful. If anger is a socially defined role, so also is a pitiless 'objectivity'. But the withdrawal of failed projections does not always require us to practise sceptical chastity (let alone pitiless objectivity). As a normally heterosexual male I have had to acquire and practise a careful discipline of not projecting my diffused amorousness onto any present woman. But in realising that they do not feel, or need not be feeling, the emotion that seems to fill *my* lived reality, I do not conclude that they are things without a life of their own that I could recognise and appreciate. Even if it is true that 'the agony of the tail end [of a cut worm] is our agony, not the worm's' (Jaynes 1976, p. 6), a thesis that I do not think is even near to being established, it does not follow that I can legitimately or sensibly conclude that because I do not 'know' or cannot 'feel in myself' what the worm feels, I somehow do know and can 'feel in myself' that the worm feels nothing. My not knowing that it is now raining in Glasgow does not mean that I know it isn't.

My inexpugnable conviction is that the creatures I encounter are aware and living creatures, with lives that I can in various measures share but which do always escape my final comprehension. 'No one can put his arm into his brother's inside' in the words of the Bantu proverb. That there is something there that is not I but that I can, to a degree, live with and in, is a projection, and a conviction, as firm as any animist's or theist's conviction of the presence of diviner spirits in rainstorm, sunshine and the stars of heaven. 'For everything that it loves, everything that it pities, love personalises' (Unamuno 1954, p. 139; see Hillman 1975, p. 15). Friendship, which is love purged of concupiscence, exists in that moment when the 'other' is at once not an 'obsequious shadow' or 'projection' of our egocentric wishes, and identified through one's own deeper self. If my friend is, as Augustine put it, 'one half of my soul' and we together are 'one soul in two bodies', it cannot be because he or she is my satellite or shadow, nor is 'my soul' what I thought it was before we were friends.

OPPOSING METHODOLOGIES

I am well aware that the dominant methodological demand of 'modern science' has been the rejection of 'projective, participatory' technique. But that rejection, when it went beyond the discipline necessary to stir us from our old dogmatic and chauvinistic slumbers, has long since become self-defeating. By withdrawing from all empathetic identification, all emotional affect (or more usually by pretending to do so) we have successively emptied the world of spirits, secondary qualities, numbers and at last our own beliefs, desires, intentions – in short, the very projective faculty that had been blamed for all our other illusions. Putnam has justly mocked this final extravagance of objectifying reason, and insisted on his epistemological right to take a stand on the personalist conviction that he really does live among friends, colleagues and creatures whom he can understand, criticise and praise (Putnam 1987, p. 15). All I would add to that credo is that we need a cosmology which makes it likely that there would be such things, and that we would have such capacities. My belief in its truth rests upon my engagement with those realities, and on the abject incoherence of all attempts to deny it.

I am also well aware that contemporary scientific rhetoricians will insist that no thesis should be accepted unless it can be supported by 'non-anecdotal' evidence (which is to say, by data revealed through carefully controlled experiments that can be repeated successfully by any qualified experimenter, whatever his or her state of mind and character). A complete rebuttal of that methodology would take another chapter. In this context I will merely point out the following difficulties. First, what is the non-

134

anecdotal evidence for the 'non-anecdotalist' principle? Second, what is the non-anecdotal evidence for the theses that one's fellow experimenters are themselves rational, responsible, honest and accurate? Are scientists themselves subjected to the would-be destructive, repeatable tests that alone could guarantee their honesty, and if they are not, what right does the non-anecdotalist have to accept their testimony? Third, is it true that 'scientific experiments' do not depend for their success on the character and unformalised intuition of the experimenters? There is surely a great deal of evidence that experimental technique is learned by imitation, socialisation, character building exercises – some of which may make it very difficult for the initiate to notice or take seriously data that other people would reckon obvious. Fourth, I have already cited non-anecdotal comparisons of the success-rate of the 'empathetic' versus the 'objectivist' techniques. Fifth, if it is wrong to accept any proposition without non-anecdotal evidence, it is equally wrong to accept the *negation* of any given proposition: once again, having no evidence that *p*, does *not* constitute evidence that non-*p*. Sixth, the usual appeal to Occam's Razor at this point (not to multiply entities beyond necessity) represents a misunderstanding of that principle, and of empathetic, participatory science. Successful participatory science is not postulating extra entities, but grasping the nature of the ones immediately present to us.

In brief, the present state of objectising science is ptolemaic: epicycles are constantly being added to our models of biological and physical nature when what we need is a Copernican realisation that we are not of any radically different kind from the things we study. Those who insist on such a radical disjunction are repeating the medieval error of supposing that there are abrupt discontinuities in the universe (as between sublunary and super-lunary matter). We know from inside what it is like to be organic, physical beings.

But the intellectual chastity which is the strength of objectivism, however badly it has been misused, deserves a second look. The peril of animism in its various forms is that it fills our world with all-too-familiar fancies. The sin of thinking that a woman is amorous in her own person merely because I am amorous, and perceive her in the light of that drug-based fantasy – no less drug-based because the drugs are naturally occurring – is matched by the sin of thinking that sheep are greedy, wolves vicious, peacocks proud, apes dishonourable mimics, merely because we find them convenient symbols of our various faults. The attempt to see them 'without emotional affect' is originally just the attempt not to mistake our clouded, moralising fables for the truth of things. The old 'enchanted' world was one where omens leered from every bush because we were quite sure that the world revolved round us. The realisation of the world's 'virile indifference and sunny selfishness', to borrow a phrase of Chesterton's (Chesterton 1961, p. 20), is liberating as well as revelatory. If we are going to be able to understand, to find ourselves inside another creature, human or otherwise, we must often first of all recoil from our easy misunderstandings.

We must not assume that a dog is 'angry', indignant, revengeful merely because he growls, any more than we should suppose that a chimpanzee is happy because she bares her teeth. The latter signal is a sign, variously, of fear and rage; the former may be no more than to say, as it were, 'keep your distance!'. Even students of animal behaviour who have been lectured all their working lives on the importance of not 'projecting' or 'anthropomorphising', regularly slip into such misleading ways. The contributors to McGuinness' volume, for example, all agreed to define aggression as 'the intention to harm another, triggered by an external stimulus' (McGuinness 1987, p. x), and went on to take it for granted that aggression so defined was to be found throughout the animal kingdom. My complaint here is not the one that, for example, Tinbergen would have felt obliged to make, that we could only 'observe' what physically happened, not how it felt to the animals (Tax and Callender 1960, p. 185). That distinction, between the observable and the non-observable, is a confused piece of outdated sceptical philosophy, especially when the 'observable' is identified with the 'physical'. What I think Tinbergen really meant, which renders his objection something more than a piece of idle scepticism, was that in speaking, as McGuinness' contributors did, of 'intentions to harm' we would be imputing a spirit to the animals which in most cases requires more grasp of logical and practical implication than they are at all likely to have, and always run ahead of the evidence of what actually happens.

In fairness to those contributors, Peter Reynolds at any rate drew a more sophisticated moral. What we have called aggression is 'the major mechanism of social affiliation as well as of social dispersal' (Reynolds 1981, p. 128). Intra-specific aggression, at any rate, does not always appear to be associated with recognisable 'anger', that impulse defined long ago, by Aristotle, as 'an impulse, accompanied by pain, to a conspicuous revenge for a conspicuous slight directed without justification towards what concerns oneself or one's friends' (Aristotle *Rhetoric* 2.1378a.30ff; see Averill 1982, p. 80). Even if we abstract from that moral and legal role the mere physiologically describable episode of rage appeased by perceived damage to an adversary, we have little reason to think that is the core of all 'aggression'. What we are seeing in intra-specific aggression, most of the time, is a jostling for spatial or hierarchical position, a technique, as Reynolds observes, whereby the relatively weaker individuals can be accommodated in the social group. What we are seeing is the 'finding-out-about-each-other' that is the root of friendship. What we are seeing, alternatively and not incompatibly, is mutual manipulation. 'No one reading de Waal's *Chimpanzee Politics* with an open mind can come away convinced of major discontinuities (between human and chimpanzee) in the underlying motivations' (Reynolds 1987, p. 128).

136

Merely to empty 'animal behaviour' of its significance for those involved incurs two great risks: the first, that we shall confuse our methodological discipline with ontological asceticism. Because we have decided not to speculate about how it feels to them we absurdly come to believe that it doesn't feel like anything (as though black-and-white films prove the world was colourless). The second danger is that, supposing ourselves to be practising objectivity, we simply describe animal doings in what we take to be the 'lowest' modes available, as instances of murderous appetite, rather than cool political manipulation, for example. Morgan, whose canon is invoked to defend the latter practice, was at least not guilty of the first: he was in fact a convinced panpsychist – which is a more rational position than either eliminative materialism or emergent property-dualism (see Rollin 1989, p. 74ff). The canon is a useful rule of thumb, a reminder that a dog may cower not from guilt nor even fear of punishment but simply from discomfort, or simply be appeasing his substitute pack-leader (Morgan 1894, p. 53; see Washburn 1917, p. 25ff). But the attribution of 'simpler' or 'lower' motivations may sound right to us exactly because that was our earliest thought, that animals are, exactly, 'animal' in being moved in ways that, finding them in ourselves, we have already christened 'animal'.

Although I have rejected the psychohistorian's suggestion that there are fundamental, untraversable discontinuities in the human emotional scene, that our ancestors had, or that foreigners have, emotions quite unlike 'our' own, I must obviously concede that we do divide up the infinite complexity of the soul in different ways, and consequently that the exact truth of the thesis that 'I am in a very bad temper' does not require that we believe in the existence of a discrete thing, 'a very bad temper' which we, or others, could not distinguish more exactly or else merge into a yet vaguer syndrome. I suppose that this is what some have meant by saying that 'an emotion is not a thing in the sense that a chair or a table is' (Plutchik 1980, p. 135). But of course the same is true, exactly, of chairs and tables and all the other furniture of the human (or rather the Western) life-world. Without its 'meaning' to us, a chair is only an odd aggregate of wood, steel, plastic, leather, cane or string. We see it as a *chair* by absorbing it into our structure of shared goals: we think it is 'really' a chair (as, perhaps, an accidentally shaped stone is not) if it was formed, from its beginning, within the moral and practical endeavour. An accidentally worn stone is not a chair, but what about a boulder selected and shaped by constant use into a comfortable form, even if the shaping was done, even if non-deliberately done, by apes? Nests are not accidental heaps of twigs, but matter formed into a practical purpose; there is no more a physical state of affairs that all nests are, than there is a physical state that all thoughts of home require. But it would be absurd to empty our minds of notions like 'nest'.

My conclusion is a simple one. We have available, in our moral sympathies, our capacity to share forms of life, our first and irreplaceable instrument for understanding what there is. 'Perhaps only through love is it possible to recognise the person of the soul' (Hillman 1975, p. 44). Whether our participatory identifications of thought or emotion are easily mapped onto a merely biochemical identification of physical state in us or in animals or not we cannot, and need not, abandon the participatory method. We do need to discipline and refine it, under the influence of two great intellectual and emotional projects: personalising love, and 'learned ignorance'. The two, I believe, point in the same direction: true love does not 'lay her own trip' on another, but waits to find the 'one soul in two bodies'; learned ignorance does not, absurdly, imagine that what we don't know is unknowable, nor that we know that p is false merely by not knowing it is true. What cosmological synthesis is eventually to be grounded in this methodology as the 'disenchanted' universe is grounded in 'scientific objectivism' is another, and even longer, story.

12

THE CONSCIOUSNESS OF ANIMALS[1]

INTRODUCTION

Common sense assures us that many non-human animals have desires, thoughts and plans much like our own. But common sense can be challenged. The chief principle of a properly scientific Enlightenment is that nothing is to be believed merely because 'common sense' would have it so, or because we *feel* its truth. Only what can be proved to the satisfaction of someone determined not to practise a potentially misleading empathy can be trusted: animals must be treated 'objectively', for the real world is one of mere, indifferent objects unaffected by our casual or conventional likes, sympathies and identifications. This 'modernism' is itself under challenge from 'post-moderns', inclined to doubt that there are any truths at all outside the sphere of what 'we' happily endorse: 'the objective world', by that account, is only another fanciful creation, and those who insist that we must only think 'objectively' are pretending to a mystical insight into 'reality itself' that post-moderns 'know' (or choose to say) is quite impossible.

It follows that any sensible examination of the problems posed by an enquiry into the consciousness, or otherwise, of animals (which is to say, non-human animals) must begin by considering the Enlightenment project that has given us modernity and, more recently, post-modernism. That project is founded on the twin postulates that knowledge is only possible if we divest ourselves of our human emotional nature, and that what is really knowable has no prescriptive force. It is founded, in fact, on the rejection of moral objectivism. My argument will be that a satisfactory solution to the question whether, and how, animals are conscious can only come by a return to moral objectivism, to the doctrine that knowledge arises from a loving attention to what is knowable, and that what is known makes its own demands on those who know. My enquiry must begin from moral philosophy rather than philosophy of mind.

MORAL OBJECTIVISM AND THE OPPOSITION

Moral naturalism – so to call a tradition of ethical thought that has been central to the last 2,000 years of civilised endeavour – has two main themes. First, that moral judgments can be really true or false, and not merely acceptable or unacceptable to this group or that. Second, that merely conventional or historically grounded distinctions are of less significance than natural ones. Thus:

1 Some acts would be wrong, some states of affairs evil, even if no one judged as much. It might be true, of course, that there could be no acts at all unless there were agents (and therefore moral judges), just as it might be true that no state of affairs would be evil unless someone or other found it disagreeable. It is a substantive (and therefore questionable) moral claim that all and only what someone or other finds disagreeable is therefore an evil; but that there are real evils, whether or not anyone does judge them evil, should not be in doubt. In the most extreme forms of moral naturalism, God himself can only observe the wrongness or the rightness of this act or that. He may create the conditions under which it has the properties that fix its moral value, but it is no more open to him to make right what otherwise would be wrong than to make 7 + 5 equal 13.[2]

2 What matters at least at the beginning of moral decision-making are those properties that are independent of human discourse. One man may be, conventionally, 'of gentle birth', and another 'of base stock', but this difference cannot be a good reason to treat them differently. Instead we should have regard to their God-given natures, what they are in origin. Merely conventional moralists of course may insist on these conventional distinctions, but what matters so far as the objective moralist is concerned must be what is true apart from such convention. Obviously enough, if it could be right to enslave one and wrong to enslave another merely because the one was *described* differently from the other, then that moral judgment at least would be true only in virtue of what 'we' said, and therefore not be objective. Objectively valid judgments can be grounded only on what is objectively true (though even objectivists will usually agree that there is a place for derivatively binding by-laws).

Many of our actual judgments are still rooted in conventional beginnings, but would-be objectivists usually then pretend that the conventions in turn reflect 'real' divisions, that, for example, gentle or Caucasian birth actually determines character or ability. Once it is clear that there are no real or natural divisions between people of a different caste, creed or colour (or none that rationally warrants different treatment when it comes to matters germane to us all), we should abandon those merely conventional discriminations. Justice is the moral entitlement of everyone, no matter where they live or what their accidental caste may be. Natural equals should be treated equally.

This sort of moral naturalism has had a poor press in recent years, and those who would relativise or historicise our moral beliefs seem to have made all the running; but those who oppose moral objectivism do not always realise all the implications of their preferred position. If there are no 'real', no natural, moral obligations, but all such obligations rest upon 'our' serious preference, then it is no longer easy to insist that only 'natural' divisions count. Where all is convention, merely conventional divisions are as good (or bad) as any. Why should it matter any longer that merely naked humans, stripped of their historical and cultural baggage, are only and entirely human? It takes a moral effort to remember this, and why should we make that effort if the only rules that bind us are our own?

There is a further problem. It may at first seem easy to distinguish the moral (which is conventional) from the merely natural (which carries no prescriptive force). We may conventionally decide that the cassowary is not a bird[3] – that is, is not to be treated like more usual birds – or that pets and pigs are treated differently. Whatever we decide will not be false. The facts of the matter, though, are otherwise: whatever it is we say or do, the cassowary is a bird (that is, cassowaries are winged things descended from the same common stock as blackbirds and penguins) and pigs need not be naturally different from the creatures we make 'pets'. We may not choose to attend to what pigs feel or fancy, but it will still be true that they feel pain when burnt, as much as pets do. But recent writers have begun to deny that facts are natural, any more than values: 'to attribute feelings to X is only to remind ourselves that it is wrong to hurt X [which is to say, respectable people don't usually approve of doing it]'.[4] Can we still insist that our conventional divisions are more rational than those of others?

In the remote past, maybe, people believed that 'weeds' or 'creepy-crawlies' named true natural kinds that were intrinsically evil. Then we began to think that these were very partial judgments, that the things we named as 'weeds' were not intrinsically weeds, nor evil. A true morality sought to discover natural kinds of a less subjective sort, the real divisions between this and that. The dogs we pet and the pigs we keep in pens are not so different (except in conventional value) that we should treat them very differently. Then we abandoned moral objectivity, including – though we did not always notice it – the obligation to treat natural equals equally and think less of all merely conventional discriminations. And finally, some few of us begin to deny even the old truth that there are natural kinds at all, that there are 'real equals' that should – on liberal views – be treated equally. We can no longer maintain the distinction between 'merely conventional' divisions and real ones. On this basis it becomes a sufficient defence of discriminatory practices that 'we' identify the victims thus and so. There are no objective rules of justice stipulating that this is wrong, nor any objective distinction between real and merely conventional distinctions. 'Rationality [in matters moral] is a myth'.[5]

The new anti-realism is in one respect more realistic than the old anti-moralism. Anti-moralists could agree that burning a pig alive would cause it pain, but deny that such an event was intrinsically wrong. Wrongness, they said, was neither a logically necessary corollary of causing-to-die-in-pain (for we could all understand, even if not admire, someone who said that acts like that were good), nor yet an identifiable property naturally occasioned by non-moral properties and having its own effects on future history. The 'wrongness', they said, was only 'our' projection. But what can it mean to say that something is in pain, if not that it is in a state worth fleeing from? And how could we decide that something was in pain except by acknowledging its screams, squirms and bloody sweats as pleas to desist? Malebranche heard a yelping dog impassively, as uttering no more than squeaking gears: to hear the yelps as evidence of pain would have been to be moved by sympathy (see Chapter 8 above). Ordinary descriptions are both factual and moral in their implications: to hold the moral implication off (with a view, maybe, to contradicting it) is to diminish our understanding even of the fact. What sort of pain is it that is not to be avoided? Can we distinguish between philosophers who deny that dogs feel pain, and ones who deny that we should ever mind? More generally: if what there is can never show us what to do, why trouble about what is? If there are no objective values, what value has the truth?

ANIMALS WITHIN THE TEXT

The new anti-realism is realistic also in this: our actual, lived worlds are structured by convention. 'Weeds', 'creepy-crawly things', 'pests', 'pets' and 'sacred cows' and 'people' are all terms at once strongly relativistic ('Everything green that grew out of the mould/Was an excellent herb to our fathers of old'[6] – but not to the average suburban gardener) and strongly prescriptive (they carry their recommendations on their faces). It is always a slight shock to realise that other peoples think us odd or filthy for those practices that seem entirely 'natural' to us – but that is merely evidence, for most of us, that they are odd or filthy. Older moral realists would often say that other people's discriminations are all superstitious – usually sublimely unaware that the speaker had his or her own absurdities. Hindus are superstitious for defending sacred cows; Koreans are bestial for killing and eating dogs.[7]

The world we live in is full of accidental and historically grounded associations and taxonomies. Churches and council chambers are more than piles of bricks, and more than buildings for crudely commercial purposes. People – even in these liberal days – are also family members and name-bearers, who learn their tasks in life from ceremonials as much as from a would-be systematic course of study. Ancient trees and hedgerows are not replaceable by plastic replicas. Horses and dogs and cows and sheep carry along with them a story dating back to neolithic times, and subtly modified in every generation by the tales we tell. Horses are imagined into being, as much as ridden: cousins to the Centaur and the Pegasus. Animals inhabit the same story as ourselves (see Hearne 1987).

Individual animals of that kind also have their own biographies. O'Donovan, commenting on Abram's sacrifice to feed three visiting angels, remarks that no one ever needed to ask 'which calf?' (O'Donovan 1987). But this is in error: many individual animals are and have been known as such, from the First Cow Audhumla (from Norse stories of the Very Beginning) to the latest champion. When the prophet Nathan confronted David with his sin, it would have been no answer for the king to have said that the poor man's ewe should be replaced: individuals are irreplaceable, even if someone, something else could play their part as well. Animals, like human beings, are identified as individuals in being attended to, in being irreplaceable for good or ill. In that sense even Alexander Beetle is an individual: not that there is or would have been a beetle of that name without a human act of naming, but that – once named and attended to – he is more than 'just an animal', more than a replaceable part. Does that naming make a difference to him? Who knows? It makes a difference to dogs and horses.

The realm of human story gives being and significance to landscape, seascape and townscape, to trees and animals and peoples. In the days when there were real distinctions to be made, of more importance than the merely fictional, it mattered that – we thought – all humans were alike in being human, all animals in being unthinking brutes. But if that vast distinction is a literary trope, we are released to notice that the world of our 'significant individuals' is populated not only by individual human beings but also by dogs, cats and horses with particular names and values; that the world contains innumerable avatars and images of the Red Bull and the Horse of Heaven. Not all insects are creepy-crawlies; some are 'singing masons building roofs of gold', the image of ideal community.

Human beings and human speech are historical inventions as well: our actual experience for long enough was of 'ourselves', the local tribes of people, dogs and horses, and of the 'others', *theria* (wild beasts) and *barbaroi* (who make noises that only vaguely sound like speech, as 'rhubarb, rhubarb'). Slowly we have invented the idea of 'humankind', a universal human essence discoverable over centuries and thousands of miles, distinct from all the other nations of the world, the only 'speaking peoples'. Other ages had no doubt that the other, non-human inhabitants of earth had voices, that their lack of human speech was only a sad disability, on a par with our own ignorance of other human and non-human tongues. The common speech was lost at Babel, but could be recovered.

An appreciation of the historical roots of our present attitudes enriches our present experience of human and non-human neighbours. Attempts to eliminate them on the plea that dogs are only canine, ancestral lands just earth, or spring flowers only 'genital and alimentary organs of plants' were always barbarous.

> Don't you see that that dreadful dry light shed on things must at last wither up the moral mysteries as illusions, respect for age, respect for property, and that the sanctity of life will be a superstition? The men in the street are only organisms, with their organs more or less displayed. For such a one there is no longer any terror in the touch of human flesh, nor does he see God watching him out of the eyes of a man.[8]

Even of a fish it is blasphemous to say that it is only a fish.[9]

A foolish work of elementary English criticism sought to 'debunk...a silly piece of writing on horses, where these animals are praised as the "willing servants" of the early colonists in Australia' (on the plea that horses are not much interested in colonial expansion). C. S. Lewis comments that its actual effect on pupils will have little to do with writing decent prose: 'some pleasure in their own ponies and dogs they will have lost: some incentive to cruelty or neglect they will have received: some pleasure in their own knowingness will have entered their minds' – but 'of Ruksh and Sleipnir and the weeping horses of Achilles and the war-horse in the Book of Job – nay, even of Brer Rabbit and of Peter Rabbit – of man's prehistoric piety to "our brother the ox" they will have learnt nothing'.[10]

If there is no truth-by-nature, or none that we need acknowledge, such reductivism is ridiculous as well as vulgar. Koreans may not be factually wrong to think of dogs as dinner: neither are we wrong to think of them as friends. Which story would we rather tell, which story choose to live in? Better: which story is already telling us? Maybe we ourselves, no less than Black Beauty or White Fang, are characters in a novel?[11]

> We enter human society, that is, with one or more imputed characters – roles into which we have been drafted – and we have to learn what they are in order to understand how others respond to us and how our responses to them are apt to be construed. ... Mythology is the heart of things.[12]

The really important supplementary is: whose is the story? Ours? No one's? Nobodaddy's? God's? Saga, tragedy or farce?

THE REACH OF EMPATHY

But can this anti-realist narration be the whole? There are some animals that feature, quite as much as humans, in the never-ending story, whether as faithful friends, or dreadful enemies. Dog and Wolf are one and the same species; so are pariah and guide-dog. White Rat and Black Rat are the same beneath the skin. Other animals are more distantly endorsed: koala bears are cuddly toys, but not so that they'd notice. It is a feature of those creatures whose ancestors our neolithic ancestors once tamed (or was the taming all one way?) that they are judged to participate in the story as something more than dummies. They act a part, no doubt, but one they understand and can exploit.

Other scholars, as well as anti-realists of the fashionable, literary kind, have denied the possibility of thought before speech. No one could think wordlessly, without a grasp of rules to identify those thoughts as sometimes incorrect or false. But this is to make the acquisition of speech a standing miracle in every growing child, and in the first beginnings of the human kind. If there never was a world outside of human language, and never a First Human (save the Very First, or God),[13] we need not bother to explain how the human, thinking, kind first came to be. But how do individuals begin to speak without ever having thought before they spoke? Must we suppose some doctrine of eternal souls who never need to learn to speak, but only to speak a given language? It seems easier to believe that, after all, unspeaking creatures, creatures that don't speak our tongues, can think and plan, that they could be characters in their own unfolding story even if they weren't in ours. Human infants could not learn to speak unless they already experienced and thought about their worlds.

Those who know them best (because they love them best) are in no normal doubt that babies, dogs and horses do respond and think. According to Searle, remember, 'only someone in the grip of a philosophical theory would deny that small babies can literally be said to want milk and that dogs want to be let out or believe that their master is at the door',[14] even though the baby has no conception of milk as such, and dogs no grasp of the indefinitely many logical implications of the proposition that so and so is at the door. The standard response that this is sentimental fancy might deserve respect if those who made it showed themselves well able to rear children or train animals.[15] Even such evidence as does exist against too 'anthropomorphic' an understanding of the wordless actually counts against the notion that they do not think. The really significant thing about Clever Hans was not that he failed at elementary maths, but that he showed a superb understanding of his human's concealed wishes.[16] Animals cannot be trained unless they understand what we are after. Understanding that, they move to manipulate us in their turn.[17]

That mutual understanding and would-be control, born in any close communication of the wordless and the wordy, may well be founded on 'shared forms of life'. Wittgenstein's too-often quoted aphorism, that 'if the lion could talk we could not understand him',[18] is implausible because lions, after all, are social mammals, predators, cousins of the familiar cat who has no difficulty speaking to us and being understood. Another remark of

Wittgenstein's is more apposite: 'what is the natural expression of an intention? – Look at a cat when it stalks a bird, or a beast when it wants to escape'.[19] If Wittgenstein could not understand that cat, how could he interpret it as 'stalking'?

One way of resolving an apparent contradiction between doctrinaire rejection of mentalistic description of the wordless and the ordinariness of just such description is to suggest that words may be used 'metaphorically'. 'The attribution of anger to infra-human animals is largely metaphorical',[20] apparently because the attribution of anger to adult humans is part of a complex social, and even legal, activity. Anti-realists of the kind I have described before can have no recourse to this move, as it involves just the distinction between literal and metaphorical meaning that is now, fashionably, rejected. There are no 'central' meanings. But other commentators, of a more realistic kind, see no reason to deny that, for example, chimpanzees show the 'full picture of human anger in its three main forms: anger [i.e. aggressive action], sulking, and the temper tantrum'.[21] And as I pointed out in the previous chapter, there are sufficient parallels between Harlow's monkeys (reared without proper parental care) and severely depressed children to make it highly probable that very similar emotional systems have been activated.[22] Even if there were no precisely homologous structures (as there probably are, given our close genealogical relationship) there would be analogous functions.[23] Similarly: the wings of bird, bat and butterfly. In all these cases we recognise what the organ or the behaviour is about, and could understand a talking beast as well as any talking person. Ethologists schooled to avoid 'anthropomorphism' resort to scare-quotation marks when writing for their peers, but rarely explain, for example, how 'rape' by an orang-utan or by a drake is different from rape.[24] Rhetorical tropes like this are ways of saving face, while the researchers still rely on their empathetic identification of what the animals are doing.[25]

'We only say of a human being and what is like one that it thinks' (so Wittgensteinians inform us on the master's authority): but this is either boringly correct (for what thinks is ipso facto like a human being) or patently false (for we actually say of many things otherwise unlike our conspecifics that they think, and cope very badly if we try to exclude this way of speaking). Wittgensteinian theory is full of dogmatic descriptions of this ordinary use or that as deviant or parasitic. Dogs (they tell us) only think, feel, get angry or affectionate or even, in the end, see, hear and smell in a 'metaphorical' sense. 'To see something', after all, is not simply to have a sensation associated with open eyes, but to have visual evidence for the belief that there is something there. Animals, lacking language, lack belief, and therefore, as Strato of Lampsacus pointed out long ago, cannot strictly *see* at all (Strato intended thus to reduce to absurdity the Stoic doctrine that some Wittgensteinians, unknowingly, endorse). If they are right, of course, animal psychologists should place words like 'see' or 'seek' within quotation marks.

146

If they are right, a great many psychological experiments (for example, on the effects of maternal deprivation on young monkeys) are ill-conceived and utterly irrelevant to human experience of such deprivation. If zoophiles are right, they *are* relevant, and, for that reason, wicked.

But maybe there are limits to our understanding, and our incorporation of the 'alien' into the humanly intelligible universe. Washburn's question (raised in Chapter 11) 'what is it like to be a wasp?'

> Anger, in our own experience, is largely composed of quickened heart beat, of altered breathing, of muscular tension, of increased blood pressure in the head and face. The circulation of a wasp is fundamentally different from that of any vertebrate. The wasp does not breathe through lungs, it wears its skeleton on the outside, and it has the muscles attached to the inside of the skeleton. What is anger like in the wasp's consciousness? We can form no adequate idea of it.[26]

So is there something it is like to be a wasp, if it is so far beyond our grasp? Why should there not be? That wasps are sometimes angry is an observation well worth remembering: that they feel emotions appropriate to their enraged behaviour (different as they must be from ours) is something I have no difficulty in imagining. Serious enquirers are regularly warned not to multiply entities beyond necessity, nor to attribute more complex or anthropomorphic modalities to what we see than are strictly needed.[27] Useful rules, but not so obvious as to justify the blank insistence that we know such creatures are unfeeling, merely because – with a sufficient hardening of the heart – we can imagine them to be unfeeling. The withdrawal of our failed projections, and the concomitant 'objectification' of the things that are left behind, should often lead to an acceptance of ignorance. The impulse to avoid that pain by saying that what we don't know is not knowledge, that our inability to prove one thing is a proof of its opposite, that what 'we' no longer 'identify' with may properly be treated as 'mere things', may often be very powerful. If anger is a socially defined role, so also is a pitiless 'objectivity'.

But the attribution of emotion to another does indeed involve that other in a definite moral universe: in identifying another's emotional state as mere crossness or anger, rather than indignation, we may be endorsing or excusing what that other does. Thus Plutchik's supposition that a whale is 'paralysed with fright' at the approach of 'killer whales'[28] is a judgment that a more Buddhistic sensibility might not endorse: maybe the whale gives herself for food? To that extent, moralistic or emotional description of 'good animals' or 'bad animals', ones that do or ones that don't do what we demand of them, is often 'sentimental' in an opprobrious sense. We would do well not to leap to too many conclusions: I doubt if a dog that savages a child is really or importantly vicious or filled with hatred, nor yet complacently filled with the loving desire to defend her master. The dog may be so far 'emotional', so

147

little able to discriminate objects independent of her own behavioral cues, as not to be emotional at all. What she is doing, often enough, is something that would – for us – be playing: the thing she plays with may, disastrously, be a human child, but for her it is only 'a thing (a toy) to be played with here-and-now', not 'the very same thing (or person)' as the friendly playmate of another moment. Of which more below.

The Wittgensteinian claim that 'dogs cannot simulate pain'[29] is some evidence that Wittgenstein knew as little about dogs as about lions, but the connection between the possibility of truth-speaking and sincerity and the possibility of play-acting is a real one. Only those who can 'pretend' to be in pain can know what they are doing (though it by no means follows that those who can't are never in pain). Only those can pretend who can play a part. It follows that Derrida is right (though deeply and perhaps culpably obscure) in his claim that false and fictional discourse is not strictly *parasitic* upon sincere or truthful discourse: truth and lie are twins.[30] But the birth of truthfulness (and fiction) precedes the birth of humankind. Bateson points out that game-playing (and pretence) is a skill more widely spread than our own species: many social mammals signal that what comes next, pretend attack or fury, is play. Some can use those very signals to distract their companions from a real attack or fraud.[31]

There is good reason to think that we can understand our fellow humans largely because we are all engaged upon a similar life, that there are innate patterns of behaviour and expression that ground our more sophisticated speeches. I can often see what someone is on about, what he or she is doing, before I think I understand their speech. Without that prior understanding nothing that they said (no noise they uttered) would be meaningful. But the same is true of other creatures than our conspecifics: there are ancestral traits we share with them, and also traits that have emerged by convergent evolution. Who doubts that cephalopods do, 'literally', have eyes, and appetites? Rorty may well be right to say that 'writhing is more important to our ability to imagine that the koala is asking us for help than what is going on in the koala. . . . So we send pigs to slaughter with equanimity, but form societies for the protection of koalas'.[32] But his imagination here is limited: others can understand our cousins' signals more astutely. Even Rorty thinks it 'paradoxical' to suppose, as Descartes did, that 'the feeling of terror which accompanies our flight has no parallel within the sheep'.[33] Where neither analogy nor homology can help us we shall be astray: true aliens would not even be as easy to describe, let alone to understand, as some (not all) science fiction writers have assumed.[34]

SENSATION, PERCEPTION, *UMWELT*

We get our grip on the intelligence of others by seeing what they are on about, and without a capacity to see the world in something like the way they do our chance of doing so is small. Often enough we get things subtly wrong. The hunting wasp that seems to be providing caterpillars for her growing young turns out to have more of an aesthetic interest: at any rate she does not care to restore a missing caterpillar to the nest before she seals it up. To state what should be obvious: this does not confirm that wasps are stupid creatures, any more than a Betelgeusean explorer's observation that humans often copulate when they can't procreate proves that we don't know or care what we are doing. The usual or expectable effect of actions is one thing, the intention of the agent is another. Though these will usually be connected, an act may be performed independently of its expectable effect, for its own sake.

Too much attention of a romantically pessimistic kind has been paid to questions about animal sensations. What is it that animals immediately sense and feel? What role do such sensations play in explaining what then happens? What difference could it make if there were systematic differences in sensational qualia, or if some animal sensed none at all? If an environmental quality can have a direct, physically measurable effect on an organism's motions, what additional purpose would be served by its being represented in that organism's sensorium at all? Do wood lice feel attracted by the dark and damp, or have dark, damp sensations? Or are they simply caused to change direction more often when they venture into dry, bright places (which they do not sense as such)? After all, we can be affected by things we do not sense, and perhaps more effectively because we do not sense them: witness bad-tempered conduct consequent on damp, hot days and their attendant salt-loss unmitigated by the cooling effect of evaporating sweat.

That there are sensations is a truism, and that some of these 'give pain'. But the painfulness is not – most fortunately – a sensation we can recall at will: we can remember being in pain, but we do not call a new sensation 'pain' because it resembles a remembered sensum. The 'private language argument' has thrown doubt on the possibility of speaking intelligibly of any sensa,[35] but even without it, it is clear enough that calling something painful can't be a matter of comparing sensa. As I remarked before: what is it to say that someone is in pain if not to recognise their screams, squirms and bloody sweats as pleas to desist? Which is not to say that this behaviour is all that 'being in pain' amounts to.

Nothing, that is, is likely to 'feel pain', and nothing is even likely to have sensa, that is not engaged in some project or other. Perception is unlike sensation, commonly so called, because our percepts are formed and directed by the ground plans of our lives. To perceive something is always to incorporate it within a view of things. Without such plans and projects creatures would indeed be limited to unanalysable sensa, momentary stimuli that had magical effects. There might indeed be little reason to expect that there 'really were' such sensa at all, since any effect they had could as easily be produced by merely physical changes. The difference between a stone that is warmed up, and an animal, is that the animal may take note of the warming (as it is represented in its sensorium) as a significant event. The animal perceives what the stone only receives.

Fortunately it is easier to discover what an animal perceives than what it merely senses. We find out about the world it lives in by identifying what it does, what routes it prefers and what priorities it has. Obviously our knowledge of what it perceives, and of what it is doing, will be incomplete if it has access to a wider (or at any rate a different) range of qualities: what strikes us as random or inane behaviour may well be a response to hidden variations, or differing goals. Clearly, we shall not know what it is doing unless we have some grasp of what its organs are. But loving attention to the creature's particularity (which is as necessary in understanding our conspecifics as in understanding baboons or bees, and sometimes more difficult) gives us hope of discovering the creature's *Merkwelt* and *Umwelt*.

The terms are Uexkuell's,[36] and signify the world of cues that are significant for a given animal, and that it notices. Different creatures do genuinely inhabit different worlds, and it takes an effort to identify what things are like for others. What is worth emphasising, and should be noticed by epistemologists, is that not all marks are merely natural. The sheep tick who waits 'patiently' for up to eighteen years until butyric acid triggers its leap from a grass stem to a sheep responds – perhaps – only to fixed stimuli. Perhaps there is no need to imagine that it senses anything at all, any more than a photoelectric cell. The chemical causes the muscles to twitch in a way moulded by millions of years of selective pressures. Any awareness of the event might really be epiphenomenal. But some marks – and we know far too little about ticks to know whether this applies to them – are actually created by the animal. Scent markers create a map embedded in the physical, a set of directions laid down by the animal and by its peers. Derrida, though not for reasons that he would or could endorse, was right to suspect that 'writing' (largely so-called) is older than mere speech. It is by the use of scent-marks and scratches that we create enduring objects. What is it to be the same lamb as the ewe has known before? For the ewe, it is to smell the same, to blend with her own smell. So when we, being vocal animals, at last begin to speak of things, we are speaking of our own markers (as well, no doubt, as markers placed 'by nature').

There does seem to be evidence that many animals have a very 'practical' perception of the world, that they are confronted not by continuing objects but by occasions for specific actions, marking out routes through immensity. We suppose that there is a physical universe surrounding us and them, a world where continuously existent objects are available for any purpose of ours but are not defined by those purposes. Male robins can be deceived into attacking any piece of red rag, but fail to respond to models that are – to our eyes – much more like male robins. Robins are no more stupid than the wasps I described before: what is 'enough like' a rival to deserve attacking is not the same for us and them. But perhaps they do not imagine robins, or male robins, at all: there are only occasions in their universe.

But of course the same is true of us. We too inhabit a world marked out for use, composed of things that are judged 'the same' by virtue of their natural and man-made significance. Would an intellectualising robin be amused to find us responding in 'the same way' to a line of lights, a scrawl of chalk, a string of vocables that all say (so we say) what 'male robins are red-breasted' says? The sameness is so obvious to us that we forget its conventionality. Again: the standard examples, in much modern philosophical discourse, of real, material objects turn out to be artefacts: as tables, chairs and houses. The point is not only that these things are made, but that they are perceived as tables, chairs and houses because 'we' choose to use them so. We live in world of *Zeug*, of implements, fenced off from our occasional imagining of a world-in-itself by our wish to complete our projects. Weeds, trees and creepy-crawlies are as conventional. Understanding other creatures' worlds (whether those creatures are of our species or not) is to share, imaginatively, in what they're doing.

OUTSIDE THE TEXT

So what is it that lies outside our text? One answer is that the 'real world' is the one and only universe revealed to an objective, scientific eye. We must exclude all morally loaded (and so all mentalistic) description if we are to approach the truth. Such a truth, of course, will have little to do with our ordinary living.

> We may if we like, by our reasonings, unwind things back to that black and jointless continuity of space and moving clouds of swarming atoms which science calls the only real world. But all the while the world we feel and live in will be that which our ancestors, and we, by slowly cumulating strokes of choice, have extricated out of this, like sculptors.[37]

Even as an ideal limit the jointless universe is lacking: in what sense, after all, is it ideal? Why should such a truth concern us, and what grounds the devotee's conviction that it is the truth? The attempt to think it through consistently must in the end require us to abandon the strange superstition that we think at all. Eliminative materialists profess to believe that neither they nor anyone else believe anything, but they thereby render their own motions unintelligible.

It seems more likely that the 'real world' be taken as the ultimate sum of life-worlds than that it be an unmeaning and strictly indescribable abyss. Uexkuell indeed concluded that astronomy itself was a biological science, concerned with points of light displayed within a human *Umwelt*. That doctrine, even though it was endorsed by Frank Ramsey,[38] does not appeal to me. If Rorty is right to identify his own position as a response to the supposed collapse of Platonism, perhaps it is time that we reconsidered that collapse. Those who would clamber from the cavern of their idiosyncratic dreams, and recognise the power of puppeteers to organise those dreams, may still hope to discover what is really real, not by rejecting what at first appears, but by surpassing it.

Both eliminative materialists and anti-realists deny that possibility, of reaching out to what is other than our dreams and finding it familiar. Both say that the folk-world and its members are only stories told by us, even if anti-realists then go on telling stories, and eliminative materialists pretend to stop. They both seek to spare themselves the possibility of error: anti-realists deny that 'we' could ever be wrong in what 'we' seriously say (for 'being wrong' is only being in the wrong, by our own standards); materialists end by denying that there is any 'we' to be right or wrong. Either way there is no division between what we think and what most truly is. But that risk, of being wrong, is the price we pay for sometimes being right. If it 'makes no sense' to wonder whether people are sentient and pigs are not (because such sentience is either a mirage or – equivalently – a projection of our arbitrary concern), we have evaded a danger, doubtless: but only at the price of surrender. We have lost that sense of Otherness that is the root of love and knowledge. Murdoch's judgment is the better path: 'we take a self-forgetful pleasure in the sheer alien, pointless [?], independent existence of animals, birds, stones and trees. . . . Good art, not fantasy art, affords us a pure delight in the independent existence of what is excellent'.[39] Art is not all that suffers when we forget that excellence. We have not learnt the right lesson from the private language argument: where there is no chance of error, nothing has been said. So we must hope to mould our thought to what is genuinely Other than our thought.

> To be fully human is to recognise everyone and everything in the universe as both Other and Beloved, and . . . this entails granting that the world is authentic and meaningful without demanding proof. . . . Animals are the only non-human Others who answer us.[40]

What is outside the text, and much to be desired? Each transformation or escape from our own private story may be welcomed, every realisation that the world is wider than our hearts. Why else have we so often imagined fairies, angels, aliens to give a new perspective on a world, our world, grown old? The great discovery we have now almost made is that there are indeed other perspectives on all our human world, that we are the objects of a patient or impatient gaze from animals that share our world and story. It is indeed a difficult task to see through the merely conventional animals with simple moral properties (inquisitive and imitative apes, greedy pigs, proud peacocks, cruel wolves). To evade those traps it is even worth adopting – temporarily – as physicalist a description of the actual behaviour of the animals as we can manage. But it would be as absurd (and perhaps as damaging) to settle for those descriptions as it would be for ardent bachelors to describe the actions of young females 'physicalistically', so as to avoid imputing motives and desires to them that are really only the males' own. To turn aside from the discovery that there are really Others in the world that we can come to know, and to pretend that pigs, dogs, pigeons, people are only pretence, only cuddly toys animated solely by the stories that we (who?) tell with them, is a radical defeat, as dreadful as the other error, which is to pretend to a romantically pessimistic doctrine that we could never ever find out real truths (except that one?). Fortunately for us (and maybe for our immortal souls) neither cats nor infants nor our adult neighbours are so tractable as to support either fancy. Yes, there really is a real world 'out there', and the fact that it is so often not what I would wish is exactly what reveals, and endears, it to me!

13

MODERN ERRORS, ANCIENT VIRTUES[1]

THE PROBLEM

The topic of animal experimentation arouses many passions. On the one hand are those who see it, straightforwardly, as torture, the deliberate inflicting of pain on defenceless creatures. On the other, those who as passionately believe that we must go on learning how animal organisms work if we are to continue to discover cures for disease and disability. Some of the latter, historically, have held that 'animals' hardly feel at all, or (if they do) it doesn't matter much. Others hold only that some pains are unavoidable if science is to progress, but that the scientists concerned will certainly be doing their best to ensure that as few and as trivial pains as possible are caused to our unwilling collaborators. The most recent British Act on the treatment of experimental subjects in the United Kingdom requires that animals judged likely to be suffering intense and long-lasting pain be killed. Often enough, neither side can quite believe that the other can be serious. Fox-hunters typically believe that hunt saboteurs are communists or worse; saboteurs typically believe that hunters are bloodthirsty yuppies or worse. So also here: experimenters think protesters are sentimental Luddites; anti-vivisectionists believe that scientists are career-conscious sadists. Both sides can *occasionally* uncover reason to suspect that they are right.

But the issue can be approached academically, with hatred and contempt for none, and it better had be if we are ever to be able to approach it politically as well. Such academic treatment has its own drawbacks. It must take place within a shared tradition of reasoned argument, and that very tradition may, historically, have built-in limitations. Patriarchalists can often sound to themselves like reasonable people just because it has been axiomatic that reason is a masculine preserve. Feminists who set themselves to argue with the enemy sometimes feel themselves at a disadvantage if they have to do so in a masculinist tongue, and respond by denouncing 'reason' as a patriarchal tool. Much the same problem faces radical zoophiles: it is 'obvious' to any reasonable person that 'animals' matter infinitely less than 'humans', and anyone who doubts that this is true cannot be serious. I remain convinced that reason transcends tradition, even though it must take shape therein, and that we ought always to suspect what 'reasonable people' say.

Experimentation is not the only – or even the most significant – area in which our relations with non-human animals need to be reconstructed. I have already mentioned parallel disputes about the rights and wrongs of hunting. Hunters in these settled islands insist upon the need to control animal populations and the relative humanity and success of hunting with hounds (as opposed to trapping, poisoning or shooting); they also associate themselves with hunters in quite different milieux, for whom hunting is a necessary stay against starvation. Those opposed to such local practices doubt the sincerity of spokesmen for field sports in making those associations: shooting and trapping somehow become humane when they in their turn must be defended against complaint; the needs of hunter-gatherers are not those of the Home Counties. But hunting, shooting, fishing (however significant they may be as totems) are also not the major cause of animal exploitation or employment. It is not unreasonable for huntsmen and experimentalists alike to comment that their victims are numbered in hundreds or thousands, while the victims (direct and indirect) of our agricultural or domestic cruelty are numbered in many millions. Huntsmen and experimentalists constitute easily defined targets: those who finance what radical zoophiles consider cruelty in and around farms are still most of the population. Even our casual kindness and projective sentimentalism, exercised on furry creatures close at hand, is often exploitative – a fact we find as difficult to face as patriarchalists do the oppressive quality of their sentimental 'respect' for women.

The point of these reminders is just this: experimentalists can usually insist that they are as likely to obey the unspoken laws of humane life as anyone else. There is little reason to suppose that there are more cruel and negligent people in the scientific world than anywhere else. There may be fewer sentimentalists, simply because people unable to control immediate impulses of unreflective kindness or distaste will not go far in the profession. But the standards scientists work to will be very much like those of society in general. Why then should they be condemned? A partial reply might draw upon the undoubted internationalism of science: the scientific community, properly enough, does not draw its standards only from one nation's mindset. Britons in the USA, for example, are regularly reminded that their own (maybe sentimental) concern for animals is not widely shared. American children, quite apart from the pervasive influence of a sentimentalised brutality enshrined in Wild West stories, are educated in school biology to discount the thought that animals can suffer pain or boredom or annoyance. Such ill-argued behaviourism is much less of a cultural force in Britain, and our national myths are of a more domestic kind. There are, after all, forces that do incline the scientifically trained to discount more of their untutored or their cultured sentiment than others. On which more below.

But the chief point I wish to insist on here is this: it may well be true that scientists mostly act upon the very same moral assumptions as non-scientists, and that their treatment of animals is no worse (and may sometimes be much better) than others'. The radical charge against experimentalists is not that they are unusually cruel or negligent, but that they act out – in a particularly noticeable form – assumptions deeply engrained in contemporary culture which are actually false or wicked. Those who are seriously and deeply concerned about the whole practice of animal experimentation (and not just about occasional and obvious abuses) challenge human culture.

So what are these assumptions, and if they are false (or even obviously false) how can they still be influencing us? It is important to remember that we are all inclined to go on acting on ideas that we actually *know* are false. One of the most difficult lessons to learn is simply to eject hypotheses that we have found are false. You may find that surprising: surely we are all honest and reasonable people here, quite ready to try out hypotheses and abandon those that we have found are wrong? Of course there will be some hypotheses of which we are so fond that we will find it hard to agree that they *are* false. But once the point is made, that they are, of course we shall abandon them. To say and believe that they are false *is* to abandon them.

Unfortunately things are not quite so simple. An idea once entertained has its own influence. We are all bedevilled by hypotheses long since proved false, that we do not wish true, which yet control our actions and beliefs. The trouble often lies with the very principle of non-contradiction, that is the principle of rational thought. We do not want to contradict ourselves, and for that very reason cannot quite give up any idea, however foolish, that we have once given room to. We prefer to devise all manner of epicycles and ad hoc inventions rather than admit that we were, simply, wrong. But even that is not the whole explanation. It just seems to be the case that we find any sort of spring-cleaning very difficult. Psychologists have tried the following experiment: the subject population are asked for their opinion on some leading figure of the day, and then told a story very much to that person's discredit. Obviously enough their opinion of the figure goes down. They are then told that the story was entirely, absolutely, false, and their opinion sought once more. It remains far more unfavourable than it was when they began. The moral, simple-mindedly, is that mud sticks. More generally: we are often moved in ways that rationally we could not defend by the lingering effects of stories that we know or believe to be false. Without an occasional dose of deliberate, sceptical enquiry, we shall continue to misdirect ourselves.

Such scepticism is a philosophical tool, and philosophers, like everyone else, are all too inclined to relapse upon the certainties born of beef and backgammon once the mood has passed. Perhaps that is inevitable, and I must accept that most of my readers will regard my attack on our present presuppositions as deliberately extreme, a device to be accepted as a way of pulling us back toward the 'norm' of *moderate* concern for animals. I doubt myself if there is any real content or foundation for that norm: my scepticism lies deeper, however uncomfortable even I may find it. Consider it possible, please, that we have all been wrong, and that the way to truth requires a really radical repentance. Unless you take that seriously you will not even gain the advantage of a moderate dose of scepticism, and still be left enacting ideas that you know are false.

THE AXIOM OF EGOCENTRISM

The first and obviously false assumption is egocentrism. It is obvious (who could seriously doubt it?) that there are entities distinct from me, who carry on existing when I do not think of them, who owe me nothing and do not think of me at all. A true account of things will not pick me out as something special, will not set the worlds in orbit round my centre. The true and only centre of the worlds is everywhere, and its circumference nowhere. Yet every day I act as if the things I do not know about (or choose to neglect), from the dripping tap to the dying Ethiopian, do not exist. Only the most rigorous employment of a sane imagination allows me to admit the obvious: that those who die in pain are no less pained because I do not think of them, that my friends exist when they are out of sight, that what I do not know about at all may yet be real.

Practical solipsism is closer to us than we usually suppose, and there have even been philosophers, and very distinguished ones, who have endorsed a full-blooded solipsism. But most of us are probably too nervous to stand quite alone. The nearest we can get to sheer, unashamed egoism is to identify ourselves with clans or castes or companies against Them. Moral behaviour begins in loyalty to just such groups, just such an insistence on 'doing good to our friends and harm to our enemies'. Our 'friends' are simply those with whom we belong, and who belong to us. If a supposed ally, one of Us, is caught considering the interests of Them (as it might be injured Argentines or class enemies or animals), We are yet more enraged. Those who give Them any thought at all are judged to have betrayed Us, and to be secretly enamoured of the alien ways We impute to Them. We know all this for nonsense, but still act as if it were true. They are 'animals', in the sense beloved of judges: uncultured egoists eager to satisfy their every impulse. Real animals are seen as symbols of the alien ways we impute to Them in considering Them animals. So anyone who wishes to give real animals a hearing must be on Their side.

But try to consider things as they would appear to an ideal observer, or to the Creator-God: why should, say, a dog, a rat, a monkey be required to live a tedious and imprisoned life, and die an agonising death so that a hominid be spared the least discomfort? Because we are hominids we may prefer (egocentrically) that non-hominids pay the price of living, but how could we persuade any ideal observer, God or disinterested jury, that our preferences have more weight than those of the dog? Why isn't that just like saying that my personal comfort must be more important, absolutely, than your vital needs?

HUMANISM, OBJECTIVE AND SUBJECTIVE

The second principle behind our doings is humanism, which purports to offer some reason for that prejudice that would or should persuade an ideal jury. The humanist revolution demanded that we attend to all members of our species, whatever their particular relation to us may be. Whereas pre-humanist societies endorsed a rigorous division between Us and Them, between our fellowship and foreigners, humanists believe it obvious that all (and only) human beings deserve the same respect. Foreigners are of no other kind than I, and all our conspecifics differ from non-human beings in deserving an absolute respect. Old-fashioned liberals identify the 'rights of man', as rights to life, liberty and property. It would be wrong on these terms to kill, control or dispossess any human being. Liberals in the sense now generally meant impose more positive duties on us all, of care for the afflicted: human rights include the right to be fed, clothed, educated and cared for (even to have annual paid holidays). In practice even such modern liberals do not admit to any enforceable duty to care for more than their fellow nationals; and old-fashioned liberals, regrettably, have not . always recognised the claims to liberty and property of those they reckon 'savages'. But humanism, in libertarian or welfare forms, has played a part in the extension of existing rights and privileges from members only of our class or sex or nation to the whole species. Where unembarrassed groupies (so to call them) think it only right to pursue Our interests at whatever cost to Them, humanists insist on taking account of Theirs, and reckon it absurd to think that what is bad when done to one of Us is somehow quite all right when done to Them.

Unfortunately for those outside the magic circle, humanism disallows even such paltry rights as had been conceded to non-humans. Hindu respect for 'sacred cows', or Jain disinclination to kill or hurt any living creature, or 'primitive' respect for 'totem animals' are easily equated with sentimental concern for pets: proofs that the animalist is personally inadequate, starved of human affection and neglectful of their 'real' human duties. Such humanism, of course, may also insist that certain styles of human living are unworthy of the name: sadistic enjoyment even of non-human pain, or negligent treatment of the animals one owns, are ways of not living up to the humanist's ideal. But it has never been easy to explain quite why such active cruelty or negligence is wrong, if only human interests matter to the rational mind. If humans matter so much more than non-humans it must be that they are of so radically different a kind that it is hard to see that 'hurting animals' is of the same kind as 'hurting humans'. Perhaps the sadist's error is just to suppose that he/she is *hurting* animals – but negligence or indifference are then no crimes.

This is the kind of humanism often deployed by experimentalists. Ethical considerations preclude invasive experimentation upon 'human beings', but not on 'animals', because all and only human beings merit rational respect: the most that animals can expect is sentimental interest of a sort that should not stand in the way of human interests. Animals either don't feel pain, or boredom, or distress, or else the 'pains' they feel are of another, and less interesting, kind than 'ours', because 'we humans' are another sort of thing, objectively, than them. A report some years ago from China suggested that biologists there were seeking to produce a human-chimpanzee hybrid which would be available as an experimental subject when 'ethical considerations' forbade the use of truly human stock. Chinese authorities, of course, show little enough concern for *human* rights, but the same strange disjunction features in Western ideology as well. It is only pure *human* nature that requires respect. Why?

One version of humanism is no more than the near-solipsism that I described before, and so no real answer to the question: Why should God prefer to hurt non-hominids? Imaginary cases may help to distinguish this variety from the more 'objective' kind: merely 'subjective' humanists do not suppose that intelligent extraterrestrials need, in moral reason, to give any weight to human interests over those of terrestrial organisms more to their taste. The medieval knight who preferred to save a lion than a snake, 'because it seemed the more natural creature', perhaps expressed a similar subjective preference for fellow mammals. Betelgeusian arachnoids might well prefer spiders, and 'we', correspondingly, need feel no qualms about the arachnoids, however civilised they are. On these terms, humanists only urge us to identify with human beings and things that look like human beings: creatures that have faces benefit from stray affections. 'Objective' humanists think otherwise, that all and only 'rational' beings (or beings of the same real kind as rational beings) deserve respect. The arachnoids ought to be treated well, and should, in reason, treat 'us' well. What matters is the mind behind the face.

Both sorts of humanist usually make two assumptions: first, that a species is a natural kind (a notion that now has very little biological backing), and second, that the human species is the unique embodiment (on Earth at any rate) of sacred reason (a notion that almost no philosophers now take seriously even if they still endorse humanistic values). After all, not all our conspecifics are actually rational, nor are they all so easily identified with. Some moralists are ready to write off imbeciles, or human beings too unlike themselves, but humanism, in whatever form, still demands that *all* our conspecifics have equal rights (whatever they are). So subjective and objective humanists alike must include in their concern all such as are of one kind with the rationally active or the sympathetic few. It is that very notion of 'one natural kind', as I have observed before, that is now suspect.

A biological species is not now thought to be a set of organisms with a shared, essential nature, such that there is or could be an organism 'typical' of the species and that other organisms may be more or less 'defective' specimens. That notion of species-membership is one that modern biologists usually call 'Aristotelian', although Aristotle himself was almost certainly not guilty of the crime (see Balme 1980). The modern notion is rather that a species is a set of interbreeding populations, and that no single specimen is more or less what the kind should be than any other. What is called the type-specimen, in textbooks, may turn out to be very 'untypical'. There is no need to think that all and only species-members have any shared character, save only that they have common ancestors and are still members of a population whose members may yet have common descendants. The matter is further complicated because a good many terms of our folk-taxonomy (as fishes, creepy-crawlies, weeds) turn out not to name scientific taxa. There are, in a real sense, no such things as fishes (for what we call 'fishes' may belong to radically unrelated groups). It is not long since scientists doubted that there were even humans.

The fact that we share ancestors and may share descendants perhaps gives some weight (psychologically) to subjective humanism. But that sort of humanism has no stronger claim than loyalty to any natural group: because our common ancestors are further off, and our shared descendants may never in fact exist, subjective humanism has less weight, in general, than closer ties. If it's all right to be partial to the claims of humans over non-humans, it must also be all right to be partial to the claims of human beings who are more like us, or better known to us. But that is to abandon the high moral ground on which humanistic moralists prefer to stand. So those who think that humanism has more moral weight must probably endorse the objective form: but that is to neglect the biological discovery. Even if all actual humans really did share some important character deserving absolute respect (say, reason), nothing says that all and only humans must, any more than it is bound to be true that every reptile has a three-chambered heart. And there is evidence, in any case, that not all our conspecifics are thus rational, and that others may be.

Consider the following analogy. 'Mammalism', so to call it, does play a part in the choices that we make: furry creatures with faces get a better deal than scaly ones (unless the furry ones are rats). But even if we elevated this subjective preference to the point of objective principle (as it might be: all moral beings must respect all creatures that are cuddly and care for their young) it would surely be odd to deny respect to non-mammals that did the same, and respect what are technically mammals even though they didn't. It would be odder still to go on being mammalists when we had found out that, strictly, there were no mammals (any more than fishes).

In brief, subjective humanism makes no general claims about the sort of things we should respect but (for that very reason) lacks the moral force regularly imputed to it. If humanism is anything more than the weak claim to mind about all those with whom we might share descendants (but not as much, no doubt, as we do about those with whom we do, or realistically might), it must claim that there is an objective duty so to mind. But what is there to mind about that all and only human beings share? Not all are really rational, and some non-humans are (by any ordinary standard) quite as rational as humans mostly are. If we have a reason beyond group-preference for wishing humans well, then it will apply to non-humans too. And it remains very unclear why an ideal observer, God, or disinterested jury would find the capacity for rational thought (whatever it is) so overwhelmingly important. Is it simply that any such jury must, if it is to judge at all, share those rational capacities, and so be compelled to respect them – and no other – on pain of denying the value of their own power to judge? It does not seem to me to be a strong argument.

UTILITARIANISM

The third principle underlying much public moralism is utilitarianism. The term has many meanings by now, including ones the movement's founders would despise. Utilitarians, to state what should be obvious, do not judge actions, people, architecture by their mere 'utility', the efficiency with which they serve some mercenary end. Real utility, in the sense utilitarians meant, includes the increase of pleasure (of all kinds, but with a learned preference for the more sociable and intellectual pleasures) and decrease of pain. Beauty is a utilitarian goal.

The nineteenth-century movement helped to secure some gains for animal welfare. What mattered, as Jeremy Bentham said, was not whether animals could talk or reason, but whether they could suffer, and the idea that they did not – however popular with animal experimenters from Malebranche to Claude Bernard, to any number of pontificating moderns – has never satisfied anyone without something to gain. Non-human animals have nervous systems and produce much the same natural opiates to counter pain as human animals. It is easy to believe that they mind less about their pains than we: just as it is easy to believe that the poor mind less about their troubles, or that Third World peasants do not need the medical care that sensitive souls like us can't live without. But historical ignorance and egoism are easily recognised too.

If pain is an intrinsic evil, something that anyone would wish to eliminate, then animal pains are too. Some versions of utilitarianism seem to speak of pain (and pleasure) as a sort of stuff, to be eliminated (or increased) no matter where or how the job is done. This crude and unreasonable theory would excuse our causing very great and lasting pain if thereby the notional total of pain was reduced or the total amount of pleasure (housed perhaps in an élite) were increased. Unfortunately for the animals in our charge, it is just this sort of utilitarianism that rules in too many experimenters' hearts. A movement that began by demanding moral respect for animals (and that was severely criticised by orthodox humanists for doing so) has since been used to defend the use of animals in painful and oppressive experiments: only so will the sum total of suffering be reduced, or the pleasures of the élite secured.

Utilitarian calculation of this kind has one stunning disadvantage (quite apart from any moral obloquy it may incur): it is wholly incalculable. Who can tell what the sum total of suffering may be or what might decrease it? Who can tell what effect a rising (human) population has? Is it a mistake to save a life if it turns out that the survivor suffered later on? Or suffered how much? Or cost the whole how much? Sensible utilitarians do two things. First, they cease to pretend to calculate the exact effect of any individual act ('act-utilitarianism') and instead act on such rules as produce best results ('rule-utilitarianism'). Second, they abandon talk of pain or pleasure as quantifiable stuff, and instead begin to talk of the real or rational preferences of the creatures affected by our acts. 'Each to count for one and none for more than one': everyone affected by the rules has as much say in what they should be. What rules, then, could or should 'we' agree on? What rules will 'we' be 'happiest' with?

I said that sensible utilitarians do this, but the truth is rather that by being sensible they cease to be utilitarian. For what we seriously prefer may not, in any clear sense, be 'what gives us most pleasure and least pain' (unless we define 'pleasure' as getting what we want). And we have no conception, prior to the votes we cast, of what would make us happy. It's not as if we knew what happiness was, and only wondered whether we'd be 'happier' as pirates or as priests, or whether a world of pirates or contented wombats would be 'happier' than one of peasants or hunter-gatherers or technicians. All forms of life have their own drawbacks and delights. The utilitarian calculation turns out only to be an extravagantly general election, and the result will turn on the prior moral choices of those allowed a vote. The first kind of utilitarianism, however absurdly, identified a goal (that world is best that has most pleasurable sensation for least cost of pain) which differed from other real and imaginable goals (as it might be, one of equable beauty or of romantic anguish). The second only offers a way of solving practical disagreements: we get the world most voters want enough. Gang-rape is only outlawed if more voters are more outraged by it than are delighted or indifferent. If enough voters already think it wrong to hurt animals it may be right to prevent such hurts; if they don't, it won't. But this tells us nothing at all about which way to vote.

Sensible utilitarians have usually lost sight, as well, of what both Bentham and Mill insisted on: that animals are voters too, or must be supposed to be. If the best outcome is the one that satisfies most voters best, and no one counts for more than one, it must seem very doubtful that the present state of things is best. How would our animals vote if they were allowed the chance? What they would vote on, remember, must be the rules under which we live. Would our victims seriously prefer to live by rules that gave their exploiters the unquestioned right to imprison, kill and torture? What advantage could they derive? One answer, that they thereby gain or keep existence (since they would not be born in such numbers if we did not intend to imprison, kill and torture them), presumably rests once more upon an unexamined use of 'totalising utilitarianism'. What advantage does the existence, under deeply unpleasant circumstances, of large numbers of their kind give to any actually existent creatures? Would any rational being choose to produce descendants as the stars of heaven if the price was that she produced them by mechanised rape, and lost them to the slaughter house or to be similarly raped, even before a natural weaning? Would it make any difference even if these descendants had occasional pleasures of a kind and intensity that free animals could not?

One further feature of utilitarian theory: whereas our ordinary maxims still distinguish acts of omission and commission, a mere concern for consequences sees no difference. If an act of mine results in someone's pain or death it makes no difference whether I directly caused that evil, or merely failed to prevent it. So experimenters claim that failing to perform admittedly invasive experiments will, over the long run, cause more evil. The argument is a lot less certain than they think, simply because we cannot predict what scientific progress would be made if we decided not to use such methods, and because few scientists have the nerve to admit that experiments on human beings (against their will, of course) would – on their terms – be likelier to result in progress. We renounce such imagined profits in the latter case, and so cannot, without additional argument, insist upon them in the other. But the principle on which they are relying is itself a suspect one, not least because it has profoundly totalitarian associations. Negative duties, not directly to cause evil, are more universal and more powerful than the positive ones, to prevent evil or cause good. At the least, there are sound reasons for us to make distinctions – but the argument here would take too long to unfold.

Some recent philosophers have attempted to argue from utilitarian principle to the conclusion that we are indeed doing wrong, and should cease torturing and killing animals. They write in Mill's and Bentham's spirit. But the very fact that other philosophers have defended the status quo on just the same principles (for any alteration in the way we live will have unpleasant consequences for those currently employed in farms, laboratories and zoos) reveals that the calculation is, as I said, incalculable. Professed utilitarians only think they reason to their conclusions by the calculus: in fact they choose their goals by other means. Utilitarianism is always and entirely an excuse – and one most used by the exploiters of our non-human kin.

OBJECTIVITY AND OBJECTIVISM

The fourth principle that affects our present reasonings is objectivism. Groupies take it for granted that what matters about things is what we call and think of them. Weeds are there to be uprooted; pets and pests and pigs are different because we give them different values. It is a profound and valuable discovery that we can look past such subjective judgments to consider what things are themselves, what they would be for an omniscient, free spirit. The virtue of objectivity is the willingness to put our prejudice aside, and see things 'as they are'. Humanists (or objective humanists) put aside the merely conventional distinctions, of class or caste, in favour of more deeply rooted 'natural' distinctions. 'When Adam delved and Eve span who was then the gentleman?' By this account we should regulate our feelings and behaviour not by conventional and changing labels, but by the real divisions of things. The trouble is, as I have pointed out, it is now very difficult to think that the human/non-human division is as clear or all-important as our predecessors thought. If we ought to treat relevantly equal cases equally we maybe ought not to do to chimpanzees what we refuse to do to human beings.

The problem is compounded by utilitarian infections. Original utilitarians thought it a matter of fact that pain was evil, and that, having the power to do so, we ought to alleviate or prevent it. But the drift of utilitarian argument is toward the thesis that 'there's nothing right or wrong but thinking makes it so'. What's wrong is what 'we' disapprove of. Emotivism is the metamoral theory (the theory about the meaning of moral judgment) that fits the moral practice of utilitarians. But emotivism simply is the thesis that moral divisions are not matters of fact to be discovered by objective thought. An 'objective observer' does nothing, and does not care one way or another. In which case objective humanism and objective utilitarianism are both false. Preferring human beings, and preferring pain-free lives, are historically grounded prejudices. Objectivism, which was once the firm intention to think real differences of more importance than conventional ones, has now become the intention to discount all moral values in reporting facts, in which case personal preference must rule in practical affairs, and we relapse, in practice, to the groupies.

The rhetoric of objectivism in its modern form has many disturbing aspects. Utilitarian calculation and objectivism together make it difficult to see why we should not use orphan or abandoned human neonates for our experimental purposes, breed pretty imbeciles for licensed pederasts and eat aborted foetuses in expensive restaurants (my apologies to all right-thinking readers for inducing nausea, but it is time that we remembered what the real possibilities are). It is doubly unfortunate, of course, that some zoophiles, intent on destroying humanistic values, have found themselves suggesting that such acts would be less wrong (might even, on some utilitarian calculation, be more right) than present treatment of non-human animals.

I shall return to that last point. But I should first point out that objectivism in its modern form rests on very dubious arguments. My objection to it is not simply that there are real evils, just as my objection to utilitarianism is not simply that it neglects real evils. Utilitarianism in all its forms is quite absurd. Modern objectivism, or emotivism, is as well. I have found that experimental scientists are especially vulnerable to its influence, but are rarely acquainted with its history or sophistical roots. Scientists, they say, are only concerned with 'facts', and moral preferences can never be grounded upon facts, nor rationally discussed. This does not seem to stop them thinking their own preferences more rational than those of zoophiles, while still denying that any such preferences are rational at all.

But what does ground the claim that there 'are no moral facts', and hence that moral judgment is only personal preference, and that scientists are somehow entitled to demand, as of right, the liberty to act upon their preferences? The arguments most commonly used are as follows. First, it always does make sense (of a sort) to deny that any particular ethical conclusion follows from any agreed factual premise. We can agree that an experiment causes pain but not agree that it should be avoided; we can agree that it may bring great advantages to the human species but not agree that it should therefore be performed. But if propositions of the form (p and q) and (p and not q) both make sense there can be no conceptual tie (of the kind obtaining between 'Joe's a bachelor' and 'Joe's unmarried') between p and q. So the connection between the 'facts' commonly held to support a particular moral judgment and that judgment is not a conceptually necessary one (if it were, the denial of it would make no more sense than the claim that one could be a married bachelor, or a round square). The only alternative generally allowed is that it be an empirical discovery that acts of such and such a kind are, as a matter of fact, always or practically always wicked. But 'being wicked' is a property quite unlike other and non-evaluative properties: it seems not amenable to laboratory controls, nor can it be recorded upon tape, nor is it transformable (in mathematical terms) into some other sort of property. We may one day discover how electromagnetism, gravity, the weak force and the strong are variations on a single theme, such that a single formula accommodates them all. But not even the most sanguine physicist believes that moral qualities could be incorporated in such a universal synthesis, as if it even could be true that faster, hotter, less acidic things alone were virtuous.

So moral laws (if they exist) are neither truths of logic, nor satisfactorily testable generalisations waiting to be subsumed in a unified general theory of the kind sought out by physicists. If those were the only alternatives, we should have to conclude (and scientists regularly do) that there are no moral laws outside the conventions of the tribe. By the same token, of course, the claim that only laws of logic and empirical generalisations have any rational status has no rational status: for it is neither a law of logic, nor an empirical discovery. In denying that there are any real moral duties, scientists abandon any right to demand logical rigour, intellectual honesty or openness to refutation. If there are no moral duties then a preference for finding out scientific truths is no more than curiosity. Logical positivism (to give this theory its old name) is not well thought of by philosophers, but retains its influence in non-philosophical circles.

A second argument against the existence of *moral* facts gets its strength simply from the way we identify 'real facts'. A fact, in contemporary rhetoric, is something that anyone must admit who approaches the data with the 'right' attitude. The right attitude in turn is understood to be one cut off from ordinary emotional responses: 'stick to the facts' means 'don't reveal your ethical opinion or your personal preference'. So facts are defined, from the beginning, as truths without an ethical dimension. Unsurprisingly, such facts carry no ethical implications. One might as well decide not to mention colours, and thence infer that all the world is colourless. But once again, the problem is that such a rule has no rational weight: how can we sensibly suppose it to be a matter of *fact* that we *should* take up this detached attitude, that we should say only what anyone could as easily say, rapist or Nazi or believing Christian? Why should those be the *only* facts? And how could they be? It plainly is not true that everyone would agree they were: and so, if we should affirm only what anyone would affirm, we should not affirm that. The objectivist identifies a *right* approach in the act of denying that there is a right approach.

A third argument against the truth of moral truisms is that people disagree even about truisms, let alone about detailed casuistry. Surely we would not disagree so much if there were a matter of fact to be discovered? But the truth is that there is much less disagreement about the truisms than objectivists pretend (though there is a lot about the application of the truisms), and that it is intolerably naive to think that matters of 'mere fact' are so easily settled.

In brief, the enormous influence of modern objectivism rests on very shaky foundations. Anyone inclined, like myself, to take an older objectivism seriously need feel few qualms: there *is* a right attitude to have if we are to see things clearly and to see them whole. That attitude does indeed require us often to put aside our idiosyncratic prejudice, to look past the creepy-crawly and find out the beetle. Moral reasoning itself often depends on trying to see things as they might be seen by anyone, and so to make no foolish exceptions for our 'friends'. But it does not follow that a claim cannot be factual unless it could be admitted to be true by anyone, no matter what his or her ethical intentions. Those who insist on seeing laboratory animals as mere 'animal preparations' or living test-tubes deny themselves the chance to see such truths as would cause difficulties for their treatment of them.

LIVING IN BEAUTY

I said that we were deeply affected by assumptions that we could easily discover were false or unreliable. Egoism, humanism, utilitarianism and modern objectivism are all principles bereft of rational support, and having most disagreeable implications. All four principles begin more plausibly. After all, the division between friends and enemies does run deep; the merely human form (irrespective of virtue, intellect or usefulness) is sacred in many traditions; pain is disagreeable, and pleasure worth pursuing; objectivity is indeed a virtue. But in every case a single useful principle is taken too seriously, as the *only* thought worth having.

I am conservative enough to think that we would gain a lot by carefully returning to the old tradition of ethical reasoning. Destructive scepticism is not the only worthwhile strategy. It is, to put it mildly, not quite sensible to refuse to believe things till they can be proved (either absolutely or to every sensible person's satisfaction). How could we ever begin or satisfactorily complete that project? We had better believe what we are told until we see good reason to reject it. Nor do I think it sensible to demand a single moral theory from which all right decisions can easily be deduced, as though we could ever relegate the pain of moral choice to pocket calculators. Morality is the record of 'our' past conclusions, the testimony of those who seriously sought to be virtuous, and to see things clearly. We ought, in general, to accept the moral truisms of our ancestors: not to do to others what we would not have them do to us, and to do for others what we would have them do for us.

So perhaps tradition is right, after all, to say that we owe less respect to animals than to humans, even if (as in many other cases) we can give no satisfactory account of that division or that duty? But tradition gives us no right to think that traditions are unalterable: refusing to change one's mind is exactly the intellectual sin I mentioned earlier. It is quite certain, for example, that our ethical traditions have given too little weight to women's interests; quite certain that the master–slave relationship has been endorsed at least since agricultural society began. There is nothing unusual, in that case, about suggesting that traditional views of animals are not merely ungrounded (which perhaps is no great fault), but demonstrably mistaken.

We are not of another, radically different kind. Ties of loyalty may bind us to particular non-humans as much as to particular humans. When we open our eyes to see the reality of another creature, and so learn to respect its being, that other creature may as easily be non-human. Those who would live virtuously, tradition tells us, must seek to allow each creature its own place, and to appreciate the beauty of the whole. It is because human beings can sometimes come to see that whole, and know their own place in it, that – in a sense – they are superior to other forms. Our 'superiority', insofar as that is real, rests not upon our self-claimed right always to have more than other creatures do (which is what our modern humanism amounts to), but on the possibility that we may (and the corresponding duty that we should) allow our fellow creatures their part of the action.

Experimentalists, perhaps, do after all stand out from the normal mass of human error. I said at the beginning that there were other areas where more harm was done to animals, by far more people. But experimentation represents our single greatest sin: the intention always to control what's going on, to evade all penalties. We experiment invasively on animal subjects because we hope to find out how things work and thereby evade the costs of pleasure-seeking and the pains of living in the real world alongside all our kindred. That impulse, to possess things perfectly, and never have to yield, is what was once identified as the first sin. The final irony is that in seeking to understand experimentally we break the thing itself. True wisdom, so tradition says, lies in acceptance.

Oddly enough, that very dictum can occasionally be found among the scientifically inclined: real scientists are often moved to enter their profession, after all, by just that happy admiration of the real world and its inhabitants. It is a strange admiration that can so often turn to destroy its focus. Perhaps, when solipsism, humanism, utilitarianism and modern objectivism are recognised as absurd perversions of the ancient virtues, experimentalists may let themselves acknowledge what the best of them already know. Our duty is to admire and to sustain the world in beauty, and not to impose on others pains and penalties we could not bear ourselves. It follows, I am very much afraid, that we should not countenance the use of any creature in an experiment likely to impair its chance of living out its life in beauty. We ought to live by those laws that an ideal observer or Creator-God would make (maybe has made) for the world: to respect the integrity of every creature, and not to seize more for ourselves and our immediate kin than would be granted under such a dispensation.

STEPHEN R. L. CLARK: PUBLICATIONS

* included in the present collection

BOOKS

Aristotle's Man (Oxford: Clarendon Press 1975; pbk 1983), 254pp.
The Moral Status of Animals (Oxford: Clarendon Press 1977; pbk 1984), 238pp.
The Nature of the Beast (Oxford: Oxford University Press 1982; pbk 1984), 136pp.
From Athens to Jerusalem (Oxford: Clarendon Press 1984), 240pp.
The Mysteries of Religion (Oxford: Blackwell 1986), 288pp.
Civil Peace and Sacred Order (Oxford: Clarendon Press 1989), 208pp.
A Parliament of Souls (Oxford: Clarendon Press 1990), 202pp.
God's World and the Great Awakening (Oxford: Clarendon Press 1991), 256pp.
How to Think about the Earth: Models of Environmental Theology, Scott-Holland
    Lectures at Liverpool, 1992 (London: Mowbrays 1993), 168pp.
How to Live Forever (London: Routledge 1995), 224pp.
Animals and Their Moral Standing (London: Routledge 1996).

CONTRIBUTIONS TO BOOKS

'How to Calculate the Greater Good', in R. Ryder and D. Paterson (eds) *Animal
    Rights* (Arundel: Centaur Press 1978), pp. 96–105.*
'Awareness and Self-Awareness', in D. Wood-Gush, M. Dawkins and R. Ewbank
    (eds) *Self-Awareness in Domesticated Animals* (Potters Bar: UFAW 1981), pp. 11ff.*
'Humans, Animals and "Animal Behavior"', in H. B. Miller and W. H. Williams
    (eds) *Ethics and Animals* (Clifton, NJ: Humana Press 1983), pp. 169ff.*
'Gaia and the Forms of Life', in R. Elliot and A. Gair (eds) *Environmental Philosophy*
    (St Lucia: University of Queensland Press 1983; Milton Keynes: Open University
    Press 1984), pp. 182ff.
'Nature and Theology', in A. Richardson and J. Bowden (eds) *New Dictionary of
    Christian Theology* (London: SCM 1983).
'Good Dogs and other Animals', in P. Singer (ed.) *In Defence of Animals* (Oxford:
    Blackwell 1985), pp. 41–51.
'Animals in Ethical Tradition', in N. Marsh and S. Haywood (eds) *Animal
    Experimentation* (FRAME 1985), pp. 1–6.
'God-Appointed Berkeley and the General Good', in J. Foster and H. Robinson (eds)
    Essays on Berkeley (Oxford: Blackwell 1985), pp. 233–53.

PUBLICATIONS

'Abstraction, Possession, Incarnation', in A. Kee and E. T. Long (eds) *Being and Truth: Essays in Honour of John Macquarrie* (London: SCM 1986), pp. 293–317.

'The Land We Live By', in *The Ecological Conscience* (BANC Occasional Papers, Gloucester 1987), pp. 7–12 (see *Civil Peace and Sacred Order*, pp. 86–8).

'The Description and Evaluation of Animal Emotion', in C. Blakemore and S. Greenwood (eds) *Mindwaves* (London: Blackwell 1987), pp. 139–49. *

The Countryside We Want: Report of the 1999 Group, C. Pye-Smith and C. Hall (eds) (London: Green Books 1988), esp. Chapter 2.

'Is Humanity a Natural Kind?', in T. Ingold (ed.) *What is an Animal?* (London: Unwin Hyman 1988), pp. 17–34.

'Abstract Morality, Concrete Cases', in J. D. G. Evans (ed.) *Moral Problems and Contemporary Moral Philosophy* (Cambridge: Cambridge University Press 1988), pp. 35–54.

'Children and the Mammalian Order', in G. Scarre (ed.) *Children, Parents and Politics* (Cambridge: Cambridge University Press 1989), pp. 115–32.

'Introducing Berkeley's Ethics', in S. R. L. Clark (ed.) *Berkeley: Money, Obedience and Affection* (New York: Garland Press 1989), pp. 1–30.

'Ethical Problems in Animal Welfare', in D. Paterson and M. Palmer (eds) *The Status of Animals: Ethics, Education and Welfare* (Wallingford, Oxon: CAB International 1989), pp. 5–14.*

'Friendship in the Christian Tradition' (with Gillian Clark), in R. Porter and S. Tomaselli (eds) *The Dialectics of Friendship* (London: Tavistock Press 1989), pp. 26–44.

'Animals', in J. O. Urmson and J. Ree (eds) *Concise Encyclopedia of Western Philosophy and Philosophers* (London: Unwin Hyman 1989), pp. 14–16.

'How to Reason about Value Judgements', in A. Phillips-Griffiths (ed.) *Key Themes in Philosophy* (Cambridge: Cambridge University Press 1989), pp. 173–90.

'Soft as the Rustle of a Reed from Cloyne (Berkeley)', in P. Gilmour (ed.) *Philosophers of the Enlightenment* (Edinburgh: Edinburgh University Press 1989), pp. 47–62.

'Reason as *Daimon*', in C. Gill (ed.) *The Person and the Human Mind* (Oxford: Clarendon Press 1990), pp. 187–206.

'Anarchists against the Revolution', in M. Warner and R. Crisp (eds) *Terrorism, Protest and Power* (Edward Elgar 1990), pp. 123–37.

'The Reality of Shared Emotion', in M. Bekoff and D. Jamieson (eds) *Interpretation and Explanation in the Study of Behavior* (Westview Press 1990), vol. I, pp. 449–72.*

'Good and Bad Ethology and the Decent *Polis*', in A. Loizou and H. Lesser (eds) *Polis and Politics: Essays in Greek Moral and Political Philosophy* (Aldershot and Brookfield, Vt: Gower Press 1991), pp. 12–22.

'Limited Explanations', in D. Knowles (ed.) *Explanation and its Limits* (Cambridge: Cambridge University Press 1991), pp. 195–210.

'The Consciousness of Animals', in R. Tallis and H. Robinson (eds) *The Pursuit of Mind* (Manchester: Carcanet Press 1991), pp. 110–28.*

'How Many Selves Make Me?', in D. Cockburn (ed.) *Human Beings* (Cambridge: Cambridge University Press 1991), pp. 213–33.

'Philosophical Anthropology', in L. C. Becker and C. B. Becker (eds) *Encyclopedia of Ethics* (New York: Garland Press 1992), vol. II, pp. 963–4.

'Descartes' Debt to Augustine', in M. McGhee (ed.) *Philosophy, Religion and the Spiritual Life* (Cambridge: Cambridge University Press 1992), pp. 73–88.

'Natural Goods and Moral Beauty', in D. Knowles and J. Skorupski (eds) *Virtue and Taste: Essays on Politics, Ethics and Aesthetics in Memory of Flint Schier* (Oxford: Blackwell 1993), pp. 83–97.

170

PUBLICATIONS

'Apes and the Idea of Kindred', in P. Singer and P. Cavalieri (eds) *The Great Ape Project: Equality Beyond Humanity* (London: Fourth Estate 1993), pp. 113–25.
'Modern, Postmodern and Archaic Animals', in B. Verschaffel and Mark Vermink (eds) *Zoology: On (Post)modern Animals: Antwerpen 93*, vol. 4 (Dublin: Liliput Press 1993), pp. 55–72 [combines parts of 'Limited Explanations' and 'Natural Goods', cited above].
'The Better Part', in A. Phillips-Griffiths (ed.) *Ethics* (Cambridge: Cambridge University Press 1993), pp. 29–49.
'Modern Errors, Ancient Virtues', in A. Dyson and J. Harris (eds) *Ethics and Biotechnology* (London: Routledge 1994), pp. 13–32.*
'Global Religion', in R. Attfield and A. Belsey (eds) *Philosophy and the Environment* (Cambridge: Cambridge University Press 1994), pp. 113–28.
'Ancient Philosophy', in A. Kenny (ed.) *Oxford Illustrated History of Western Philosophy* (Oxford: Oxford University Press 1994), pp. 1–53.
'Herds of Free Bipeds', in C. Rowe (ed.) *Reading the Statesman, in proceedings of the Third Symposium Platonicum* (Sankt Augustin: Academia Verlag 1995), pp. 236–52.
'Enlarging the Community', in Brenda Almond (ed.) *Introducing Applied Ethics* (Oxford: Blackwell 1995), pp. 318–30.
'Alien Dreams – Kipling', in D. Seed (ed.) *Anticipations, in Essays on Early Science Fiction and its Precursors* (Liverpool: Liverpool University Press 1995), pp. 172–94.
Contributions to *Oxford Companion to Philosophy*, T. Honderich (ed.) (Oxford: Clarendon Press 1995).
'Environmental Ethics', in P. Byrne and L. Houlden (eds) *Companion Encyclopedia of Theology* (London: Routledge 1995), pp. 843–70.
'Tools, Machines and Marvels', in R. Fellows (ed.) *Philosophy and Technology* (Cambridge: Cambridge University Press 1995), pp. 159–76.
'Plotinus: Body and Soul', in Lloyd P. Gerson (ed) *Cambridge Companion to Plotinus* (Cambridge & New York: Cambridge University Press 1996), pp 275–91.
'Philosophy' (with Barry Dainton), in C. Mullings, M. Deegan, S. Ross, S. Kensa (eds), *New Technologies for the Humanities* (East Grinstead: Bowker-Sauer 1996), pp. 319–37.

BOOKS (EDITED)

Berkeley: Money, Obedience and Affection (ed.) (New York: Garland Press 1989), 230pp.

ARTICLES

'The use of "man's function" in Aristotle', *Ethics* 82, 1972, pp. 269ff.
'God, good and evil', *Proceedings of the Aristotelian Society* 77, 1977, pp. 247ff.
'Animals and Philosophy', *The Vegetarian* July 1977, p. 17.
'The Case against Killing', *Resurgence* 8, 4, pp. 20–1, 1977.
'Animal Wrongs', *Analysis* 38, 1978, pp. 147–9.
'The Rights of Wild Things', *Inquiry* 22,1979, pp. 171ff.*
'The Rights of Animals', *Open Mind* 9, 1980, pp. 24–8.
'Prawa Zwierzat' (tr. Z. Nierada), *Etyka* 18, 1980, pp. 77–86.
'The lack of a gap between Fact and Value', *Aristotelian Society, Supplementary Volume* 54, 1980, pp. 245ff.
'God's Law and Morality', *Philosophical Quarterly* 32, 1982, pp. 339–47.
'Aristotle's Woman', *History of Political Thought* 3, 1982, pp. 177–91.

PUBLICATIONS

'Sexual Ontology and the Group Marriage', *Philosophy* 58, 1983, pp. 215–27.
'Waking-up: a Neglected Model for the After-life', *Inquiry* 26, 1983, pp. 209ff.
'Just War Theory', *The Philosopher*, October 1983, pp. 2–12.
'Morals, Moore and Macintyre', *Inquiry* 26, 1984, pp. 425–45.
'Slaves and Citizens', *Philosophy* 60, 1985, pp. 27–46.
'Hume, Animals and the Objectivity of Morals', in *Philosophical Quarterly* 25, 1985, pp. 117–33.*
'The Rights of the Wild and the Tame', *Chronicles of Culture* 9, 8, 1985, pp. 20–2.
'Olaf Stapledon, Science-fiction philosopher', *Times Higher Education Supplement* 19 September 1986, p. 16.
'Richard Dawkins's *Blind Watchmaker*', *Times Literary Supplement* 26 September 1986, 4356, pp. 1047–9.
'Olaf Stapledon: Philosopher and Fabulist', *Chronicles of Culture* 10,12, 1986, pp. 14–18.
'Christian Responsibility for the Environment', *Modern Churchman* 38,1986, pp. 24–31.
'Icons, Sacred Relics, Obsolescent Plant', *Journal of Applied Philosophy* 3, 1986, pp. 201–10.
'The One Incomprehensible Thing', R. E. Burge (ed.) *Religion and Science: Proceedings of a Symposium at Windsor Great Park* (London: King's College 1987), pp. 44–57.
'Having Opinions', *Chronicles of Culture* 11, 4, 1987, pp. 13–15.
'Animals, Ecosystems and the Liberal Ethic', *Monist* 70, 1987, pp. 114–33.*
'God's Law and Chandler', *Philosophical Quarterly* 37, 1987, pp. 200–6.
'The City of the Wise', *Apeiron* 20, 1987, pp. 63–80.
'How to Believe in Fairies', *Inquiry* 30, 1988, pp. 337–55.
'Robotic Morals', *Cogito* 2, 1988.
'Cupitt and the Divine Imagining', *Modern Theology* 5, 1988, pp. 45–60.
'Utility, Rights and the Domestic Virtues', *Between the Species* 4, 1988, pp. 235–46.*
'A View of Animals and How They Stand', *Animal–Human Relationships: Some Philosophers' Views* (RSPCA 1988), pp. 4–5.
'Ethics and the Peaceable Kingdom', 10th Frey Ellis Memorial Lecture 1988 (London: Vegan Society).
'The Spiritual Meaning of Philosophy', *Chronicles of Culture* 13,9, 1989, pp. 14–19.
'Mackie and the Moral Order', *Philosophical Quarterly* 39, 1989, pp. 98–144.
'On Wishing There were Unicorns', *Proceedings of the Aristotelian Society* 90, 1990, pp. 247–65.
'Notes on the Underground', *Inquiry* 33, 1990, pp. 27–37.
'World Religions and World Orders', *Religious Studies* 26, 1990, pp. 43–57.
'Retrospective 1988–45', *Between the Species* 4, 1990.
'A Disposition for Destruction?', *Argument* 1, 1990, pp. 9–16.
'The Teaching of Ethics', *Humane Education Newsletter* 2, 1, 1991, pp. 4–6.
'New Issues: Eradicating the Obvious', *Journal of Applied Philosophy* 8, 1991, pp. 121–5.
'Taylor's Waking Dream: No-one's Reply', *Inquiry* 34, 1991. pp. 195–215.
'Orwell and the Limits of Language', *Philosophy* 67, 1992, pp. 141–54.
'Where have all the Angels gone?' *Religious Studies* 28, 1992, pp. 221–34.
'Philosophy Lists', *Computers and Texts* 3, 1992, pp. 7–8.
'Paul Davies's *The Mind of God*', *Times Literary Supplement* 26 June 1992, 4656, pp. 6–7.
'Minds, Memes and Rhetoric', *Inquiry* 36, 1993, pp. 3–16.
'Social, Moral and Metaphysical Identities', *Personalist Forum* 8, 1992, pp. 159–62.

PUBLICATIONS

'New Issues: Philosophy and Popular Cosmology', *Journal of Applied Philosophy* 10, 1993, pp. 115–22.
'Olaf Stapledon (1886–1950)', *International Science Reviews* 18, 1993, pp. 112–19.
'Does the Burgess Shale have Moral Implications?' *Inquiry* 36, 1993, pp. 357–80.
'Companions on the Way', *Philosophical Quarterly* 44, 1993, pp. 90–100.
'The Possible Truth of Metaphor', *International Philosophical Studies* 2, 1994, pp. 19–30.
'Extraterrestrial Intelligence, the Neglected Experiment', *Foundation* 61, 1994, pp. 50–65.
'New Issues: Genetic and Other Engineering', *Journal of Applied Philosophy* 11, 1994, pp. 233–8.
'Substance', *Proceedings of the Aristotelian Society, Supplementary Volume* 95, 1995, pp. 1–14.
'Objective Values, Final Causes', *Electronic Journal of Analytical Philosophy* 3, 1995, pp. 65–78 (http://www.phil.indiana.eddu/ejap/).
'Ecology and the Transformation of Nature', *Theology in Green* 3, 1995, pp. 28–46.
'Status and Contract Societies: the Non-human Dimension', *National Geographical Journal of India* 41, 1995, pp. 225–30.
'Conservation and Animal Welfare', *Chronicles of Culture* 20, 6, 1996, pp. 13–16.
'Commentary on Stephen Braude's "Multiple Personality and Moral Responsibility"', *Philosophy, Psychiatry and Psychology* 3, 1996, pp. 55–8.
'Nations and Empires', *European Journal of Philosophy* 4, 1996, pp. 65–80.
'Thinking about How and Why to Think', *Philosophy* 71, 1996, pp. 385–404.
'Minds, Memes and Multiples', *Philosophy, Psychology and Psychiatry* 3, 1996, pp. 21–8.

REPRINTS AND TRANSLATIONS

La Naturaleza de la Bestia, tr. J. J. Utrillo (Mexico: Fondo de la Cultura Economica 1987).
'God, Good and Evil', in J. Houston (ed.) *Is it Reasonable to Believe in God?* (Handsel Press 1984).
'Ethics and the Peaceable Kingdom', *The Vegan* Autumn, 1988, p. 7.
'Icons, Sacred Relics, Obsolete Plant' (extracts), *A Better Country: Magazine of the Society for Rural Theology* 1988.
'Retrospettiva', tr. P. Cavalieri, *Etica e Animali* 2, 1988, pp. 80–4.
La Morale dei Robot, tr. A. Tutino, *Prometeo* 8, 1990, pp. 68–73.
'Remarks on Animals and Morality' in A. Linzey and T. Regan (eds) *Animals and Christianity* (New York: Crossroad 1988), pp. 143–4, 201–2.
'Animalismo "Debole"', *La Nuova Ecologia* March, 1991, pp. 68–71.
'Amando il Mondo Vivente', tr. P. Cavalieri, *Cenobio* 40, 1991, pp. 33–47.
'Moderne, Postmoderne en Archaische Dieren', tr. E. Bettens in B. Verschaffel and M. Vermink (eds) *Zoologie: Over (Post-) moderne Dieren: Antwerpen 93*, vol. 4, (Amsterdam: J. M. Meulenhoff 1993), pp. 79–98.
'Philosophy Related Resources on the Internet' (with Peter Morville) in L. Rosenfeld, J. James and M. Vander Holk (eds) *The Internet Compendium* (New York and London: Neal-Schuman Publishers 1995), pp. 231–52 (http://www.liv.ac.uk/~srlclark/list.html).
'La Contribution de Stephen Clark à la Philosophie sur Internet' in J. Lanteigne (ed.) *Horizons Philosophiques* 6, 1996, pp. 95–109 (http://www.liv.ac.ul/~srlclark/philos.html).

PUBLICATIONS

FORTHCOMING

'Nationalism and the Environment', in J. O'Neill (ed.) *Values and the Environment* (Edinburgh: Edinburgh University Press).

'Objectivism and the Alternatives', in E. Morscher, O. Neumaier, P. Simons (eds) *Applied Ethics and its Foundations*.

'Countryside', in A. Linzey and P. Clarke (eds) *Dictionary of Theology* (London: Routledge), pp. 373–6.

'Holism', in A. Linzey and P. Clarke (eds) *Dictionary of Theology* (London: Routledge), pp. 767–70.

'Libertarianism', in A. Linzey and P. Clarke (eds) *Dictionary of Theology* (London: Routledge), pp. 955–7.

'Is Nature God's Will?', in A. Linzey (ed.) *Animals in Christian Religion*.

'Berkeley's Philosophy of Religion', in K. Winckler (ed.) *Cambridge Companion to Berkeley*.

'Natural Integrity and Biotechnology', in J. A. Laing and D. S. Oderberg (eds) *Human Lives* (London: Macmillan).

'Making up Animals', in A. Holland and A. Johnson (eds) *Biotechnology and Ethics*.

'Platonism and the Love of Place', in Tim Chappell (ed.) *Metaphysics of Environmentalism*

'How Chesterton Read History', *Inquiry* 40, 1997.

Other Minds, Other Worlds: Alien Intelligence in Science Fiction and Philosophy (Liverpool: Liverpool University Press).

Biology and Christian Ethics (Cambridge: Cambridge University Press).

NOTES

1 INTRODUCTION

1 Almond (1995), pp. 318–30.
2 Singer and Cavalieri (1993), pp. 113–25.
3 For my fullest argument against utilitarianism see 'Natural Integrity and Biotechnology', in *Human Lives* Jacqueline A. Laing and David S. Oderberg (eds) (Macmillan 1996).
4 see, especially, *From Athens to Jerusalem* (Oxford: Clarendon Press 1984), *Civil Peace and Sacred Order* (Oxford: Clarendon Press 1989), and *How to Think About the Earth* (Mowbrays 1993).
5 Some of the following material first appeared in 'Christian Responsibility for the Environment', in *Modern Churchman* 38, 1986, pp. 24–31.
6 On which see my *How to Think About the Earth* (Mowbrays 1993), and 'Global Religions', in R. Attfield and A. Belsey *Philosophy and the Natural Environment* (Cambridge: Cambridge University Press 1994), pp. 13–28.
7 Ps-Jerome's Commentary on Mark 1.13 (J. P. Migne's *Patrologia Latina* 30.595): see *Moral Status of Animals*, p. 105.
8 Haring (Mercier Press 1963), II, p. 362.
9 Frye 1982, p.76.

2 HOW TO CALCULATE THE GREATER GOOD

1 R. Ryder and D. Paterson (eds) *Animal Rights* (Centaur Press 1978), pp. 96–105. A paper by H. LaFollette and N. Shanks 'Utilizing Animals', in *Journal of Applied Philosophy* 13, 1995, has since argued this more completely.
2 see Rosenfield 1941, pp. 16ff, 52.
3 P. Singer (1975), pp. 83f, quoting *Bulletin of the National Society for Medical Research* 24 (10) October 1973. West German law was well in advance of ours on this point (see Ryder 1975, p. 141).

3 THE RIGHTS OF WILD THINGS

1 *Inquiry* 22, 1979, pp. 171ff. This issue of *Inquiry* was devoted to the general problem of our treatment of animals.
2 Ritchie 1916, pp. 107f, reprinted in Regan and Singer (1976), pp. 181ff; see also Martin 1976.

3 Nozick 1974, p. 39.
4 Harman 1975; see my 'The lack of a gap between fact and value', in *Aristotelian Society Supplementary Volume* 54, 1980, pp. 245ff.
5 My original reference was to a working paper 'Can animals be moral agents?': this grew into a book *The Nature of the Beast* (Oxford: Oxford University Press 1981).
6 Jenyns *Free Enquiry into the Nature and Origin of Evil* (1793); see S. Johnson (1984), pp. 220ff.
7 Siskind (1973), p. 154 (an opinion of the Sharanhua).
8 my *The Moral Status of Animals* (Oxford: Clarendon Press: 1977), pp. 11ff.
9 Regan 1975, Frey 1977, Regan 1977.
10 J. Rachels 'Do Animals have a Right to Liberty?', Regan and Singer 1976, p. 221.
11 Maynard Smith 1982, p. 144 (after N. B. Davies).
12 van Lawick Goodall (1971); see Harris (1975), after N. A. Hagnon (1968) – who has since been criticised for exaggerating the extent to which the Yanomamo differ from the rest of us.
13 Darling and Leopold 1953, pp. 170f; see MacFadyen (1963), p. 274.
14 Nozick 1974, p. 29.
15 J. Kleinig 1978, p. 42.
16 Sandys-Wunsch 1978, pp. 120f; the present act, of 1986, offers greater protection to primates than the act of 1876. Its terms, and the decision procedure followed by the Home Office Inspectorate, have still not been tested in the courts.
17 Turner 1964; see also Lynam 1975.
18 I acknowledge that this calculation is intrinsically ridiculous, but – in that case – so is utilitarianism; see my 'Natural Integrity', in D. S. Oderberg and J. S. Laing (eds) *Human Beings* (London: Macmillan 1996).
19 Plutarch 'On the Eating of Flesh', 994b.
20 Cornford 1908, p. 15.
21 Clark 1977, p. 183: those who have misunderstood have read carelessly, but I must accept some share of the blame for having written unclearly.
22 Clark 1977, p. 196.
23 Jolly 1970; see Wilson 1975, p. 568.
24 Morgan 1972, p. 206. For the record, some male readers don't.
25 Wilson 1975, p. 247.
26 Part of the problem is political: those bandits that we call the upper classes, nobles, gentry like to model themselves on ideological images of eagles, lions and other pretty predators.
27 Herodotus *History of the Persian War*, 2. 64; see also Chapter 6 of this volume.
28 Dawkins 1976, p. 11.
29 Plutarch 'On the Good Luck or Good Character of Alexander', 329ab.
30 Wilson 1975, p. 247.
31 Wilson 1975, p. 356.
32 Downs 1960.
33 See Ingold 1974, pp. 523ff.
34 Plutarch *Sollertia Animalium*, 962a; see my 'Children and the Mammalian Order', in G. Scarre (ed.) *Children, Parents and Politics* (Cambridge: Cambridge University Press 1989), pp. 115–32.
35 Justinian *Institutiones*, I. 2.
36 Leopold 1966, p. x; see Clark 1977, pp. 31f.
37 Passmore 1974, p. 116.

38 Aristotle *Metaphysics*, 12. 1075a,16ff.
39 See my 'Nations and Empires', *European Journal of Philosophy* 4, 1996.
40 Koran 6. 39.
41 Nozick 1974, p. 109.
42 Nozick 1974, p. 110; Hanula and Hill (1977) follow Stone (1974) in urging that guardians could speak for the inviolable rights of animals in the minimal state, but do not consider what rights wild things may have against each other.
43 Dawkins 1976, p. 10.

4 AWARENESS AND SELF-AWARENESS

1 'Awareness and Self-Awareness', in D. Wood-Gush, M. Dawkins and R. Ewbank (eds) *Self-Awareness in Domesticated Animals* (Potters Bar: UFAW 1981), pp. 11ff.
2 I now have a higher opinion of Descartes' arguments here: see 'Descartes Debt to Augustine', M. McGhee (ed.) *Philosophy, Religion and the Spiritual Life* (Cambridge: Cambridge University Press 1992), pp. 73–88; and 'Substance', *Proceedings of the Aristotelian Society Supplementary Volume* 95, 1995, pp. 1–14.
3 I have argued the point at greater length in *From Athens to Jerusalem* (Oxford: Clarendon Press 1984).
4 I argued this at a meeting of the Thyssen Foundation: the result was later published as a chapter of *From Athens to Jerusalem*.
5 See my response to Mary Midgley, 'The Lack of a Gap between Fact and Value', *Aristotelian Society Supplementary Volume* 54, 1980, pp. 245ff.
6 *New Scientist* 30 June 1977; more detailed reports suggest that no clear grammatical sentence was produced by Koko in this conversation, but it may be that she did intend to convey what her trainer understood.

5 HUMANS, ANIMALS AND 'ANIMAL BEHAVIOUR'

1 H. B. Miller and W. H. Williams (eds) *Ethics and Animals* (Clifton, NJ: Humana Press 1983), pp. 169ff: originally written for the conference on Ethics and Animals at Virginia State Polytechnic.
2 On which see Chapter 8 of this volume.
3 *Conquest*, January 1970, quoted in Ryder 1975, pp. 146f.
4 Indeed, I would now say that it was wholly unfair: Stoic *'apatheia'* is not a lack of compassion, but a refusal to be governed by passions that deflect us from a real recognition of need.
5 See also Clark, 1975, pp. 191ff.
6 Attributed to K. Lorenz, but without exact location.
7 Later reports suggest that the Gombe chimpanzees also indulge in infanticide and tribal warfare.
8 See Clark 1977, pp. 145ff.
9 Though there is good reason to think that cats do suffer considerable pain from the operation, which is the surgical removal of the top joint of their digits.
10 In a paper 'God, Good and Evil', in *From Athens to Jerusalem*, and in the three volumes of *Limits and Renewals*.
11 Ascribed to Zeno by Plutarch, *De Alexandri Fortuna aut Virtute*, 329ab.
12 I have since come to think that 'stewardship' is a thoroughly misleading notion: 'stewards' are what brigands claim to be when they have got tired of using overt violence on their prey. See *How to Think about the Earth*.

13 See Clark, 1975, pp. 84ff.

6 HUME, ANIMALS AND THE OBJECTIVITY OF MORALS

1 *Philosophical Quarterly* 25, 1985, pp. 117–33. A shorter, more discursive version of this paper appears in Singer 1985 as 'Good Dogs and Other Animals'. Related ideas are discussed in 'Good and Bad Ethology and the Decent Polis', in A Loizou and H. Lesser (eds) *Polis and Politics: Essays in Greek Moral and Political Philosophy* (Aldershot and Brookfield, Vt: Gower Press 1991), pp. 12–22; and 'Herds of Free Bipeds', in C. Rowe (ed.) *Reading the Statesman: Proceedings of the Third Symposium Platonicum (Academia Verlag: Sankt Augustin 1995)*, pp. 236–52.
2 David Hume, *Treatise* (1988), p. 467.
3 Herodotus, *Histories* 2.64.
4 Dio Chrysostom 10. 29; Chrysippus, Diogenes Laertius *Lives of the Philosophers* 7. 188.
5 Diogenes Laertius 6. 22.
6 *Treatise* 2. 1. 22: pp. 324ff.
7 Plutarch, Gryllus 987 ff.: *Moralia* (1968), pp. 501ff.
8 Aristotle, *Politics* 1.1253a29, see 1252a3f.
9 Aristotle, *Historia Animalium* 8.589alff, *Politics* 8.1333b18f.
10 Aristotle, *Nicomachean Ethics* 9.1170b10ff.
11 *NE* 9.1169b17 ff.
12 Machan (1975), p. 83; see pp. 71ff.
13 Justinian, *Institutions* 1.2.
14 Morris 1843, p 185.
15 Williams 1965, pp. 93ff.
16 Bischoff 1975, pp. 37ff, Lévi-Strauss 1969, pp. 14ff.
17 Boswell 1953 p. 309 (20.7.1776), p. 1227 (20.4.1784), p. 464 (31.3.1772).
18 *NE* 7.1149a10.
19 Cf. my 'Slaves and Citizens', *Philosophy* 60 (1985).
20 Ericson 1981, p. 387.
21 Lorenz 1966, pp. 115ff.
22 Temerlin 1975; see Bischoff 1975.
23 Bygoff 1972, pp. 410ff; see Kummer 1978, pp. 35ff.
24 Cherfas 1980, pp. 303ff.
25 Lorenz 1966, p. 174: Of the gander who mates with a goose without the triumph ceremony: 'he does not love her in the least'. See also Lorenz 1981, pp. 89ff on 'functionally determined concepts'.
26 Barash 1977, p. 160.
27 van Lawick-Goodall 1970, p. 169.
28 Steiner 1973, p. 263: the claim is a priori, rather than one founded on any real understanding of what elephants do. It may be completely false.
29 van Lawick-Goodall 1971.
30 Harman 1975, p. 5.
31 Berkeley, *Alciphron* 3: (1948), vol. 3, p. 129.
32 Berkeley, *Alciphron* 1: (1948) vol. 3, p. 63.
33 Aristotle, *Eudemian Ethics* 8.1248b17ff.

7 ANIMALS, ECOSYSTEMS AND THE LIBERAL ETHIC

1 *The Monist* 70, 1987, pp. 114–33. This issue of *The Monist* was devoted to a discussion especially of Tom Regan's arguments for animal rights. An earlier version of this paper was read to a Social Ethics Conference at St Martin's Lancaster (April 1984). I also profited from discussion at the universities of Bristol, Glasgow, Manchester, Keele, East Anglia and Liverpool, and Bolton College of Higher Education.

2 See Chapter 4 above.

3 It is now clear that 'Chief Seattle's Speech', as it is now remembered, was not spoken by Seattle (see Callicott 1989, p. 204). It remains a rousing piece of rhetoric.

8 THE DESCRIPTION AND EVALUATION OF ANIMAL EMOTION

1 C. Blakemore and S. Greenwood (eds) *Mindwaves* (Oxford: Blackwell 1987), pp. 39–49. Originally written for a lecture series at Oxford University.

2 Spinoza 1982, 3p57s.

3 Balme 1980; see my 'Is Humanity a Natural Kind?' in T. Ingold (ed.) *What is an Animal?*.

4 Spinoza 1982, 4p20d.

5 ibid., 4p37s1.

6 ibid., 4p45s.

7 ibid., 1p36s.

8 ibid., 4p37s.

9 ibid., 4p68s. Spinoza's Christology, while unorthodox, is not unfamiliar: see my *God's World and the Great Awakening* (Oxford: Clarendon Press 1991).

10 Spinoza 1982, 3p2s.

11 Spinoza 1982, Letter 19, p. 237.

12 See papers by Schubert and Thema Rowell in Schubert and Masters (1991).

13 Spinoza 1982, Letter 78, p. 254.

14 Kant 1963, p. 164; see Chapter 5 of this volume.

15 Liddell 1956, p. 6.

16 ibid., p. 15.

17 ibid., p. 53.

18 ibid., p. 42.

19 ibid., p. 19.

20 ibid., p. 38.

21 Lorenz 1983, p. 90.

22 It is interesting (and also puzzling) that those scientists present when I first gave this paper were more concerned to insist (against what they believed to be my Spinozistic doubts) that animals do indeed have harems, commit rape and are sometimes genuinely angry, than to defend experimental (ab)use of such sensitive creatures.

23 see my 'Morals, Moore and MacIntyre', *Inquiry* 26, 1984, pp. 425–45.

24 Spinoza 1982, 3AD18.

25 ibid., 4p50d.

26 Liddell 1956, pp. 22f.

9 UTILITY, RIGHTS AND THE DOMESTIC VIRTUES

1 *Between the Species* 4, 1988, pp. 235–46. Written for the Wolfson Lecture Series in 1986. Raymond Frey's published paper was not a reply to mine. An earlier response to Frey was 'Animal Wrongs', in *Analysis* 38, 1978, pp. 147–9: I there pointed out that the so-called 'marginal cases' argument for animal rights was not a 'scholastic' one, but a way of drawing attention to the real presences of the creatures we abuse.

2 And one I have explored further in a paper originally composed for the Banner Working Party (created by the Ministry of Agriculture Food and Fisheries) to discuss the new technologies used in the breeding of farm animals. A later version is in press as 'Natural Integrity and Biotechnology', in David Oderberg and Jacqueline Laing (eds) *Human Lives* (London: Macmillan forthcoming).

3 When I made this claim in *The Moral Status of Animals*, one (utilitarian) reviewer professed to be insulted, as if I had accused him of having disreputable motives for his conclusions. On the contrary, I think his motives are likely to be excellent: it is his theory that I find disreputable.

4 I have made some, cautious attempts in this direction in *A Parliament of Souls* (Oxford: Clarendon Press 1990).

5 On which see my 'Objective Values, Final Causes' in *Electronic Journal of Analytical Philosophy* 3, 1995.

10 ETHICAL PROBLEMS IN ANIMAL WELFARE

1 D. Paterson and M. Palmer (eds) *The Status of Animals: Ethics, Education and Welfare* (CAB International 1989), pp. 5–14. Members of the original audience were chiefly veterinary practitioners and animal welfare officers.

2 Jones 1891, p. 36.

3 Maximus Confessor 1985, p. 69.

11 THE REALITY OF SHARED EMOTION

1 M. Bekoff and D. Jamieson (eds) *Interpretation and Explanation in the Study of Behavior* (Boulder, Col.: Westview Press 1990), vol. I, pp. 449–72. This was first delivered as part of a lecture series organised by the editors at Colorado State University in Boulder, Colorado.

2 See my *God's World and the Great Awakening* (Oxford: Clarendon Press 1991), and 'Extraterrestrial Intelligence: the Neglected Experiment' in *Foundation* 61, 1994.

12 THE CONSCIOUSNESS OF ANIMALS

1 R. Tallis and H. Robinson (eds) *The Pursuit of Mind* (Manchester: Carcanet Press 1991), pp. 110–28. This volume contains a variety of papers attacking anti-realism, post-modernism and other less than reasonable fashions.

2 See my 'God's Law and Morality', *Philosophical Quarterly* 32, 1982, pp. 339–47; and 'God's Law and Chandler', *Philosophical Quarterly* 37, 1987, pp. 200–6.

3 Bulmer 1967 (discussing the taxonomy preferred by the Karam people of New Guinea). Other Karam folk-taxa include flying birds and bats (*yakt*), dogs, pigs, rats from homesteads and gardens (*kopyak*), frogs and small marsupials and

rodents other than *kopyak (as)*, tadpoles, weevils and snails. I doubt if our own folk-taxonomy is much more rational.

4 Dombrowski (1984), p.129, summarising Rorty (1979), pp. 182–92. Words within square brackets are my own summary of what conventionalism must mean.

5 Rorty 1979, p. 190.

6 Kipling 1927, p. 547.

7 The two condemnations, to be fair, are not entirely incompatible. Some would say that what was relevant was simply pain. Sacred cows, because nobody kills them, suffer protracted deaths; Korean dogs perish by slow strangulation.

8 Chesterton 1962, p. 70.

9 ibid., p. 58.

10 Lewis 1943, pp. 12f.

11 see my 'On Wishing There Were Unicorns', *Proceedings of the Aristotelian Society* 1989–90.

12 MacIntyre 1981, p. 201.

13 On which see *God's World and the Great Awakening* (Oxford: Clarendon Press 1991), pp. 118ff.

14 Searle 1983, p. 5. Leahy offers a particularly rich example of such self-blinding: 'to say of the cat "it believes that the laces are tied" is to hold that the cat believes the sentence "the laces are tied" is true' (Leahy 1991, p. 51, after R. G. Frey).

15 see Hebb 1946.

16 Hearne 1987, pp. 5, 115.

17 see Mugford 1981, Kiley-Worthington 1990.

18 Wittgenstein 1958, p. 223g.

19 ibid., p. 165e: 647.

20 Averill 1982, p. 282.

21 Hebb 1972, p. 202.

22 Plutchik 1980, p. 107.

23 Lorenz 1981, p. 90.

24 There might well be a difference, namely that human rapists, but probably not drakes or orang-utans, may be moved by hate as much as lust. But the act is still rape even if this is not so.

25 See Crocker 1984.

26 Washburn 1917, pp. 3f.

27 See Rollin 1989 for an historical account of these maxims and their bad effects on the study of animal psychology.

28 Plutchik 1980, p. 105.

29 Wittgenstein 1958, p. 250.

30 Derrida 1982, pp. 321ff.

31 Bateson 1973, pp. 150ff.

32 Rorty 1979, p. 190. I do not quite understand who 'we' may be: I have a lot more sympathy for pigs than for koalas, and it is not true that only 'cuddly animals' are protected or preserved by people wide-awake enough to realise their duties.

33 Rorty 1979, p. 53.

34 Bloor 1983, pp. 74–6, remarks that Wittgenstein's observation is founded in a 'quite proper sense of the biological basis of social life'. If lions were really alien beings, we would indeed find it difficult or impossible to communicate.

35 Unless there is an omnipresent and omniscient God who shares our sensa: true Cartesians never did believe in the 'privacy' of our own subjectivity. But that is another story.
36 Uexkuell 1926, 1957.
37 James 1890, p. 288.
38 Uexkuell 1926, pp. 35ff; Ramsey 1931, p. 291: 'I don't really believe in astronomy, except as a complicated description of part of the course of human and possibly animal sensation'.
39 Murdoch 1970, p. 85.
40 Hearne 1987, p. 264.

13 MODERN ERRORS, ANCIENT VIRTUES

1 A. Dyson and J. Harris (eds) *Ethics and Biotechnology* (London: Routledge 1994), pp. 13–32. Originally written for a lecture series in the Centre for Ethics in Manchester University. It is the descendant of several earlier papers to similar audiences, notably 'Animals and Philosophy', *The Vegetarian* July 1977, p. 17; 'The Case against Killing', *Resurgence* 8, 4, 1977, pp. 20–1; 'The Rights of Animals', *Open Mind* 9, 1980, pp. 24–8; and 'Animals in Ethical Tradition', in N. Marsh and S. Haywood (eds) *Animal Experimentation* (FRAME 1985), pp. 1–6.

BIBLIOGRAPHY

Almond, B. (ed.) (1995) *Introducing Applied Ethics* (Oxford: Blackwell).

Attfield, R. (1983) *The Ethics of Environmental Concern* (Oxford: Blackwell).

Austin, P. (1885) *Our Duty to Animals* (London: Kegan, Paul).

Averill, J R. (1982) *Anger and Aggression* (New York: Springer-Verlag).

Balme, D. E. (1980) 'Aristotle's biology was not essentialist', *Archiv für Geschichte der Philosophie* 62, pp. 1ff.

Barash, D. F. (1977) *Sociobiology and Behaviour* (New York: Elsevier).

Barker, E. (1915) *Political Thought in England* (London: Williams and Norgate).

Bates, R. (1977) 'Why Medicine has a Health Problem', *The Listener* 98, 4 August 1977, pp. 130f.

Bateson, G. (1973) *Steps Towards an Ecology of Mind* (Paladin: London).

Berkeley, G. (1948) *Collected Works* A. A. Luce and T. E. Jessop (eds) (Edinburgh: Thomas Nelson & Sons).

Bischoff, N. (1975) 'Comparative Ethology of Incest Avoidance', in R. Fox (ed.) *Biosocial Anthropology* (London: Tavistock), pp. 37ff.

Bloor, D. (1983) *Wittgenstein: a Social Theory of Knowledge* (London: Macmillan).

Boswell, J. (1953) *Life of Johnson* (Oxford: Clarendon Press).

Bradley F. H. (1897) *Appearance and Reality* second edn (Oxford: Oxford University Press).

Bridgman P. W. (1936) *The Nature of Physical Theory* (Princeton, NJ: Princeton University Press).

Bruce, A. B. (1899) *The Moral Order of the World in Ancient and Modern Thought* (London: Hodder & Stoughton).

Bulmer, R. (1967) 'Why the Cassowary is not a Bird', *Man* 2, pp. 5–25.

Bygoff, J. D. (1972) 'Cannibalism among Wild Chimpanzees', *Nature* 238, pp. 410ff.

Callicott, J. B. (1989) *In Defence of the Land Ethic* (New York: SUNY Press).

Chagnon, N. A. (1968) *Yanomamo: the Fierce People* (New York: Holt, Rinehart & Winston).

Cherfas, J. (1980) 'Voices in the Wilderness', *New Scientist* 86, pp. 303ff.

Chesterton, G K. (1961) *Orthodoxy* (London: Fontana).

—— ([1929]1962) *The Poet and the Lunatics* (London: Darwen Finlayson).

Chisholm R. (1957) *Perceiving* (Ithaca, NY:: Cornell University Press).

Churchland, P. M. (1984) *Matter and Consciousness* (Cambridge, Mass.: MIT Press).

Churchland, P. S. (1986) 'Replies to Critics', *Inquiry* 29, pp. 241–72.

Cornford, F. (1908) *Microcosmographia Academica* (Cambridge: Bowes & Bowes).

Crocker, D. R. (1984) 'Anthropomorphism: Bad Practice, Honest Prejudice?'

Georgina Ferry (ed.) *The Understanding of Animals* (Oxford: Blackwell), pp. 304–313.

Darling, F. F. (1970) *Wilderness and Plenty* (Boston: Houghton Mifflin).

Darling, F. F. and Leopold, A. S. 'What's Happening in Alaska?', *Animal Kingdom* (New York) 55, 1953, pp. 170f.

Dawkins, R. (1976) *The Selfish Gene* (Oxford: Clarendon Press).

Dawkins, M. (1981) 'Welfare of animals', in D. McFarland (ed.) *Oxford Companion to Animal Behaviour* (Oxford: Oxford University Press), pp. 598–60.

Deren, M. (1975) *The Voodoo Gods* (London: Paladin).

Derrida, J. (1982) *Margins of Philosophy* tr. A. Bass (Brighton: Harvester).

Diamond, C. (1978) 'Eating Meat and Eating People', *Philosophy* 53, pp. 465–80.

Dombrowski, D. A. (1984) *The Philosophy of Vegetarianism* (Amherst, Mass.: University of Massachusetts Press).

Donne, J. (1929) *Complete Poetry and Selected Prose* J. Hayward (ed.) (London: Nonesuch Press).

Dover, K. (1975) *Greek Popular Morality* (Oxford: Blackwell).

Downs, J. F. (1960) 'Domestication: an Examination of the Changing Social Relationships between Man and Animals', *Kroeber Anthropological Society papers* 22, pp. 18–67.

Elliot, R. (1984) 'Rawlsian Justice and Non-human Animals', *Journal of Applied Philosophy* 1, pp. 95–106.

Epictetus (1946) *Discourses* tr. W. A. Oldfather (London: Heinemann).

Ericson, C. (1981) 'Mate Selection', in D. MacFarland (ed.) *Oxford Companion to Animal Behaviour* (Oxford: Oxford University Press).

Findlay, J. N. (1963) *Meinong's Theory of Objects and Values* (Oxford: Clarendon Press).

Frey, R. G. (1977) 'Interests and Animal Rights', *Philosophical Quarterly* 27, pp. 254ff.

—— (1980) *Interests and Rights* (Oxford: Clarendon Press).

—— (1983) *Rights, Killing and Suffering* (Oxford: Blackwell).

Fromm E. (1974). *The Anatomy of Human Destructiveness* (London: Cape).

Frye, N. (1982) *The Great Code* (London: Routledge & Kegan Paul).

Godlovitch, R. (1971) 'Animals and Morals', *Philosophy* 46, pp. 23ff.

Gordon, R M. (1989) *The Structure of Emotions* (Cambridge: Cambridge University Press).

Gregg, A. (1955) 'A medical aspect of the population problem', *Science* 121, pp. 681–2.

Hanula, R. W. and Hill, P. W. (1977) 'Using Metaright Theory to ascribe Kantian Rights to Animals within Nozick's Minimal State', *Arizona Law Review* 19, pp. 242ff.

Hargrove, E. C. (1980) 'Anglo-American land-use attitudes', *Environmental Ethics* 2, pp. 121ff.

Haring, B. (1963) *The Law of Christ* tr. E. G. Kaiser (Cork: Mercier Press).

Harman, G. (1975) 'Can Moral Relativism be Defended?', *Philosophical Review* 84, pp. 3ff.

Harré, R. (1984) *Personal Being* (Cambridge, Mass.: Harvard University Press).

Harris, M. (1975) *Cows, Pigs, Wars and Witches* (London: Hutchinson).

Hayward, J. W. (1987) *Shifting World, Changing Minds* (Boston and London: Shambhala).

Hearne, V. (1987) *Adam's Task: Calling Animals by Name* (London: Cape).

Hebb, D. O. (1946) 'Emotion in Man and Animal', *Psychological Review* 53, pp. 88–106.

—— (1972) *Textbook of Psychology* third edn (Philadelphia, Penn.: W. B. Saunders).

Hillman, J. (1975) *Re-visioning Psychology* (New York: Harper & Row).

Hume, D. (1888) *Treatise of Human Nature*, L. A. Selby-Bigge (ed.) (Oxford: Clarendon Press).

—— (1962) *Enquiries* L. A. Selby-Bigge (ed.) (Oxford: Clarendon Press).

Humphreys, N. K. (1974) 'Vision in a Monkey without Striate Cortex', *Perception* 3, pp. 41–55.

Ingold, T. (1974) 'On Reindeer and Men', *Man* 9, pp. 523ff.

James, W. (1890) *The Principles of Psychology* (London: Macmillan).

Jaynes, J. (1976) *The Origin of Consciousness in the Breakdown of the BiCameral Mind* (Boston: Houghton-Mifflin).

Jenyns, S. (1793) 'A Free Inquiry into the Nature and Origin of Evil', in *Works*, second edn (London: Cadell).

Johnson, S. (1984) 'Review of Jenyns' "Free Inquiry"', in *Samuel Johnson*, D. Greene (ed.) (Oxford: Oxford University Press).

Jolly, C. J. (1970) 'The Seed-Eaters: a New Model of Hominid Differentiation Based on a Baboon Analogy', *Man* 5, pp. 5–26.

Jones, H. (1891) *Browning as a Philosophic and Religious Teacher* (Edinburgh: Thomas Nelson).

Kallen, H. M. (1969) 'The Book of Job', in N. N. Glatzer (ed.) *The Dimensions of Job* (New York: Schocken Books), pp. 17ff.

Kant, I. ([1930]1963) *Lectures on Ethics* tr. L. Infeld (London: Methuen).

Kenny A. (1973) *Wittgenstein* (London: Allen Lane).

Kiley-Worthington, M. (1990) *Animals in Circuses and Zoos: Chiron's World?* (Basildon: Little Eco-Farms Publishing).

Kipling, R. (1927) *Collected Verse 1885–1826* (London: Hodder & Stoughton).

Kleinig, J. (1978) 'Human Rights, Legal Rights and Social Change', E. Kamenka and A. Ehr-Soon Tay (eds) *Human Rights* (London: E. Arnold).

Kohak, E. (1984) *The Embers and the Stars* (Chicago: University of Chicago Press).

Kummer, H. (1978) 'Aspects of Morality among Non-Human Primates', in G. S. Stent (ed.) *Morality as a Biological Phenomenon* (Berlin: Dahlem), pp. 35ff.

Lawrence, J. (1798) *A Philosophical and practical Treatise on Horses and the moral duties of man towards the brute creation* (T. N. Longman: London): 2nd edition (1802) London: H. D. Simonds; 3rd edition (1810) London: Sherwood, Neely & Jones.

Leahy, M. P. T. (1991) *Against Liberation: Putting Animals in Perspective* (London: Routledge).

Lee, D. (1959) *Freedom and Culture* (New York: Prentice-Hall).

Leopold, A. (1966) *Sand County Almanac* (New York: Oxford University Press).

Lévi-Strauss, C. (1969) *The Elementary Structures of Kinship* tr. J. H Bell, J. R. von Sturmer and R. Needham (London: Eyre & Spottiswoode).

Lewis, C. S. (1943) *The Abolition of Man* (London: Bles).

—— (1953) *The Silver Chair* (London: Bles).

Liddell, H. (1956) *Emotional Hazards in Animals and Men* (Springfield, Ill.: C. C. Thomas).

Locke, J. (1963) *Two Treatises of Government* P. Laslett (ed.) (Cambridge: Cambridge University Press).

Lorenz, K. Z. (1966) *On Aggression* tr. M. Latzke (London: Methuen).

—— (1981) *The Foundations of Ethology* (New York: Springer-Verlag).

Lovejoy, A O. (1930) *The Revolt against Dualism* (Chicago: Open Court Publishing).

Lovelock, J. (1974) *Gaia: a New Look at the Earth* (Oxford: Oxford University Press).

—— (1991) *Healing Gaia* (New York: Crown Publishers).

Lynam, S. (1975) *Humanity Dick: a Biography of Richard Martin* (London: Hamilton).

McCall, G. J. (1977) 'The Social Looking-Glass', in T. Mischel (ed) *The Self* (Oxford: Blackwell), pp. 250ff, 274ff.

McCloskey, H. J. (1965) 'Rights', *Philosophical Quarterly* 15, pp. 115ff.

MacFadyen, A. (1963) *Animal Ecology* second edn (London: Pitman).

McGuinness, D. (ed.) (1987) *Dominance, Aggression and War* (New York: Paragon House).

Machan, T. R. (1975) *Human Rights and Human Liberties* (Chicago: Nelson-Hall).

MacIntyre, A. (1981) *After Virtue* (Oxford: Blackwell).

—— (1983) *Ecological Ethics and Politics* (New Jersey: Rowman & Littlefield).

Martin, M. (1976) 'A Critique of Moral Vegetarianism', *Reason Papers* 3, pp. 13ff.

Mathews G. B. (1978) 'Animals and the Unity of Psychology', *Philosophy* 53, pp. 88–106.

Maximus Confessor (1985) *Selected Writings* tr. G. C. Berthold, intro. J. Pelikan (London: SPCK).

Maynard Smith, J. (1982) *Evolution and the Theory of Games* (Cambridge: Cambridge University Press).

Menzel E. W. (1973) 'Chimpanzee Spatial Memory Organization', *Science* 182, pp. 943–5.

Midgley M. (1978) *Beast and Man* (Ithaca, NY: Cornell University Press).

Mill, J. S. (1852) 'Dr Whewell on Moral Philosophy', *Westminster Review* (reprinted in *Dissertations and Discussions* (1859), vol. II, pp. 450ff).

—— (1962) *On Utilitarianism* M. Warnock (ed.) (London: Fontana).

Mises, L. von (1949) *Human Action* (London: Hodge & Co.).

Monod, J. (1972) *Chance and Necessity* (London: Collins).

Morgan, C L. (1894) *Introduction to Comparative Psychology* (London: Walter Scott).

Morgan, E. (1972) *The Descent of Woman* (London: Souvenir Press).

Morris, J. B. (1843) *Towards the Conversion of the Hindus* (London: J. G. F. and J. Rivington).

Moyer, K. E. (1987) 'Biological Basis of Dominance and Aggression', in *Dominance, Aggression and War* D. McGuinness (ed.) (New York: Paragon House), pp. 1–34.

Mugford, R. A. (1981) 'The Social Skills of Dogs as an Indication of Self-awareness', in D. G. M. Woodgush, M. Dawkins and R. Ewbank (eds) *Self-Awareness in Domesticated Animals* (Potters Bar: UFAW), pp. 40ff.

Murdoch, I. (1970) *The Sovereignty of Good* (London: Routledge & Kegal Paul).

Naess, A. (1973) 'The Shallow and the Deep, Long-range Ecological Movement', *Inquiry* 16, pp. 95ff.

—— (1979) 'Self-realization in Mixed Communities of Humans, Bears and Wolves', *Inquiry* 22, pp. 231ff.

Nagel T. (1979) *Mortal Questions* (Cambridge: Cambridge University Press).

Nicholson, E. B. (1879) *The Rights of an Animal* (London: Kegan Paul).

Nieli, R. (1987) *Wittgenstein: From Mysticism to Ordinary Language* (Albany, NY: SUNY).

Nozick, R. (1974) *Anarchy, State and Utopia* (Oxford: Blackwell).

O'Donovan, O. (1987) *Begotten or Made* (Oxford: Clarendon Press).

Onians, R B. (1951) *The Origins of European Thought* (Cambridge: Cambridge University Press).

Otto, W. F. (1962) *Mythos und Welt* (Stuttgart: Klett).

Pacheco, A. (1985) 'The Silver Spring Monkeys', in *In Defence of Animals* P. Singer (ed.) (Oxford: Blackwell), pp. 135ff.

Passmore, J. (1974) *Man's Responsibility for Nature* (Duckworth: London).

Philo (1930) *Complete Works* tr. F. H. Colson and G. H. Whitaker (London: Heinemann, Loeb Classical Library; New York: Putnam's).

Philokalia (1979) Vol. 1, tr. G. E. H. Palmer, P. Sherrard and K. Ware (London: Faber).

Plutarch (1968) *Moralia* vol. 12, tr. H. Cherniss and W. C. Helmhold (London and Cambridge, Mass.:).

Plutchik, R. (1980) *Emotion: A Psychoevolutionary Synthesis* (New York: Harper & Row).

Primatt, H. (1839) *The Duty of Humanity to Inferior Creatures* A. Broome (ed.) (London).

Prior, A. (1968) *Papers on Time and Tense* (Oxford: Clarendon Press).

Putnam, H. (1987) *The Many Faces of Realism* (La Salle, Ill.: Open Court).

Rachlin H. and Green L. (1972). Cited by P. F. Secord 'Making Oneself Behave', in T. Mischel (ed) (1977) *The Self* (Oxford: Blackwell) pp. 250ff.

Ramsey, F. P. (1931) *Foundations of Mathematics* (London: Kegan Paul).

Rand, A. (1967) *Capitalism: the Unknown Ideal* (New York: New American Library).

Raphael, D. D. (1974) 'The Standard of Morals', *Proceedings of the Aristotelian Society* 96, pp. 1ff.

Regan, T. (1975) 'The Moral Basis of Vegetarianism', *Canadian Journal of Philosophy* 5, pp. 181ff.

—— (1977) 'Frey on Interests and Animal Rights', *Philosophical Quarterly* 27, pp. 335ff.

—— (1983) *The Case for Animal Rights* (London: Routledge & Kegan Paul).

—— (1984) 'Honey Dribbles down your Fur', *Bowling Green Studies in Applied Philosophy* 6, pp. 138ff.

—— (1986) 'The Bird in the Cage', *Between the Species* 2, pp. 90–9.

Regan, T. and Singer, P. (1976) (eds) *Animal Rights and Human Obligations* (Englewood Cliffs, NJ: Prentice-Hall).

Reynolds, P. C. (1981) *On the Evolution of Human Behaviour* (Berkeley, Cal.: University of California Press).

—— (1987) 'Animal Intelligence and Human Instinct', in *Dominance, Aggression and War* D. McGuinness (ed.) (New York: Paragon House), pp. 119–30.

Reynolds V. (1976) *The Biology of Human Action* (Reading: Freeman).

Ritchie, A. M. (1964) 'Can Animals See?', *Proceedings of the Aristotelian Society* 64, pp. 221–42.

Ritchie, D. G. (1916) *Natural Rights* third edn (London: Allen & Unwin).

Robinson, H. M. (1982) *Matter and Consciousness* (Cambridge: Cambridge University Press).

Rollin, B. E. (1989) *The Unheeded Cry* (Oxford: Oxford University Press).

Rorty, R. (1979) *Philosophy and the Mirror of Nature* (Princeton, NJ: Princeton University Press).

Rosenfield, L. C. (1941) *From Beast-Machine to Man-Machine* (New York: Oxford University Press).

Rothbard, M. N. (1973) *For a New Liberty* (New York: Macmillan).

—— (1982) *The Ethics of Liberty* (New Jersey: Humanities Press).

Ryder, R. (1975) *Victims of Science* (London: Davis Poynter).

Said, E. (1979) *A New Language for Psychoanalysis* (New Haven, Conn.: Yale University Press).

Salt, H. (1980) *Animals' Rights* intro. P. Singer (London: Centaur Press).

Sandys-Wunsch, G. (1978) *Animal Law* (London: Shaw & Sons).

Sartre, J. P. (1962) *A Sketch for a Theory of the Emotions*, tr. P. Mairet (London: Methuen).

Scarre, G. (ed.) (1989) *Children, Parents and Politics* (Cambridge: Cambridge University Press).

Schafer, R. (1976) *A New Approach to Psychoanalysis* (New Haven, Conn.: Yale University Press).

Schubert, G. and Masters, R. D. (eds) (1991) *Primate Politics* (Carbondale and Edwardsville, Ill.: Southern Illinois University Press).

Searle, J. R. (1983) *Intentionality* (Cambridge: Cambridge University Press).

Seattle ([1854] 1976) *Chief Seattle's Testimony* tr. D. Smith (London: Pax Christi and Friends of the Earth).

Sextus Empiricus (1933) *Outlines of Pyrrhonism I* tr. R. G. Bury (London: Heinemann).

Singer, P. (1976) *Animal Liberation* (London: Cape).

—— (ed.) (1985) *In Defence of Animals* (Oxford: Blackwell).

Singer, P. and Cavalieri, P. (eds) (1993) *The Great Ape Project* (London: Fourth Estate; New York: St Martin's Press).

Siskind, J. (1973) *To Hunt in the Morning* (New York: Oxford University Press).

Smith, A. (1976) *The Theory of Moral Sentiments* D. D. Raphael and A. L. Macfie (eds) (Oxford: Clarendon Press).

Smith N. (1978) 'The Evolution of Behavior', *Scientific American* 239, 3, pp. 176–92.

Sperry, R. (1983) *Science and Moral Priority* (Oxford: Blackwell).

Spiegelberg, H. (1972) *Phenomenology in Psychology and Psychiatry* (Evanston, Ill.: Northwestern Universities Press).

Spinoza, B. (1982) *Ethics and Selected Letters* tr. S. Shirley (Indianapolis: Hackett).

Spooner, L. (1886) *Letter to Grover Cleveland* (Boston: Tucker).

Sprigge, T. L. (1984) 'Non-human Rights: an Idealist Perspective', *Inquiry* 27, pp. 439ff.

Steiner, H. (1973) 'Moral Agents', *Mind* 82, pp. 263–5

Stich, S. (1983) *From Folk Psychology to Cognitive Science* (Cambridge, Mass.: MIT Press).

Stone, C. D. (1974) *Should Trees Have Standing?* (Los Altos: William Kaufmann Inc).

Tax, S. and Callender, C. (eds) (1960) *Evolution after Darwin, Volume III: Issues in Evolution* (Chicago, Ill.: University of Chicago Press).

Temerlin, M. (1975) *Lucy: Growing up Human* (Palo Alto, Cal.: Science & Behavior).

Tinbergen, N. (1968) 'On War and Peace in Animals and Men', *Science* 160, pp. 1411ff.

Turner, E. S. (1964) *All Heaven in a Rage* (London: Michael Joseph).

Uexkuell, J. von (1926) *Theoretical Biology* tr. D. L. Mackinnon (London: Kegan Paul).

—— (1957) 'A Stroll Through the Worlds of Animals and Men', in C. H. Schiller (ed.) *Instinctive Behaviour* (New York: International University Press), pp. 5–80.

Unamuno, M de (1954) *The Tragic Sense of Life* tr. J. G. Crawford Fletch (New York: Dover Publishing).

Van Lawick-Goodall, J. (1970) *Innocent Killers* (London: Collins).

—— (1971) *In the Shadow of Man* (London: Collins).

Walshe, F. (1968) 'Personal Knowledge and Concepts in the Biological Sciences', in *Intellect and Hope* T. A. Langford and W. H. Poteat (eds) (Durham, N. Carolina: Duke University Press), pp. 275–314.

Washburn, A. L. (1917) *The Animal Mind* second edn (New York: Macmillan).

Whewell, W. (1852) *Lectures on the History of Moral Philosophy in England* (London: John W. Parker & Son).

Wilkes, K. (1978) *Physicalism* (London: Routledge & Kegan Paul).

—— (1988) *Real Persons* (Oxford: Clarendon Press).

Williams, L. (1965) *Samba and the Monkey Mind* (London: Bodley Head).

Wilson, E. O. (1975) *Sociobiology* (Cambridge, Mass.: Harvard University Press).
Wittgenstein, L. (1958) *Philosophical Investigations* tr. G. E. M. Anscombe (Oxford: Blackwell).
Yeats, W B. (1961) *Essays and Introductions* (London: Macmillan).

INDEX

accidie 129
Act of 1876 21
Act of 1986 154
agribusiness 15, 108
altruism 26, 53, 57
American Sign Language 37
Amerindians 81, 98, 118
anaesthesia 43
anger 34, 92, 127f., 130, 132,
  136f., 146
animal experimentation, *see* vivisection
animism 49, 133f.; *see also* panpsychism
anthropomorphism 2, 47f., 60, 145
anti-realism 3, 33, 121, 124ff., 139,
  142, 144ff.; *see also* 31, 97ff.
apprehension 91, 95
Aquinas 121
arachnoids 159
Ardrey 25
Aristophanes 51, 124
Aristotle 27, 44, 49, 53f., 57, 80, 87,
  121, 133, 136, 160; *see also* 69
Attfield 74
Augustine 43, 134
Aurelius 81, 108
Austin 43
autonomy 9f., 20, 74, 83, 158
Averill 128, 136

baboons 12, 18, 25, 29, 51, 67, 78,
  115, 129
Babylon 6
Balme 160
Barker 76
Bates 13
Bateson 148
beastliness 42ff., 59f.
beauty 69, 161, 167f.; *see also* 80

behaviourism 35
belief 112, 126, 131
Benthamites 11, 99, 161
Berkeley 68, 80, 83ff., 108, 110
blackbirds 16, 78, 103, 141
blind sight 132
Bradley 48
Bridgman 32, 34
British beasts 28, 85, 105
Bruce 45f.
Buddhism 131
Burke 28
butterflies 18, 50, 127, 146
Buytendjik 132

calculus, *see* utilitarianism
canary 132
cannibalism 73, 102, 117, 164
Cartesians 2, 9, 32, 48f., 80, 89, 142
cassowary 141
cats 16f., 19, 21, 25, 40, 51, 85, 106,
  130, 145f., 153
cattle 35, 47, 98, 104ff., 142f.; *see also*
  115, 118, 144
causality 14
chairs 137
Cherfas 39
Chesterton 135f., 144
child abuse 55, 64, 78, 97
children 10, 33, 43, 45, 49, 61, 83, 85,
  106, 108, 113, 127
chimpanzees 9, 17f., 24, 29, 35, 37,
  39f., 51, 62, 65, 90, 98, 102, 118,
  127, 129f., 136f.
China 159
Chisholm 33
Churchland, Paul & Patricia 122ff.,
  129, 131

Clever Hans 104, 145
'colourless world' 82, 137, 166; see also
    48, 134f.
communities 27, 29, 109
conscience 59, 62, 67
consciousness 31ff., 82, 90, 126,
    132, 139
conservation 28, 116
Cornford's Wedge 23
cows, see cattle
cruelty 17, 70, 156
cuckoos 26, 53; see also 61
Cynics 56f.

Daniel 4
Darling 27, 53
Dawkins, M. 95
Dawkins, R. 26, 29, 53
death 45f., 74, 103, 114
declawing cats 51
deformities 58f.
depression 127, 129, 146
Derrida 148, 150
Descartes 32f., 37, 48, 107, 148
Deuteronomy 5, 8
Diamond 47, 107
difference 3, 105
Diogenes 56
disasters 27f., 65
dogs 17, 26, 35, 40, 55f., 58, 91, 106,
    110, 115, 117f., 120, 127, 136,
    141ff., 147f., 157
domestication 26, 58ff., 75, 106f.,
    115f., 120
donkeys 5, 100, 102
Donne 54
doubt 40, 62
Dover 47

Earth's Household 27, 53, 108
egoism 57f., 70f., 88, 95, 157
electrical shocks 91f.
Elliot 85
emergence 36; see also magic
emotions 42ff., 87, 112, 121ff., 130ff.
empiricism 31f., 92f.; see also 111, 121f.
environmentalism 73, 81, 109f.; see also
    conservation
Epictetus 44ff., 50, 130
Esdras 2
Evagrius 129, 131
evidence 33

evolution 36f., 41, 53, 59, 98, 110
extra-terrestrials 10, 25, 159
Ezra 7

Fall of Adam 88, 130
feminism 52, 154; see also 88, 94
fighting 61
Findlay 131
fixed action patterns 60
folk psychology 125ff.
foxes 45, 78, 83, 154
FRAME 13
Fraser Darling, see Darling
Frey 73, 97ff., 105, 109
friends 57, 120, 134, 136, 157, 166
Fromm 40
Frye 5f.
functions 93f., 124, 127

Galileo 111
Gandhi 43
geese 63f., 178
genes 26, 53
genocide 12, 19, 114, 120
Gerard 122
goats 91ff.
Godlovitch 19
Goodall 40, 50, 64f.
Gordon 130
gorillas 40
Great City 68, 80ff., 105f., 108
Gregg 82

Hamilton 45
Hargrove 79
Harman 17, 65
Harr 129
Hayward 128
Hearne 3, 107, 143, 152
Hebb 34, 127, 130, 146
Hegel 38
Heidegger 81
hell 6
herms 128
hierarchy 136
Hillman 132, 134, 138
Hobbes 61, 71, 75, 78, 88f.
holism 82
horses 87, 90, 104, 106, 143f.; see also
    115
Hosea 4
human evolution 24f., 117

humanism, *see* speciesism
Hume 55ff., 75, 90; *see also* 156
Humphreys 38
hunting 21, 24, 52, 107, 116, 155
hybrid 159

ignorance not knowledge 134, 138
incest 55ff., 90
Ingold 34
inherent value 81
interests 18
intuitionism 13
Inuit 19, 21, 103
invisible hand 60, 75
Isaiah 5ff.
Israel 6f.

James 122, 151
Jaynes 129, 133; *see also* 137
Jefferson 81
Jenyns 17
Jeremiah 6, 8
Jesus Christ 4, 88
Job 5, 144
Johnson 59ff.
Judgement 8, 111
justice 71f., 77, 85, 113, 132, 140
Justinian 27, 51, 57

Kallen 5
Kant & Kantians 10, 16, 18, 42, 47, 67,
   91, 101f.
Kenny 33
killing 10, 77, 84, 99, 115, 163; *see
   also* death
kindliness 17, 25, 65, 107, 155
Kipling 108, 142
Kleinig 21
Kohak 110
Koran 28
Koreans 117, 142, 144
kumpans 38f.

lamb 6, 92, 95
language 2, 33f., 37, 49, 69, 106, 123,
   126, 129f., 143, 145
Lapps 34
Lawrence 79
laws of manners 17, 21, 70ff., 77, 101
learning to speak 145
Lee 81
Leopold 4, 41, 73, 80, 109

Leviticus 5, 111
Lewis 47, 50, 144
libertarianism 70ff., 158f.
Liddell 87, 91ff.
lions 6, 52, 145, 148, 181
Locke 75f., 79, 109
logic 37, 127, 145, 165
Lorenz 48, 62, 64, 93, 127
love 128, 138ff.
Lovejoy 121; *see also* 134
Lovelock 82

macaques 40
McCall 37
McCloskey 18, 70f., 74, 76f., 78
McGuinness 136
Machan 57, 70
MacIntyre 79, 81, 144
Maclean 129
magic 90, 96, 124f.
Malebranche 142, 161
maps 38, 60, 150
marginal cases 102
materialists 122ff., 131, 133, 151
Matthews 34
mazes 38
meaning 122, 133
meat-eating 15, 23, 43f., 57, 100
mental states 31f., 48f., 81ff., 89, 122f.,
   131, 146, 151
Menzel 38
metaphors 8, 32, 128f., 146
mice 17, 20, 23f., 56
Midgley 33, 49
Mill 11, 72, 99, 163
mind and body 31ff., 89, 122ff.
minimal state 29, 74, 177; *see also* 101f.
Mises 75
monkeys 79, 127, 146f., 157; *see also*
   macaques, vervet
Monod 50
Moore 94
moral facts 31, 36, 41, 55ff., 66ff., 93ff.,
   97ff., 117, 140, 142, 165ff.
Morgan, E. 25
Morgan, L. 137; *see also* 147
Morris 58f.
Moyer 128
Murdoch 152

Naess 73, 75
Nagel 36

Nathan 5, 117, 143
'naturalistic fallacy' 94, 165
natural kinds 124, 141; see also species
natural law 27, 50ff., 57
nature vs culture 4, 6, 25, 50, 56f., 122f., 128, 137, 140ff., 164f.
Nazis 97, 114, 123, 166; see also 95, 119
nesting material 66
Nicholson 79, 102
Nieli 123
Nozick 10, 16, 20, 29

objectivity 47f., 50, 68, 133, 135, 139, 147, 152f., 164
O'Donovan 143
Oedipus 56
omissions 11, 20, 58
Onians 129
Orient 129
Other 3, 129, 152
Otto 132
ox, see cattle

Pacheco 79
pain not a sensation 149f.
panpsychism 36; see also 133
parental feeling 26f., 49, 61, 69, 106, 113
Passmore 27
Pavlov 91
perception 150
persons 11, 38, 104, 125
Philo 81
philosophical method 1f., 112f., 126, 134, 155f.
pigeons 40, 153
pigs 35, 91, 141f., 148, 152, 164, 181
pity 43, 59, 88f., 94, 96
Plato 44, 51, 62, 80, 111, 129, 152
Plutarch 22, 49, 56
Plutchik 126f., 130, 137, 147
points of view 25; see also consciousness
predators 16ff., 52, 58, 103
prejudices 112
pretence 148
Primatt 83
principles 1, 13
Prior 14
prisons 115
private language 33, 149, 182
probabilities 12, 14

property 18, 64, 74ff., 79, 99, 107, 119f.
prostitution 64
prudence 40f., 76
psychosis 92, 117
Putnam 134

quod natura omnia animalia docuit 27, 51, 57

Rachlin & Green 40
rainbow 6
Ramsey 151f.
Rand 71
rape 28, 44, 90, 97, 118, 146, 162f., 166, 181
Raphael 10
rats 37f., 116, 145, 157
realism 121
Regan 18, 70ff., 77, 82, 99ff.
reindeer 34
replaceability 99
Research Defence Society 13, 45
Revelation 4, 6
Reynolds, P.C. 129f., 136
Reynolds, V. 41
rights 2f., 9ff., 16ff., 70ff., 98f.
Ritchie, A.M. 49
Ritchie, D.G. 16ff.
robins 150
Robinson 124
Rollin 137
roles 38f.
Rorty 121f., 148, 152
Rosenfield 108
Rothbard 73f., 98
rules of war 61ff., 75, 103

Sabbath 5, 111
sacrifice 7, 10
Said 129
saints 3f.
salmon 60
Salt 16, 21f., 101
Sartre 96
savages 59ff., 75
Schafer 132
scepticism 33, 94, 113, 125, 133, 136, 155ff., 167
scientific method 31ff., 111, 134ff., 139, 165; see also objectivity
seals 115f.

Searle 127, 145
Seattle 82, 179
self-awareness 36ff., 62f., 67
self-evidence 32
self-ownership 78f., 83f.; *see also* egoism
sentiment 43, 51, 67, 76, 79, 117f., 123
sex in temples 25, 56
Sextus Empiricus 125
sexuality 42f., 59, 87, 91, 118, 128, 133, 149, 153
sheep 5, 7, 91f., 95, 130, 135, 143, 150
side-constraints 20, 101
Singer 2, 98ff.
slavery 21, 27, 59, 74ff., 95, 115, 140, 167
Smith, A. 109
Smith, N. 50
social contract 34, 85
social insects 26, 90, 143
Socrates 113; *see also* Plato
solipsism 32, 79, 82, 157
Sophocles 129
sparrows 4
species 26, 68, 84, 87, 95, 98f., 106, 111, 118f., 160
speciesism 25f., 51, 98; *see also* 68, 118, 158ff.
Sperry 73, 110
Spiegelberg 132
Spinoza 43, 74, 87ff., 93, 130
Spooner 71
Sprigge 77, 81f.
squirrels 116
Steiner 65
Stich 122f., 126, 131
Stoicism 5, 26, 42ff., 68, 106, 146; *see also* 109
Stone 74
stories 143f., 152, 155f.
strangers 106
Strato 146
subjects of a life 74, 101, 103
supermantises 65f., 117f.
symbolism 44, 157

Taub 79, 86
taxation 71
Temerlin 62
temptation 40
territoriality 50, 61, 128
tick 38, 150
Tinbergen 132, 136

tools 126, 151
tripartite brain 129
truth 2, 121ff., 134, 148

Uexkuell 35, 38, 150
Umwelt 35, 61, 150f.
Unamuno 134
utilitarians 2, 9ff., 16, 19f., 42ff., 70, 72, 84, 99ff., 161ff., 180
utility monsters 21

Van Lawick-Goodall, *see* Goodall
veganism 23
vegetarianism 23, 43f., 100
vervet monkeys 39
veterinary practitioners 119f.
vetos, *see* side constraints
virtue 88, 90
vivisection 13, 18, 21, 72, 91ff., 102, 108, 110, 123, 154
voodoo 128

Waal 136
Walshe 122
war, *see* rules of war
Washburn 133, 137, 147
wasps 39, 60, 65, 67, 133, 147, 149
Weil 119
welfare rights 20ff., 71ff., 101, 119, 158
whales 29, 77, 85, 103, 147
Whewell 42
Whyte 126
wild animals 16ff., 84, 104
Wilkes 124, 133
Williams 58
Willis 3
wills 9f., 76f.
Wilson 25, 49
witches 123
Wittgenstein & Wittgensteinians 2, 123, 130, 145f., 148
wolves 6, 22, 44, 62, 135, 145
woodlice 60, 149
World State 27f.
worms 133f.

Yanomamo 19
Yeats 132

zebra 17
Zeno 26
Zeus 81, 108, 124